Theatres of Contagion

Methuen Drama Engage offers original reflections about key practitioners, movements and genres in the fields of modern theatre and performance. Each volume in the series seeks to challenge mainstream critical thought through original and interdisciplinary perspectives on the body of work under examination. By questioning existing critical paradigms, it is hoped that each volume will open up fresh approaches and suggest avenues for further exploration.

Series Editors
Mark Taylor-Batty
University of Leeds, UK
Enoch Brater
University of Michigan, USA

Selected Titles

Christoph Schlingensief: Staging Chaos, Performing Politics and Theatrical Phantasmagoria by Anna Teresa Scheer
ISBN 978-1-350-00105-3

Political Dramaturgies and Theatre Spectatorship: Provocations for Change by Liz Tomlin
ISBN 978-1-474-29560-4

Postdramatic Theatre and Form
edited by Michael Shane Boyle, Matt Cornish and Brandon Woolf
ISBN 978-1-350-04316-9

Social Housing in Performance: The English Council Estate on and off Stage by Katie Beswick
ISBN 978-1-474-28521-6

Theatre in the Dark: Shadow, Gloom and Blackout in Contemporary Theatre
edited by Adam Alston and Martin Welton
ISBN 978-1-4742-5118-1

Watching War on the Twenty-First-Century Stage: Spectacles of Conflict by Clare Finburgh Delijani
ISBN 978-1-3500-9941-8

Fiery Temporalities in Theatre and Performance: The Initiation of History by Maurya Wickstrom
ISBN 978-1-4742-8169-0

Robert Lepage/Ex Machina: Revolutions in Theatrical Space by James Reynolds
ISBN 978-1-4742-7609-2

Theatres of Contagion

Transmitting Early Modern to Contemporary Performance

Edited by
Fintan Walsh

Series editors
Mark Taylor-Batty and Enoch Brater

methuen | drama
LONDON • NEW YORK • OXFORD • NEW DELHI • SYDNEY

METHUEN DRAMA
Bloomsbury Publishing Plc
50 Bedford Square, London, WC1B 3DP, UK
1385 Broadway, New York, NY 10018, USA
29 Earlsfort Terrace, Dublin 2, Ireland

BLOOMSBURY, METHUEN DRAMA and the Methuen Drama logo
are trademarks of Bloomsbury Publishing Plc

First published in Great Britain 2020
Paperback edition first published 2021

Copyright © Fintan Walsh and contributors, 2020

Fintan Walsh and contributors have asserted their right under the Copyright,
Designs and Patents Act, 1988, to be identified as authors of this work.

For legal purposes the Acknowledgements on p. xii constitute
an extension of this copyright page.

Series design by Louise Dugdale
Cover image: Re-Member Me by Dickie Beau, photograph by Tristram Kenton

All rights reserved. No part of this publication may be reproduced or
transmitted in any form or by any means, electronic or mechanical,
including photocopying, recording, or any information storage or retrieval
system, without prior permission in writing from the publishers.

Bloomsbury Publishing Plc does not have any control over, or responsibility for,
any third-party websites referred to or in this book. All internet addresses given
in this book were correct at the time of going to press. The author and publisher
regret any inconvenience caused if addresses have changed or sites have
ceased to exist, but can accept no responsibility for any such changes.

A catalogue record for this book is available from the British Library.

A catalog record for this book is available from the Library of Congress.

Library of Congress Control Number: 2019947829

ISBN: HB: 978-1-3500-8598-5
PB: 978-1-3502-1551-1
ePDF: 978-1-3500-8600-5
eBook: 978-1-3500-8599-2

Series: Methuen Drama Engage

Typeset by Integra Software Services Pvt. Ltd.

To find out more about our authors and books visit
www.bloomsbury.com and sign up for our newsletters.

Contents

List of Figures	vii
Notes on Contributors	viii
Acknowledgements	xii

Introduction

1 Contagious Performance: Between Illness and Ambience *Fintan Walsh*   3

Part One   Infectious Bodies and Behaviours

2 Viral Hamlet: History, Memory, Kinship *Fintan Walsh*   23
3 'A plague o' both your houses': Auditory Contagion and Affective Frequencies in Musical and Intercultural Theatres *Marcus Cheng Chye Tan*   41
4 'Look not upon me, for thine eyes are wounding': Infectious Sights in Shakespeare's Theatre of Contagion *Shani Bans*   56
5 Catching a Feeling: A Practice-based Inquiry into Affective Contagion in Elizabeth Inchbald's *The Massacre* *Rebecca McCutcheon*   71

Part Two   Sites of Contamination and Containment

6 Plague Inc.: Theatre's Engagement with Mechanisms of Contagion and Containment *Kirsten E. Shepherd-Barr*   89
7 'Is there a doctor in the house?': The Myth and Reality of Audience Psychogenic and Neurological Responses to the Theatre of Horror *Julius Green*   105
8 'I don't know why she's crying': Contagion and Criminality in Clean Break's *Dream Pill* and *Little on the inside* *Molly McPhee*   121
9 Nomadic Contagion and the Performance of Infrastructure in Dale Farm's Post-eviction Scene *Lynne McCarthy*   136

Part Three Conducting Emotions, Moods and Minds

10 The Paradox of Immersion: Mechanisms of Contagion and Separation in Punchdrunk's *Sleep No More* Ana Pais ... 155
11 Outer and Inner Contagions *Mark Pizzato* ... 170
12 Theatre, Appification and VR Apps: Disability Simulations as an Intervention in 'Affective Realism' *Liam Jarvis* ... 186

Index ... 202

List of Figures

2.1	Dickie Beau lip-synching in silhouette on stage and across prerecorded video. Photo by Robin Fisher, courtesy of Almeida Theatre	28
2.2	Dickie Beau dressing and undressing mannequins with old theatre costumes. Photo by Robin Fisher, courtesy of Almeida Theatre	29
5.1	The performance space at Dilston Grove. Photo courtesy of photographer Jamie Smith	79
9.1	Open sewage flows between the bund walls at Dale Farm, 2012. Photo by Lynne McCarthy	143
9.2	Dale Farm overgrowth, 2012. Photo by Lynne McCarthy	146
12.1	Screenshots from 'On the Road', in the *A Walk Through Dementia* app. Courtesy of Alzheimer's Research UK	189
12.2	Data gathered from Alzheimer's Research UK's survey of *A Walk Through Dementia* app user. Reproduced courtesy of Alzheimer's Research UK	196

Notes on Contributors

Shani Bans is a PhD candidate in the English Department at UCL, where she is currently completing her thesis, 'Optics in Shakespeare and His Contemporaries', supported by the Arts and Humanities Research Council.

Julius Green received an MA in history from Corpus Christi College, Cambridge, and was Fellow Commoner of the College in 2014. He is a Fellow of Birkbeck Centre for Contemporary Theatre, and at Birkbeck he taught the MA course in Creative Producing for seven years. Julius is a lecturer and member of the Advisory Panel for the National Film and Television School's MA in Creative Business for Entrepreneurs and Executives, and teaches on the Central School of Speech and Drama's MA course in Creative Producing. He has over 250 plays and musicals to his credit as a theatre producer, has served on the Board of Management of the Society of London Theatre and the Board of Directors of the Edinburgh Festival Fringe Society, and is a director of the Academy of Circus Arts. Julius is a regular columnist for *The Stage* newspaper and his book *How to Produce a West End Show* was published in 2012. His second book, *Agatha Christie – A Life in Theatre*, was published in 2015 and his next book, *Stars and Spies* (in collaboration with MI5's official historian Professor Christopher Andrew), will be published in 2020. He is a member of the Society for Theatre Research and the Circus Research Network and is the archivist for the record-breaking London production of *The Mousetrap*.

Liam Jarvis is a researcher-theatre maker and Lecturer in Drama at the University of Essex in the Literature, Film and Theatre studies (LiFTs) department. Since 2007, he has been Co-director of Analogue theatre company. His co-authored devised work includes the published works *Beachy Head* and *2401 Objects* which have been performed throughout the UK/Europe. Most recently, *Sleepless* was presented as a co-production with Shoreditch Town Hall and Staatstheater Mainz (Germany) in 2016. Analogue's digital installation *Transports* recently used Raspberry Pi and wearable technologies to enable participants to embody experiences of tremor in collaboration with Parkinson's UK and volunteers living with young-onset Parkinson's disease. Liam's research and teaching has focused on affect, immersion, embodiment and performance in digital maker culture and he has published numerous book chapters as well as articles and reviews in journals such as *Performance Research*, *International Journal of*

Performance Arts and Digital Media and *Studies in Theatre and Performance*. His new research monograph, *Immersive Embodiment: Theatres of Mislocalised Sensation,* will be published in 2019.

Lynne McCarthy is a lecturer in Applied Theatre at University of East London. Her research engages with people-property relations in current cultural practices with a particular focus on the interactions of artists with home-made space and evictions dealing specifically with the subjectivities of social tenants and nomads. This research aims to articulate contemporary modes of cultural possession. Additionally, McCarthy undertakes research practices with the feminist collective Speaking of IMELDA on Irish reproductive justice. Her research has appeared in *Contemporary Theatre Review*'s 'Interventions' and *Research in Drama Education*.

Rebecca McCutcheon is a researcher and director based in London who makes performances in a range of settings, from theatres to disused train stations to palaces to alleyways. Her work often attends to unheard stories, and is concerned with how sites can catalyse relationships between different groups. McCutcheon is Artistic Director of Lost Text/Found Space, a performance company which makes site-based works with unperformed texts by women, creating new contemporary connections to lost voices.

Molly McPhee is a doctoral candidate in theatre at the Victorian College of the Arts, University of Melbourne, Australia. For six years (2009–15) she was involved in the development and production of over fifteen new plays as a member of Clean Break Theatre Company, touring to theatres, custodial and community settings around the UK. Her research investigates carceral imagination and carceral seepage at the theatre, developing a framework of 'miasmatic performance' to describe the inter- and extralegal porosities of social stigma, prison, public health and policing as they emerge within performance practice and audience exchange. Her publications include 'Miasmatic Performance' for *Performance Research* (July 2018), 'Stigma: The Work of the Straightener' (Erewhon exhibition catalogue, 2016), and a forthcoming chapter in *Applied Theatre: Women and the Criminal Justice System*, edited by Caoimhe McAvinchey. She was educated at Pomona College, California Institute of the Arts (MFA Critical Studies) and the University of Hamburg, where she was a Fulbright grant researcher.

Ana Pais is a FCT postdoctoral fellow at Centro de Estudos de Teatro, School of Arts and Humanities, University of Lisbon. She holds a PhD in theatre studies entitled *Commotion: Affective Rhythms in the Theatrical Event* from the University of Lisbon. Since 2000, she has been participating in national and international conferences. Between 2003 and 2004, she worked as a theatre critic for the most distinguished Portuguese newspapers as well as a dramaturge in both theatre and dance projects in Portugal. She is the author of *Discourse of Complicité – Contemporary Dramaturgies* (2004) and of several articles. From 2005 to 2010, she was Assistant Professor at Escola Superior de Teatro e Cinema (Lisbon). As part of her postdoc project, she curated the discursive and performative event *Projecto P! Performance na Esfera Pública* (Lisbon, 10–14 April 2017).

Mark Pizzato is Professor of Theatre and Film at the University of North Carolina at Charlotte, USA. He is the author of *Edges of Loss: From Modern Drama to Postmodern Theory* (1998), *Theatres of Human Sacrifice: From Ancient Ritual to Screen Violence* (2005), *Ghosts of Theatre and Cinema in the Brain* (2006), *Inner Theatres of Good and Evil: The Mind's Staging of Gods, Angels and Devils* (2011), and *Beast-People Onscreen and in Your Brain: The Evolution of Animal-Humans from Prehistoric Cave Art to Modern Movies* (2016). Dr Pizzato also co-edited, with Lisa Perdigao, *Death in American Texts and Performances* (2016) and wrote the forthcoming textbook *Mapping Global Theatre History* (2019).

Kirsten E. Shepherd-Barr is Professor of English and Theatre Studies at the University of Oxford and a Fellow of St Catherine's College. Her main areas of interest lie in the interactions between science and theatre on which she has published *Theatre and Evolution from Ibsen to Beckett* (2015) and *Science on Stage: From Doctor Faustus to Copenhagen* (2006; paperback 2012) as well as numerous articles and book chapters. She also specializes in modern drama and the role of theatrical performance in histories of modernism. Publications in this area include *Modern Drama: A Very Short Introduction* (2016) and *Ibsen and Early Modernist Theatre, 1890–1900* (1997), as well as *Twenty First-century Approaches to Literature: Late Victorian into Modern*, co-edited with Laura Marcus and Michèle Mendelssohn (2016).

Marcus Cheng Chye Tan is Assistant Professor of Drama and Higher Degrees Programme Leader at the National Institute of Education, Nanyang Technological University Singapore. He researches primarily in intercultural theatre, performance soundscapes, sound and music in theatre, virtual performativities, and Southeast Asian theatre. He is author of *Acoustic Interculturalism: Listening to Performance* (2012) and has had articles published in journals such as *The Drama Review, Theatre Research International* and *Contemporary Theatre Review* in these areas. Marcus is also Associate Editor of the *Journal of Interdisciplinary Voice Studies*, co-convenor of the Music Theatre Working Group, International Federation for Theatre

Research, and dramaturge for a Singapore theatre company, Dark Matter Theatrics. Marcus is currently editing a book on contemporary politics and performance in Southeast Asia.

Fintan Walsh is Reader in Theatre and Performance in the Department of English and Humanities at Birkbeck, University of London, and Co-director of Birkbeck Centre for Contemporary Theatre and Director of Birkbeck Gender and Sexuality (BiGS). His books include *Queer Performance and Contemporary Ireland: Dissent and Disorientation* (2016), *Theatre & Therapy* (2013), and *Male Trouble: Masculinity and the Performance of Crisis* (2010). He is editor or co-editor of numerous books and journal issues and is Senior Editor of *Theatre Research International*.

Acknowledgements

The early stages of this project benefited from financial support provided by Birkbeck's Wellcome Trust Institutional Strategic Support Fund, and I would like to thank the awarding body for its contribution. It enabled the hosting of a two-day conference on the topic at Birkbeck in May 2017, where some of the chapters in this volume began as panel presentations, lectures or performances. I'm grateful to all those who contributed to the conference and to those who helped organize it, including Birkbeck Centre for Contemporary Theatre Fellows Dickie Beau, Rachel Mars, Martin O'Brien and David Slater and colleagues Louise Owen, Emily Senior, Matthew Weait, Jo Winning, Sue Wiseman and Gill Woods. Special thanks are due to Louise, who enriches everything on which we collaborate, and to Gill for reading a portion of the manuscript and sharing her early modern expertise. Of course I'm grateful to all those who have contributed to this volume, graciously persisting through the editorial process. For their editorial guidance and support, thanks to Mark Dudgeon and Lara Bateman at Methuen Drama and series editors Enoch Brater and Mark Taylor-Batty. Sincere thanks to copy-editors, especially Leah Sidi for her invaluable assistance in preparing the manuscript for publication.

Fintan Walsh
London, 2018

Introduction

1

Contagious Performance: Between Illness and Ambience

Fintan Walsh

The age of globalization is the age of universal contagion.
　　　　　　　　　Michael Hardt and Antonio Negri, *Empire* (2000)

European theatre is 'beginning to infect' British theatre, David Hare charged in 2017, with theatre makers spoiling the health of dramatic writing and the once vigorous state of the nation play (Sweet 2017: 69). Hare's comments built on the commonly shared belief that theatre is a contagious cultural phenomenon, in no small part due to its capacity to draw bodies closely together in the event of live performance. While on the surface Hare's remarks were angled at theatre practice, especially at a perceived waning of dramatic writing in favour of more experimental performance modes, they were more fundamentally targeted at the globalized cultural climate that enabled international styles and models to affect and cross-fertilize more traditional British forms. Hare's criticisms generated some media controversy at the time of their publication, when they found themselves amplified by chiming with other sentiments largely emanating from the UK and the United States. In the wake of the Brexit vote and Trump's presidency, for instance, political discourse became dominated with calls for distinct and stable cultural boundaries, impervious to corrupting external influences, especially migrants. Theatre's contagiousness, in Hare's formulation, is also a matter of sociopolitical cause and consequence, insofar as it is cultivated by too much contact amongst diverse individuals, places and cultures.

　　In the same year, Neil Bartlett's *The Plague* opened at the Arcola Theatre, London. Bartlett's play is a theatrical adaptation of Albert Camus's 1947 novel of the same title, set in the Algerian city of Oran, in which a mysterious illness spreads throughout the population. On a narrative level, the novel addresses the devastation of real plagues throughout history, but on an allegorical plain, it investigates the rapid spread of fascism throughout a community, likened to pathogens passing between bodies. (Indeed, Eugène

Ionesco's play *Rhinoceros* (1959) would later critique fascism from a similar perspective, by depicting characters metamorphosing into rhinoceroses to capture its herd-like psychological structure.) Bartlett's play is presented as a public inquiry, in which five witnesses recall the events they have seen, from the relative safety of its aftermath. Here both plague and its fascist analogy still stand, but in erasing all references to a specific time and place, the play allows for more contemporary resonances too. We hear in Bartlett's writing echoes of the AIDS epidemic which came well after Camus's novel, and which aligns with the queer politics of much of Bartlett's other work, but also a critique of populist ideologies on the rise throughout the world at the time of the play's production as fascist germs. As the voices of characters Grand, Tarrou and Rambert resound in chorus to the question of what the plague really is: 'Life's a plague' (Bartlett 2017: 66). But if life is a plague, theatre is a form in which destructive forces can be summoned for scrutiny, and epidemiology dramaturgically interpreted and modelled. As the doctor Rieux describes her own contribution to the inquiry at the end of the play, theatre can be a place to speak up and bear witness, to remember and affirm: 'I decided to not be one of the people who keep silent, but to speak up and bear witness [...] there is more to admire about people than to despise or despair of' (Bartlett 2017: 67). With joy always under threat, as Rieux continues to observe (68), we are led to believe that theatre might even sow the seeds of collective pleasure. Here joy is pitched as a remedy for suffering, theatre as an antidote to fascism.

With these reference points, I introduce three different ideas of theatrical contagion central to this volume. In the first, via Hare, theatre is imagined as a culturally corrupting force, often spreading from the East to the West; in the second, via *The Plague*, theatre endeavours to represent disease and its psycho-medical impact; and in the third, by the end of the same play, it is capable of countering the worst effects of illness and any suspicions of contamination through the invigorating exchange of information, feelings and culture. These same ideas appear at different turns throughout this book, with authors testing the claims across a diverse range of theatre and performance practices, from the early modern to contemporary periods.

The primary aim of this book is to investigate theatre's status as a contagious cultural practice by questioning its role in the spread or control of medical, psychological and affective conditions and phenomena. We might envisage these along a sliding spectrum, running from illness to ambience, the former denoting bodily disease and the latter experienced environment and mood. In between these points hover a range of physiological, psychological and affective experiences that pass – or seem to – between people, cultures and things. That they *seem* to is as important as any certainty that they do, for the fantasy of and desire for contagion are often as powerful as any biological or chemical fact. As many of the essays collected here demonstrate, with contagion the literal and the metaphorical, the real and suggestive, often overlap and blur.

While discrete chapters pursue specific concerns, the book is devoted to exploring a number of key questions, which weave throughout its pages: (1) how has contagion been understood to happen and operate?; (2) what are its real and imagined effects?; (3) how have these effects been a source of distress and pleasure for theatre makers, audiences and various authorities?; and finally (4) what does theatrical contagion suggest about the real and imagined work of our cultural borders and structures of social-political organization? Ultimately, arguments in the book broadly contend that theatre is a cultural practice in which all sorts of matter, behaviours, illnesses, conditions, emotions, affects, moods, ideas, social and cultural phenomena pass around and between bodies and their environments – or are imagined or willed to – and are sometimes guarded against.

In terms of touch

As a term which defies boundaries, 'contagion' has developed different meanings and applications across a range of disciplines. In this volume it is variously approached as metaphoric, speculative and real, drawing on perspectives from medicine, neuroscience, psychology, anthropology, philosophy, law and affect theory. Despite being a subject of wide disciplinary concern, contagion is primarily associated with the domains of medicine and biology, especially pathologies. In medicine, contagion is usually taken to mean something contracted by physical contact, while infection occurs airborne. But central to both terms is the idea that matter, whether seen or unseen, moves around and between bodies. Perhaps for this reason, the sheer idea of contagion has long held power for makers and audiences of theatre, where bodies wilfully come to encounter others in close proximity. At the theatre, some form of contagion is often what is feared as well as what is deeply desired.

While contagion is explored from different disciplinary perspectives in this book, many chapters stay close to its etymological definition, which is rooted in notions of touch. The Latin *contāgiōn-em*, for example, incorporates *con* (with, together) and *tangere* (to touch). Whatever its precise causation, or its seemingly positive, negative or ambivalent effects, we can agree that contagion always draws attention to the impact of touch, no matter how surface or deep. And as Roland Barthes reminds us in *Camera Lucida*, we do not touch only with the hand but may also do so with the eye (Barthes [1980] 1982). Indeed, all senses have this haptic potential in their capacity to draw us into closer contact with the objects of our apprehension. Priscilla Wald discusses some of the meanings which gather around contagion to argue that the word 'tells us about the many ways in which we are in contact; it shows us whom we have touched both literally and figuratively, or more to the point, it blurs the distinction between them' (Foreword in Nixon and Servitje 2016: vi). To think about theatre and contagion, I suggest, is always to consider their enmeshment in the realities and fantasies of touch.

To approach the world through the prism of contagion is at one level to consider how everything is constructed through the exchange of matter, and the effects and affects of that process; to think across, as Jane Bennett suggests, 'the quarantines of matter and life' (Bennett 2010: vii). This is a broad axiom shared by scientific disciplines from astrophysics to biology, whose modern manifestations can be traced to the Renaissance era. Astrophysics tells us this about the universe at large, and biological branches (including medicine, neuroscience and genetics) offer a similar but more schematic story of human physiology, attesting to the ways other bodies, especially genetic relatives, shape our own. In the past decade or so, theories of epigenetics have freshly posited that our genes may not just carry physical data but memories and traumas experienced by our ancestors (e.g. Yehuda et al. 2016). Scientific studies of mirror neurons have claimed that in seeing behaviours performed, our brains act as if we have performed them ourselves (e.g. Prochazkova and Kret 2017), potentially explaining a whole range of imitated behaviour which has been widely speculated about at least since Plato's *Republic* (c. 380 BCE).

For much of the twentieth century, ideas of intergenerational transmission were less likely to have been heard within medicine than Freudian psychoanalysis, whose conceptualization of psychic life has always been haunted by the intersubjective and sometimes intergenerational dynamics of memory, desire, transference, doubling and repetition. In more mainstream sociology and psychology, notions of emotional contagion, imitation and imprinting form the building blocks of psycho-social life. For phenomenologists and affect theorists, what can feel like the contagious distribution of physical sensation is the effect of bodily matter bristling against worldly experience. These disciplines all accede, in different ways, to how the circulation and exchange of matter construct ourselves and our worlds, while offering a vast and varied vocabulary for understanding how contagion and its corollaries operate.

I am necessarily simplifying disciplinary complexity and nuance with this overview to fashion a working sense of how contagion is understood across different disciplines. But while this comprehension is important, these definitions alone do not account for how contagion morphs under the influence of power and desire, which are crucial to understanding cultural processes and practices. For it is only when contagion is somehow longed for or resisted that we glimpse its hold on the human imagination and societies, and the ways in which it shapes our sense of self and other(ness), particularly in terms of identity, community and belonging. Of course, theatre is created by the desire and power of multiple invested parties, and it is often also a crucible for their dissection. How power and desire shape different disciplinary understandings of contagion is central to many of the essays gathered in this volume.

While contagion's dream is of unity and transformation, its nightmare is of indistinction and destruction. As Roberto Esposito tells us, because of its inherent concern with boundary formation and management, contagion appears as a subject across a swathe of disciplines, often to account for how 'what was healthy, secure, identical to itself, is now exposed to a form of contamination that risks its devastation' (Esposito 2011: 2). Thinking contagiously reminds us that we are amalgams at atomic and experiential levels and that our physiology, psychology, emotional and social lives are forever influenced by our contact with each other and the world. Thinking contagiously through theatre, we not only see disciplinary walls start to crumble, but the centrality of the body to this folding and unfolding. For this reason, contagious inquiry has the capacity to unravel both intellectual boundaries and ideas of liberal Western subjectivity that imagine the individual as autonomous, sealed and bounded.

Plagues of history

The book's subtitle can be read in a number of ways. First, it signifies the volume's concern with contagion as a mode of transmission within the temporal parameters of the study. Second, it marks the early modern period as a time during which contagion became a topic of heightened concern for theatre makers and audiences, and the world around them. Third, it captures the significant amount of exchange between the early modern and contemporary period, particularly evidenced via contemporary productions, adaptations or responses to early modern work invested in ideas of contagion. Part of the challenge in editing this book has been to manage interdisciplinary study across a long historical sweep, but there is no way to neatly contain contagion. As many essays reveal, any analysis of the term rapidly introduces numerous other disciplines, and many of its contemporary cultural iterations quickly draw us back to early modern concerns. At some level, contagion is always about the transmission of history.

Since the sixteenth century the word 'contagion' has been in regular circulation in literary and medical texts, largely as a result of outbreaks of smallpox, syphilis, typhus, malaria and especially the bubonic plague. Plague had erupted across Europe since the fourteenth century ending with the Great Plague of London in 1665–6. Its effect was not only to decimate populations but to raise awareness of the vulnerability of the body to poor hygiene and illness, as well as to death.

A number of medical and politically attuned writers responded to the plague during this time. Published in 1603 in London, Thomas Lodge's *Treatise of the Plague* mapped the spread of disease throughout the city. The Italian physician, poet and scholar Girolamo Fracastoro published two treatises on the subject of contagion: the epic poem *Syphilis, or, A Poetical History of the French Disease* (*Syphilis sive Morbus Gallicus*) in 1530 and *De Contagione et Contagionis Morbis et eorum Curatione Libri Tres* in 1546. These texts challenged the prevailing Gallenic humoral theory of disease transmission, which held that an imbalance of the four humors created illness, by arguing that disease was communicated by the body's intake of external infectious agents.[1] In this way they prefigured advancements in nineteenth-century germ theory, which makes itself present in the work of Henrik Ibsen and George Bernard Shaw (see Kirsten E. Shepherd-Barr's chapter). Around the same time, a number of political tracts emerged which drew analogies between the body and the state, including William Averell's *A Mervailous Combat of Contrareties* (1588) and Edward Forset's *A Comparative Discourse of the Bodies Naturall and Politique* (1606).

These latter texts blur medical and cultural understanding by positioning the state as an entity which requires protection from external agents, which for the incipient British Empire often included other cultures and trading partners, colonized and enslaved peoples, and foreign enemies and migrants, including the expanding Jewish community in parts of Western Europe. For this reason, Michael Hardt and Antonio Negri argue that globalization is coterminous with the advent of 'universal contagion' (Hardt and Negri 2000: 136). As the world became more connected than ever before in the early modern period, anxieties around the spread of illness, ideas and cultures also grew. Of course these persist in contemporary concerns around open borders and free movement, which have precipitated nationalist agendas such as Brexit and US migration policies under Trump, including the president's promise to build a wall on the US-Mexico border. In discussing the wall, Trump routinely blurs the political, cultural and medical, describing Mexicans as being responsible for introducing 'tremendous infectious disease' as well as moral and criminal corruption.[2] But the desire to spread and share, history teaches us, also precipitates the impulse to defend. As Esposito puts it, 'the greater the vulnerability of the body politic must have appeared, the more urgent the need became to hermetically seal the orifices that had opened up in its frontiers' (2011: 123).

The early modern interest in contagion, therefore, is closely connected to the appetites of empire and its entwinement with medical discourse. But as Donna Haraway has pointed out, in the paranoid colonial imagination, the colonized was often figured as the invader. Haraway writes: 'In the face of the disease genocides accompanying European "penetration" of the globe, the "coloured" body of the colonized was constructed as the dark source of infection, pollution, disorder, and so on, that threatened to overwhelm white manhood (cities, civilization, the family, the white personal body) with its decadent emanations' (Haraway 1991: 223). The legacy of this projection persists in the present day, which Haraway observes amongst discourses of parasitic diseases and AIDS. But we can also see this inverse figuration apply to a whole range of processes of social othering, where minorities of all kinds are figured as contagious forces, which concerns many of the essays in this collection. The particular ethnic and racial dimension to this othering is foregrounded in chapters by Molly McPhee (Chapter 8) and Lynne McCarthy (Chapter 9).

The response of medicine and law to the perceived endangerment of its various bodies by external agents takes the form of immunity and defence. This language pervades contemporary Western political discourse when migrants and refugees are described as infectious (again, we can look to Trump) or moving in swarms (as according to David Cameron).[3] We see this vocabulary extend to pathologizing minorities too, including outside a Western context, such as when China's ruling Communist Party began interring its Muslim Uighur population in 2017 for indoctrination, likening the Islamic faith to 'being infected by a disease' (Sigal 2018). Immunity and defence are legal concepts, inherited from ancient Rome, which were invoked by emerging modern medicine in the seventeenth and eighteenth centuries with new understanding of how disease spread and could be controlled. It is within this context, set against the waning of sovereignty, that the human body becomes the locus of biopolitical control. As Michel Foucault reminds us in his elaboration of bio-power, as the body becomes a key site of knowledge since the eighteenth century, it also becomes something to be disciplined and controlled (Foucault [2004] 2007). Developments in modern medicine at this time begin to politicize the body at a cellular level.

Epidemiology and dramaturgy

The creation of purpose-built theatres in the mid-sixteenth century, where large audiences would pack in tightly together, presented a particular problem for the spread of illness, disease and influence but concomitantly a fascination with that potential. While theatres were often closed down to guard against plague's spread, with London playhouses shut for prolonged periods in 1581–2, 1592–3, 1603–4, 1608–9, 1609–10, 1625, 1630, 1636–7 and 1640 (Gurr 1992: 78), drama still conspired to produce contagion as a potent and persistent category of inquiry. Even though in the late twentieth century Susan Sontag would caution against illness as metaphor for its obscurantist tendencies (Sontag 1978), ideas of plague and contagion were frequently deployed figuratively in the early modern period to account for the spread of emotions and ideas amongst performers and audiences.

We find references to plague and contagion in Thomas Dekker's play *The Whore of Babylon* (1607), and references abound in Shakespeare's corpus, including *Hamlet, Romeo and Juliet, Julius Caesar, The Tempest, Timon of Athens* and *King Lear*, which are variously discussed in my own essay (Chapter 2), Marcus Cheng Chye Tan's contribution (Chapter 3) and Shani Bans's chapter (Chapter 4). And as Ana Pais informs us, the toxic emotions and atmospheres of *Macbeth* are the starting point for Punchdrunk's *Sleep No More* (Chapter 10). As a site in which bodies were presented, desired, policed, interrogated and viewed by large groups in proximity, the theatre became a significant arena for bodily study more generally. At the heart of this inquiry on stage was often an examination into where the body stopped and the world began, as well as an exploration of theatre's capacity to translate its corporeal investigations, even of illness, into spectacle and pleasure. In part owing to the imagined power of this close bodily display and impact, the anti-theatrical pamphleteers often attacked theatre's capacity for moral contagion. As in John Rainolds's charge, 'the manners of all spectators commonly are hazarded by the contagion of theatrical sights' (Rainolds [1599] 2004: 177).

The early modern period was not the first time contagion became a concern of the theatre or indeed that the epidemiological and dramaturgical became intertwined. Some of the oldest plays of Greek theatre were preoccupied with plague, most likely responding to the great plague of Athens towards the end of the fifth century BCE, as accounted for by Thucydides ([431 BCE] 1972). The language of disease pervaded fifth-century dramas such as Euripides's *Hippolytus* (428 BCE) and Sophocles's *Oedipus Rex* (429 BCE) and *Women of Trachis* (date unknown), such that many scholars see these works as directly responding to the plague. But if tragedians were interested in plague they were also curious about theatre's potential for healing, as in part indicated by the construction of the Sanctuary of Asklepios next to the Theatre of Dionysus, which was devoted to curative practices.

In *Poetics* (c. 335 BCE [2013]) Aristotle gestures towards this beneficent dimension of tragedy in his elaboration of its cathartic function. Central to his formulation is the idea that tragic poetry is an art that imitates life and that it is the audience's encounter with this imitation that can lead to emotional purgation or purification. In this, Aristotle's aesthetic and dramaturgically sensitive model counters the sociopolitical and moral reservations of Plato. In Book X of the *Republic* Plato argues that imitative arts should be removed from the just city because they risk corrupting it by confounding distinctions between reality and illusion. For René Girard, drawing on psychoanalysis and anthropology, desire, death and violence are contagious and contaminative, and cultures develop rites and rituals around them, such as Greek tragedy, to protect their effects from spreading and undoing established social relations ([1972] 2005). Desire, as mimetic, is learned from others, who run the risk of becoming rivals in competing for the same objects and thus precipitating violence.

In *Inner Experience*, Georges Bataille is also interested in the relationship between contagion and the sacred, associating the former with the violent transmission of affect, which overflows and undoes the rational and enclosed subject. This spread of affect is a feature of sacrifice – out of which tragedy emerged and which in a sense it enacts – whereby violent exposition has the effect of releasing and soliciting affective discharge. The power of 'dramatic art', for Bataille, is its capacity to trade in 'non-discursive sensation', capable of rippling through audiences or, as Bataille puts it, 'to chill – as by contagion' (Bataille [1954] 1988: 13).

More fundamentally, Bataille saw contagion as the structuring principle of subjectivity. In his writing we find a picture of the self as mobile, kinetic and porous. 'What you are stems from the activity which links the innumerable elements which constitute you to the intense communication of the elements among themselves', Bataille writes. 'These are contagions of energy, of movement, of warmth, or transfers of elements, which constitute inevitably the life of your organized being' (94). Teresa Brennan would describe this phenomenon as the transmission of affect, in which 'the emotions or affects of one person, and the enhancing or depressing energies these affects entail, can enter into another' (Brennan 2004: 3), even infusing or absorbing external atmospheres. And one of the ways we might understand theatre, by Brennan's definition, is as 'the *deliberate* creation of an atmosphere' (16).

Given its importance to theatre history and some critical and cultural theory, the little sustained attention contagion has received within theatre and performance studies is surprising. In her recent book *Viral Performance: Contagious Theaters from Modernism to the Digital Age* (2018), Miriam Felton-Dansky intervenes this dearth. However, her study considers notions of the viral in relation to a selection of performance works from the 1960s to the present, exploring how viral dramaturgies draw on emerging media to develop new modes of quick dissemination and produce new models of action.

It is in the writings of Antonin Artaud, to whom Felton-Dansky also looks, that theatre's contagious dimensions and possibilities have received their most sustained consideration, and these appear in chapters by Shepherd-Barr (Chapter 6) and Mark Pizzato (Chapter 11). At its best and most powerful, theatre could be like the plague, according to Artaud. By this he appears to mean that its dynamic energies and affects could spread amongst performers and audiences, confounding both linguistic and corporeal boundaries, bodily organization and cultural hierarchy. The value of this contagion would be to puncture conventions of Western rationality and authority, finding sense in new languages of experience and sensation. In appealing to non-Western cultures for his ideas, however affirmatively, Artaud also makes himself vulnerable to charges of cultural fetishization. In the essay 'The Theater and the Plague', published in *The Theater and Its Double*, Artaud suggests that the theatre as plague 'releases conflicts, disengages powers, liberates possibilities' (Artaud [1938] 1958: 31). While the essay is clearly invested in the contagious power of the theatre as plague, Artaud suggests that the essence of such theatre is less to do with contagion but with 'revelation': 'the bringing forth, the exteriorization of a depth of latent cruelty by means of which all the perverse possibilities of the mind, whether of an individual or a people' (Artaud [1938] 1958: 30).

Mary Douglas introduces her seminal anthropological study *Purity and Danger* as 'a treatise on dirt and contagion' ([1996] 2002: x). Douglas observes how societies produce taboos to regulate what they deem unclean or polluting, coaxing the ambiguous into the realm of the sacred. Douglas's ideas in part inform McCarthy's reading of the Dale Farm eviction site in Chapter 9. What Douglas discerns as the threat of contagion is figured as something of a promise or potential in the work of Bataille and Artaud. In a similar vein, Gilles Deleuze and Félix Guattari celebrate a contagious view of the world for its anti-hierarchical potential: 'We oppose epidemic to filiation, contagion to heredity, peopling by contagion to sexual reproduction, epidemics, battlefields and catastrophes' ([1980] 2002: 266), they write. Indeed, Deleuze and Guattari draw on Artaud's notion of the Body without Organs to try and elaborate a model of anti-Oedipal subjectivity ([1980] 2002: 165–84), which has proved an important concept for making and interpreting twentieth-century body-based performance art.

While Artaud is interested in the kinetic and affective power of theatre as plague, his ideas are founded in historical circumstance. 'The Theater and the Plague' begins with a dream of plague set in 1720 with a premonition of the outbreak of plague in Marseille a matter of weeks later. It spirals back to discuss plague in the fourteenth and sixteenth centuries before leaping forward to the nineteenth. Indeed, Stanton B. Garner, Jr. maintains that Artaud's thinking was directly inspired by advancements in germ theory in the nineteenth century, including the work of Louis Pasteur. But crucially, Artaud finds in disease and medical invention a vocabulary for describing the psychic, emotional and affective power of theatre. This movement between disease and experience, or what I describe here as the slide between illness and ambience, is central to many of the essays gathered in this collection too.

Overview

This book cannot document all the ways in which theatre and contagion are intertwined. However, it aims to supply ample historical, cultural and intellectual context towards understanding the relationship, and chapters can be approached as diverse and provocative exemplars. While the collection focuses mainly on Western culture, chapters by Tan and Pizzato take in non-Western traditions and implications too. The book is organized around three themes, which roughly move chronologically from the early modern to the contemporary period with plenty of cross-fertilization between chapters and divisions.

'Infectious Bodies and Behaviours' features chapters that examine the body as a site of contagion in the early modern period and in some contemporary adaptations or responses. My own essay explores the relationship between contagion and queer kinship through the figure of Hamlet, focusing on Dickie Beau's *Re-Member Me* (2017). Beau's production uncovers how queerness and Hamlet have often been silent bedfellows by revealing how many leading actors who played the role transpired to be gay men. His observations eventually focus on the largely forgotten final performance of Scottish actor Ian Charleson as Hamlet at the National Theatre in 1989, a role he played while effectively dying of AIDS. Reading Beau's production in light of the legacy and ghosts of *Hamlet*, I suggest that Beau develops a dramaturgy of contagion to link the past with the present, transmitting queer culture but also nourishing kinship networks.

Marcus Cheng Chye Tan's chapter focuses on a musical adaptation and an intercultural variation of Shakespeare's *Romeo and Juliet* to examine sound as a form of contagion. Tan explores how music's frequencies work in performance to affectively infect bodies, compelling them to physically engage, move and act. Sound, Tan tells us, is the primary actant in musical theatre, and his chapter argues that its deployment in the adaptations under focus disrupts the conventional signifying properties of Shakespeare. Staying with Shakespeare, Shani Bans addresses ocular metaphors of transmission, infection and contagion across a number of plays including *King Henry VI Part 2, As You Like It* and *Twelfth Night*. Bans examines these tropes in relation to early modern medical theories of vision and architecture. Her essay argues that in Shakespeare's theatre, contagion evolves from referring to a lover's infectious gaze to account for the theatre space as a site of multiple transmissions.

Rebecca McCutcheon's chapter is also rooted in the early modern period with the sectarian massacres of Huguenots by Catholics in 1572. This event is the subject of Elizabeth Inchbald's 1792 play *The Massacre*, which McCutcheon argues is particularly attuned to the infectious effects of mob behaviour. The contagious effects of mob behaviour in theatre are perhaps most readily associated with Arthur Miller's *The Crucible* (1953) in which the late seventeenth-century Salem witch trials serve as an allegory of the persecutions of McCarthyism. But McCutcheon's contribution recovers an important earlier precursor, which anticipates the pioneering crowd behaviour studies of Gabriel Tarde (1890) and Gustav Le Bon (1895). She also discusses her own practice-based site-specific investigation into the play, *A Testimony and a Silence*, at Dilston Grove, London, in 2014. This production sought to reimagine the play's negative contagion as affirmative affect that led audiences into a deeper understanding of violence, the site and its historical referent.

It was in the eighteenth century that Franz Anton Mesmer developed a theory of animal magnetism, or mesmerism, which held that invisible forces connected and influenced animate entities and that these could be manipulated towards healing. Mesmerism was criticized on many grounds, including for its showmanship, although in this it laid the foundation for the development of stage hypnosis. Inchbald was dubious about the medical claims of mesmerism and sends them up in her farce *Animal Magnetism* (1788), an adaptation of Dumaniant's highly popular 1786 farce *Le Médecin Malgré Tout le Monde*. But while critical of mesmerism, in McCutcheon's chapter we see Inchbald preoccupied with the power of group feeling on and off stage.

The second part, 'Sites of Contamination and Containment', builds on the site-specific analyses initiated by McCutcheon's chapter to examine how theatre as a form and a place works to contaminate or contain. We move from the eighteenth to the nineteenth century to consider how germ theory, science and medicine impacted naturalist theatre and theatres of horror.

Athena Vrettos argues for 'the ubiquity of contagion as a master narrative in Victorian culture' (1995: 178), and Allan Conrad Christensen maintains that this was both literal and metaphoric (2005: 4). The outbreaks of major epidemics initially contributed to this concern (influenza, smallpox, measles, whooping cough, typhoid and cholera), prompting debates among proponents of germ theory (who claimed that specific diseases were spread by specific germs), infectionists (who believed that disease was spread indirectly) and miasmists (who incorrectly held that disease was spread by bad air). But the slippage between the medical and the metaphorical could be discerned amongst the moral concerns of the Contagious Diseases Acts (1864, 1866 and 1869), which began with an inquiry into venereal diseases in the armed forces and resulted in the internment of prostitutes in hospitals. This gendered dimension to the Victorian imagining of contagion can be discerned in the first act of Ibsen's *A Doll's House* (1879) in which Torvald Helmer grounds the dysfunction of his household in Nora's contaminative dishonesty: 'A fog of lies like that in a household, and it spreads disease and infection to every part of it,' he says. 'Every breath the children take in that kind of house is reeking with evil germs [...] Practically all juvenile delinquents come from homes where the mother is dishonest' ([1879] 2008: 33). While Ibsen continues to expose a more complex worldview, Torvald would have us blame Nora from the outset.

Kirsten E. Shepherd-Barr's chapter locates nineteenth-century theatre's interest in scientific transmission in notions of heredity, in Ibsen and August Strindberg, and breastfeeding on stage in plays by James A. Herne and Eugène Brieux. She argues that nineteenth-century theatre blurs the line between medical and social contagion, laying the ground for Artaud's thinking in the twentieth century. This fascination continues to the present day, Shepherd-Barr maintains, in the prevalence of epidemic fantasies in computer games.

Julius Green's chapter takes us from the nineteenth to the twenty-first century in his analysis of the Théâtre du Grand-Guignol and its legacy. Green discusses the reported faintings at this famed theatre and speculates that a key reason may have been a phobic response to the sight of stage blood. Green links this phenomenon to contemporary theatre practice, including Lucy Bailey's notoriously bloody 2014 production of *Titus Andronicus* at Shakespeare's Globe, London. While attending to medical matters, Green also considers the impact of ambient factors and the performance space, and the role of theatrical managers, publicists and make-up artists in manipulating audience expectations and reactions.

We move from fainting audiences to an incarcerated woman crying with Molly McPhee's chapter. McPhee examines the contagious metaphors that structure law and carceral states. Her chapter discusses Clean Break Theatre

Company's *Dream Pill* and *Little on the inside* to show how the productions explore the perceived contagiousness of crime and theatre's capacity to rethink this formulation. In her analysis, Clean Break's dramaturgy works to deepen our awareness of how contagious language shapes our responses to criminality and incarceration.

The interplay of law and contagion is also a concern of Lynne McCarthy's chapter. McCarthy focuses on the aftermath of an Irish Traveller eviction at Dale Farm in the UK in 2011 to argue that metaphors of contagion are central to the state's vilification of Travellers, while illuminating how these became realized in the production of bunding around the site to stop the flow of pollutants. For McCarthy, bunding is a form of statecraft – which has clear resonances with stagecraft – that physically sequesters and architecturally compounds the state's framing of Travellers as toxic.

The discourses of feeling, emotion and affect which have gained prominence in theatre and performance studies in the past two decades are a concern of the third part, 'Conducting Emotions, Moods and Minds'. Chapters in this division are particularly interested in the role of contemporary immersive and digital practices in the production and transmission of these phenomena and their implication in the production of atmosphere and the shaping of mental life. Elaine Hatfield, John T. Cacioppo and Richard L. Rapson propose that 'emotional contagion is best conceptualized as a multiply determined family of social, psychophysiological, and behavioral phenomena' (1994: 7), and this section is equally invested in this broad-based understanding of emotional, affective and somatic experience. Similarly, but emphasizing the viral form of contemporary networks, Tony D. Sampson distances contagion from disease 'to explore new exploitable social assemblages of affective contagious encounter' (2012: 3). We can detect this phenomenon at play in this section too, in which a sense of affective or cognitive contagion contours different forms of performative encounter.

The transmission of affect is a particular concern of Ana Pais's chapter, which focuses on Punchdrunk's *Sleep No More*. Pais explores how sound design functions as an agent of affective contagion in the immersive performance, while also attending to its strategies of separation such as masks and suspense. Pais's analysis illuminates how immersive performance often pivots on the interplay between strategies of containment and separation.

Mark Pizzato's chapter is concerned with how emotional contagion is conceived in neuroscience, as well as in Western and non-Western dramatic theories. His essay maps analogies and connections between these diverse disciplines and discourses to explore the brain's staging of consciousness and circulation of feeling in the theatre. Also drawing on neuroscience, Liam Jarvis's final chapter frames smartphone apps as quasi-theatrical spaces in which we perform virtually. Jarvis is interested in how apps can shape experience for neurodiverse or neurologically disordered people through the production of affective realism. His chapter focuses on Alzheimer's Research UK's *A Walk through Dementia* VR app (2016), which embeds users in a series of first-person simulations of dementia symptoms. While sensitive to the benefits of such encounters, Jarvis also challenges easy assumptions of simulation as disseminated knowledge or empathy and queries the ethical implications of these practices.

Conclusion

While this introduction opened with anxieties of contagion, I hope the volume ultimately affirms the subject's centrality to making and understanding vital theatre and performance practice. Contagion, we will see, is a persistent subject of artistic, personal, disciplinary, political and ethical concern, and the essays look to a wide range of forms to develop arguments on these matters, while considering the bleeds between drama, theatre, performance, digital practices and architecture. The chapters expose theatre as a space of touch and exchange, ricocheting between the bodily, psychological, affective and ambient, blurring those distinctions and the perceived borders separating the real and imaginary, the literal and metaphorical. In theatres of contagion, we see how the thrill of contact is often chased by the fear of too much. Both outcomes speak to theatre's capacity to stage encounters with the unseen, unknown and uncontained, and the risks that potential introduces. And the essays demonstrate the importance of letting discourses from diverse disciplines, including sciences and humanities, cross-pollinate one another to advance our understanding.

The greater hope for this book is that it will help illuminate how contagion is deeply implicated in the discourses and practices of sociopolitical formation when it is routinely evoked and weaponized in language, imagery and law as a category or aesthetic to abject and other. Theatre and performance can serve as a microcosm of these manipulations, sometimes exposing them to direct critique and occasionally presenting what is perceived to be negative about contagion as ultimately affirmative – even performance's greatest gift. What is fundamentally at stake in discussions of theatre's contagiousness, the essays collectively explore, is the porousness of the body to the world and the ethical implications of this position or perception. How should we be responsible to and for that which constructs and contours our being? How might theatre help us to understand our divisions and distinctions, and more importantly, our most intimate and radical connections?

Notes

1 Humoral theory dominated medical understandings of illness and disease transmission from the classical to early modern period. Largely associated with Hippocrates (ca. 460–370 BCE), it posited that an imbalance of the four humours – black or melancholy bile, yellow or red bile, blood and phlegm – produced sickness.
2 On 16 June 2015, Trump launched his presidential campaign by warning that Mexican migrants were 'bringing crime, they're rapists', and on 5 July 2015 he issued a widely reported statement that Mexicans were responsible for 'tremendous infectious disease … pouring across the border'.
3 For example, on 19 June 2018, President Trump tweeted: 'Democrats [...] want illegal immigrants, no matter how bad they may be, to pour into and infest our Country, like MS-13.' Speaking about the Calais crisis in an interview for ITV aired on 30 July 2015, then UK Prime Minister David Cameron spoke of 'a swarm of people coming across the Mediterranean'.

References

Aristotle ([c. 335 BCE] 2013), *The Poetics of Aristotle*. Available online: https://www.gutenberg.org/files/1974/1974-h/1974-h.htm (accessed 24 September 2018).

Artaud, A. ([1938] 1958), *The Theater and Its Double*, trans. Mary Caroline Richards, New York: Grove Press.

Barthes, R. ([1980] 1982), *Camera Lucida: Reflections on Photography*, trans. Richard Howard, New York: Hill and Wang.

Bartlett, N. (2017), *The Plague* (after *La Peste* by Albert Camus), London: Oberon Books.

Bataille, G. ([1954] 1988), *Inner Experience*, trans. Leslie Anne Boldt, Albany: State University of New York Press.

Bennett, J. (2010), *Vibrant Matter: A Political Ecology of Things*, Durham and London: Duke University Press.

Brennan, T. (2004), *The Transmission of Affect*, New York: Cornell University Press.

Camus, A. ([1947] 2001), *The Plague*, trans. Robin Buss, London: Penguin Books.

Christensen, A. C. (2005), *Nineteenth-century Narratives of Contagion: 'Our Feverist Contact'*, London and New York: Routledge.

Dekker, T. (1607), *The Whore of Babylon*, London: Nathaniel Butter.

Deleuze, G. and F. Guattari ([1980]2004), *A Thousand Plateaus*, London and New York: Continuum.

Douglas, M. ([1996] 2002), *Purity and Danger*, London and New York: Routledge Classics.

Esposito, R. ([2002] 2011), *Immunitas: The Protection and Negation of Life*, Cambridge: Polity Press.
Euripides (2003), *Medea and Other Plays*, London: Penguin Books.
Felton-Dansky, M. (2018), *Viral Performance: Contagious Theaters from Modernism to the Digital Age*, Evanston: Northwestern University Press.
Forset, E. (1607), *A Comparative Discourse of the Bodies Naturall and Politique*, London: John Bill.
Foucault, M. ([2004] 2007), *Security, Territory, Population: Lectures at the Collège de France 1977-1978*, ed. Michel Senellart, Basingstoke and New York: Palgrave Macmillan.
Fracastoro, G. ([1530] 1686), *Syphilis, or, A poetical History of the French Disease Written in Latin by Fracastorius; and Now Attempted in English*, trans. Nahum Tate, London: Jacob Tonson.
Fracastoro, G. ([1946] 1930), *De Contagione et Contagiosis Morbis et eorum curatione*, Libri III, trans. W. C Wright, New York: G. P. Putnam.
Garner, Stanton B., Jr. (2006), 'Artaud, Germ Theory, and the Theatre of Contagion', *Theatre Journal*, 58: 1-14.
Girard, R. ([1972] 2005), *Violence and the Sacred*, trans. Patrick Gregory, London and New York: Continuum.
Gurr, A. (1992), *The Shakespearean Stage 1574-1642: Third Edition*, Cambridge: Cambridge University Press.
Haraway, D. J. (1991), *Simians, Cyborgs, and Woman: The Reinvention of Nature*, London and New York: Routledge.
Hardt, M., and A. Negri (2000), *Empire*, Cambridge, MA: Harvard University Press.
Hatfield, E., J. T. Cacioppo and R. L. Rapson (1994), *Emotional Contagion*, Cambridge: Cambridge University Press.
Ibsen, H. ([1879] 2008), 'A Doll's House', in *Henrik Ibsen: Four Major Plays*, Oxford: Oxford World Classics.
Ionesco, E. (1960), *Rhinoceros, and Other Plays*, trans. Derek Prouse, New York: Grove Press.
Le Bon, G. ([1895] 1960), *The Crowd: A Study of the Popular Mind*, New York: Viking Books.
Miller, A. ([1953] 2000), *The Crucible*, London: Penguin Books.
Nixon, K. and L. Servitje, eds (2016), *Endemic: Essays in Contagion Theory*, London: Palgrave Macmillan.
Plato ([c.380 BCE] 1994), *Republic*, trans. with intro. Robin Waterfield, Oxford: Oxford University Press.
Prochazkova., E. and M. E. Kret (2017), 'Connecting Minds and Sharing Emotions through Mimicry: A Neurocognitive Model of Emotional Contagion', *Neuroscience and Behavioral Reviews*, 80 (September): 99-144.
Rainolds, John ([1599] 2004), 'The Overthrow of Stage-Plays', in Tanya Pollard (ed.), *Shakespeare's Theater: A Sourcebook*, 170-8, Oxford: Blackwell.

Sampson, T.D. (2012), *Virality: Contagion Theory in the Age of Networks*, London and Minneapolis: University of Minnesota Press.

Sigal, S. (2018), 'China Is Treating Islam Like a Mental Illness', *The Atlantic*, 28 August. Available online: https://www.theatlantic.com/international/archive/2018/08/china-pathologizing-uighur-muslims-mental-illness/568525/ (accessed 12 September 2018).

Sontag, S. (1978), *Illness as Metaphor*, New York: Farrar, Strauss and Giroux.

Sophocles (2001), *The Complete Plays*, trans. Paul Roche, New York: Signet Classics.

Sweet, J. (2017), *What Playwrights Talk about When They Talk about Writing*, New Haven, CT: Yale University Press.

Tarde, G. ([1890] 1903), *The Laws of Imitation*, trans. Elsie Clews Parsons, New York: Henry Holt and Company.

Thucydides ([431 BCE] 1972), *History of the Peloponnesian War*, trans. Rex Warner, Harmondsworth: Penguin Books.

Vrettos, A. (1995), *Somatic Fictions: Imagining Illness in Victorian Culture*, Stanford: Stanford University Press.

Yehuda, R., N. P. Daskalakis, L. M. Bierer, H. N. Bader, T. Klengel, F. Holsboer and E. B. Binder (2016), 'Holocaust Exposure Induced Intergenerational Effects on FKBP5 Methylation', *Biological Psychiatry*, 80 (5): 372–80.

Part One

Infectious Bodies and Behaviours

2

Viral Hamlet: History, Memory, Kinship

Fintan Walsh

A chorus of overlapping voices announces the opening of Dickie Beau's *Re-Member Me*: 'I remember ... I can't remember ... If he remembers ... I've forgotten ... one of the many things I've forgotten ... probably provoked by memory ... Must I remember?'[1] Resounding like a ghostly incantation at the Almeida Theatre, London, where the production was first staged in 2017, these words evoke a séance in which the voices of deceased or long-standing players in UK theatre are conjured in the present to query the compulsory invocation of the past. These figures' comments have been cut from recorded interviews – some found, some conducted by Beau himself – as they reflect on their careers, in particular the experience of playing Hamlet or watching the play performed. Relayed over an hour-long performance, these observations circle around the largely forgotten and final performance of Scottish actor Ian Charleson (1949–90) as Hamlet in Richard Eyre's production at the National Theatre in 1989, a role he played while effectively dying of AIDS. In Beau's production, directed by Jan-Willem Van Den Bosch, the ghost's injunction 'remember me' reverberates more as question than a demand. It queries the same words uttered in Robert Icke's production of *Hamlet*, which it was originally programmed to precede,[2] and ripples across the theatre industry and British culture, including the nation-wide events which surrounded it to mark the fiftieth anniversary of the Sexual Offences Act 1967. Spun as an interrogative, verbally and dramaturgically interwoven, Beau's production asks us to consider how certain forms of cultural remembrance and production operate by wilfully forgetting or inoculating against others, in particular queer histories.

This chapter examines how Beau's production finds form in Charleson's illness to elaborate a dramaturgy of contagion that insists the past infects the present. On a visual level, we see this impulse play out in Beau's precise lip-synching, as well as via his imitative speech and gestures. Structurally, we can discern it in the swirl of gossip,[3] ephemera, objects and history that contour the project, as well as amongst the voices, bodies, places, times, feelings and images that crisscross the stage and digital media, creating a sense of psychical and theatrical possession. This form works to temper some of the deleterious effects of biological and cultural destruction due to AIDS by staging surprise cultural connections and transmissions that carve a place for Charleson within queer culture, and for both Charleson and queer culture within UK and Western theatre traditions. Understood in this context, remembrance emerges as both a mode of thinking and doing – the passing and piecing together of bodies, relationships and histories in unpredictable new ways. Ultimately the chapter argues that Beau's approach offers compelling ways for thinking more broadly about medical and cultural interplay by demonstrating the latter's capacity to translate death, disappearance and amnesia into life-sustaining engagements with history, memory and kinship production.

Queer commemoration

In the year of *Re-Member Me*'s premiere, the commemoration of queer cultural history was highly topical in the UK, given that 2017 marked the fiftieth anniversary of the Sexual Offences Act 1967, which partially decriminalized sexual acts between men.[4] Programming by numerous institutions reflected an effort to engage with LGBTQ history and culture. Across television and radio, for instance, the BBC's Gay Britannia season included a wide range of programmes exploring queer history and culture. Tate Britain hosted a major David Hockney exhibition from February to May, which overlapped with Queer British Art 1861–1967, which ran from April to October. In July, the National Theatre marked Pride month and the fiftieth anniversary with a season of Queer Theatre, which featured an array of rehearsed readings, talks, exhibitions and screenings. *Angels in America* took over the Lyttleton stage from April to August before transferring to Broadway, having had its UK premiere in the same theatre in 1992. Opening in Soho Theatre in November, David Hoyle's *Diamond* reflected on LGBTQ life and politics in the UK since the 1950s, refracted through the performer's own biography. Matthew Lopez's *The Inheritance* had its world premiere at the Young Vic in March 2018, whose title in part refers to its meditation on the relationship between a generation of gay men anguished by the AIDS crisis and contemporary one that is not. The commemorative impulse seemed to peak with the announcement in early 2018 of plans to open Queer Britain – the national LGBTQ+ museum.

The desire to celebrate the partial decriminalization of gay male sex ran simultaneous to the urge to reflect upon some of the more painful and unresolved aspects of queer cultural history. Large cities in the UK, though especially London, were devastated by the AIDS crisis in the 1980s and 1990s, including the theatre communities in which gay men worked. According to NHS statistics, in 1994 or earlier, there were 26,939 recordings of HIV, 11,516 of AIDS and 8,901 of related deaths, with 88 per cent of HIV diagnoses being amongst males prior to 1982 (Harker 2010). Across queer communities in the West, incorporating the history of the AIDS crisis into successive generations' sense of the past has been a fraught affair, in part because of a desire to leave the past behind, made possible by changes in societal attitudes and law and advancements in antiretroviral treatment. Indeed, the justification for any attachment to this morbid past at all has been thrown into question in more recent years with the development of pre-exposure prophylaxis (PrEP) medication, which has already contributed to the dramatic drop in HIV acquisition (Public Health England 2017: 2).[5] When, from the vantage point of the present, the future of queer culture does not seem so tragically inclined as its past, some question the value of keeping that history alive. Should the dawn of immunity from disease (for some at least) warrant immunity from its remembrance and cultural legacy?

Remembering the dead

Dickie Beau (Richard Boyce) is a London-based performer and theatre maker whose work has ranged from club drag to theatre and film acting. His individual practice is founded in an unruly archaeological method that responds to found materials – voice recordings, digital cuts, recovered footage, text, images and objects – reorganizing them in surprising, often weird ways to afford them new life in the present. Beau's three other main productions to date – *Blackouts: Twilights of the Idols* (2011), *Lost in Trans* (2013) and *Camera Lucida* (2014) – are all concerned with remembering the dead via their obscure remains by letting their voices speak through the performer's meticulously ventriloquizing lips. Beau describes his mode as a type of playback theatre, which draws on drag and spiritualist traditions to channel lost or forgotten lives, with the aim of serving as 'a live performing archive of the missing' (Beau 2016a).

Many are missing in *Re-Member Me* with none but Beau present on stage. The performer draws on interviews he conducted with actor Ian McKellen and directors Eyre and Sean Mathias, alongside other recordings featuring the actor John Gielgud, Beau's former agent John Wood, and John Peter, former chief drama critic at *The Sunday Times*, as they comment on

Hamlet or those who performed the title role. In addition to McKellen and Gielgud, other famous actors mentioned in the production who played the prince include Simon Russell Beale, Kenneth Branagh, Alan Cummings, Daniel Day-Lewis, Ralph Fiennes, Mel Gibson, Jeremy Northam, Peter O'Toole, Michael Pennington, Jonathan Pryce, Roger Rees, Alan Rickman, Mark Rylance, Jonathan Slinger and Ben Whishaw. According to Beau, by drawing on all these figures and voices his aim was to create 'a human Hamlet mix-tape [...] Part documentary theatre, part twenty first century séance' (Beau 2016b).

The opening conceit is that Beau feels he will never get to play Hamlet, a role which leading actors often pass through and imprint.[6] Expressed against a rendition of the Village People's 'YMCA' (followed by a snippet of Barbara Streisand's 'Papa Can You Hear Me?'), while wearing rainbow sweatbands, Beau's campness and queerness are given to undermine his capacity to be a leading man. However, the production proceeds to foreground how many of the actors who have played the role were in fact gay men – Beale, Charleson, Cummings, Gielgud, McKellen, Rees, Whishaw, and Andrew Scott on the contemporaneous Almeida run – suggesting a persistent if often concealed or tacit connection between queerness and Hamlet. But there is nothing subtle about Beau's sexuality on stage, and in his performance of not being Hamlet, he allows for the queerness of the lineage to be seen while implicitly positioning himself within it.

Charleson's final performance as Hamlet forms the centrepiece of the production. A successful actor in his lifetime, Charleson arrived to play Hamlet fresh from acclaimed recent performances as Brick in Tennessee Williams's *Cat on a Hot Tin Roof* and Eddie in Sam Shepard's *Fool for Love*. But Charleson's memory has largely been forgotten within UK and queer theatre culture, partly because he died so young of AIDS-related illness and partly because his performance was over-shadowed by taking on the role from Day-Lewis (following a short stint by Jeremy Northam) who left the production mid-run, to claims he saw his own father on stage (some reports maintained he originally made and later retracted the claim for being misconstrued, and the official reason eventually given was exhaustion).[7] Charleson only played the part from 9 October to 13 November, and seeing as he was visibly sick at the time, his family requested that the National Theatre did not make any photographs available to the public following his death.[8] Despite his obvious illness, most audiences did not know that Charleson was so unwell, or that Hamlet would be his final role, dying as he did eight weeks after he left the production. But for a small number of people, including his friend McKellen, this knowledge made Charleson's feat all the more momentous and Hamlet's meditation on mourning and death particularly powerful. Charleson's Hamlet was, to all intents and purposes, dying in front of the audiences' eyes.

McKellen relays Charleson's life and final performance in greatest colour and detail. A gifted young actor, Charleson was involved in the early years of gay activism in the UK. Immediately prior to playing Hamlet in 1989, he played Greta in Martin Sherman's *Bent* for one night only at London's Adelphi Theatre to raise money for the founding of Stonewall, his body reported to have been covered with Kaposi's sarcoma at the time (Benedict 1995).[9] McKellen recalls concerns amongst friends who knew Charleson was sick that he should not take on the part as there would be nowhere to hide in a role like Hamlet. During rehearsals Charleson underwent chemotherapy and radiation and had an operation for a chronic sinus infection, which many reviews reported, without mention of the underlying cause.[10] Charleson also suffered sight problems, and cast members and friends observed his weight loss and facial disfigurement (see Davidson 1999).[11] But for McKellen, Charleson's sickness sort of infected his performance by infusing Hamlet's mortal preoccupations with Charleson's own. 'It was revelatory,' McKellen's voice tells us, via Beau's lips, 'an actor talking from his own experience about the prospect of death'.

In his published diaries, Eyre writes that when Charleson agreed to take on the role in August 1989, they did not discuss his HIV-positive status (which he received early in 1986), but that it was 'there as an unspoken subtext' (2003: 82). According to fellow cast member Judith Coke, Charleson performed his dying with intent: 'he made the deliberate choice to play the part of a dying man – or, at least, a man in love with death, because he was in a unique position to do so' (quoted in Davidson 1999: 173). Coke even recalls Charleson say of himself: 'I bet I'm the best qualified Hamlet they'll see – I'm not coming back from the bourn, either, and I want to see the truth of it' (Davidson 1999: 173).

Recalling Charleson deliver the line 'Oh that this too too solid flesh would melt,' the voice of actor Suzanne Bertish describes how he collapsed on the floor of the Olivier stage, to which the audience responded with a standing ovation. 'Oh. I remember that. At the end, and I have never seen this, in England, for a Shakespeare ... at the end two thirds of the audience just stood. Not a few people. Just stood! They knew they had witnessed something deeply profound,' she says. This had the effect of rupturing the integrity of the play's representational mode, as unlike other actors, Charleson was effectively dying himself. According to McKellen, this made Charleson's delivery all the more impactful: 'You know, you play Hamlet, we all know he's going to jump up at the end and take the curtain call and go off to a club. Turn up and give this performance again tomorrow. But with Ian … He's dying in front of our eyes.' Charleson took the knowledge of this own imminent death, McKellen suggests, 'and gave that to Hamlet', making for an extraordinary performance, standing ovations and critical acclaim.

The voices recounting Charleson are either lip-synched by Beau on stage or sound across screens with prerecorded footage. Occasionally Beau stands front of stage, other times he mimes in silhouette (Figure 2.1). He dresses and undresses mannequins standing in for the cast of Hamlet at one point, using costumes retrieved from previous productions, surrounded by medical screens (Figure 2.2). In this moment, Charleson's illness is added to Hamlet's layered performance history, and Beau's theatre practice framed as both surgical and replete with care. As if representing Charleson's death, and foreshadowing his own, Beau places a mannequin in a medical stretcher. If *Hamlet* is, as Marvin Carlson asserts, the 'most haunted of all Western dramas' (2001: 4), Beau's production is explicitly and markedly so with every performer mentioned, speaking and present, already a spectre or one in the making – including Beau.

Figure 2.1 Dickie Beau lip-synching in silhouette on stage and across prerecorded video. Photo by Robin Fisher, courtesy of Almeida Theatre.

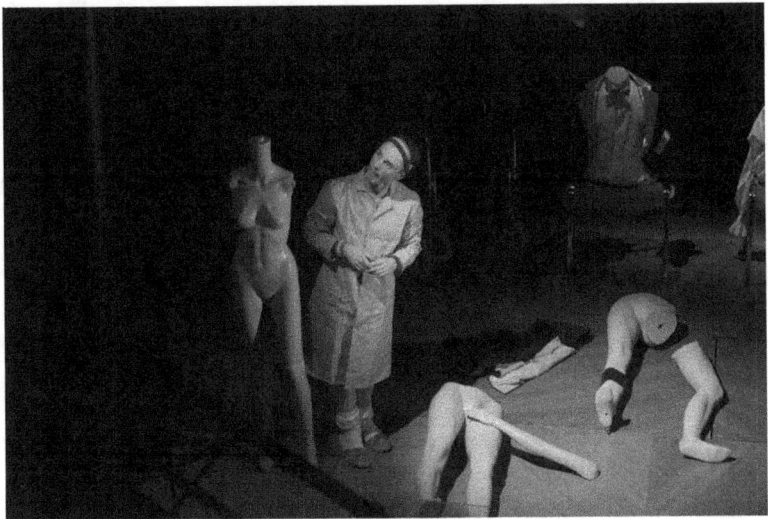

Figure 2.2 Dickie Beau dressing and undressing mannequins with old theatre costumes. Photo by Robin Fisher, courtesy of Almeida Theatre.

Dramaturgies of contagion

When Shakespeare's Hamlet speaks directly of contagion in Act 3, Scene 2, he too is reflecting on the persistent influence of the dead on the living. Preparing for revenge, the protagonist's soliloquy likens his time of action to 'when churchyards yawn and hell itself breathes out / Contagion to this world' (3.2.379–80). This comparison imagines a noxious portal between life and death that no one can escape, and indeed it stirs Hamlet's own desire to 'drink hot blood' (3.2.380). The word 'contagion' appears again in Act 4, Scene 7, when Laertes announces his plans to take Hamlet's life with a poisoned sword. This reference sits alongside many other allusions to corruption and contamination in the play, and it is poison which is largely responsible for the drama's infamous mound of corpses. But here contagion may also operate as a veiled reference to the bubonic plague which had erupted intermittently across Europe since the fourteenth century with devastating effects, ending with the Great Plague of London in 1665–6. (Indeed, this period was the main focus of *Ten Plagues* (2011), a song cycle written by Mark Ravenhill and performed by Marc Almond, which appeared to insinuate connections between the seventeenth century epidemic and the AIDS crisis.) A number of major outbreaks occurred during Shakespeare's own lifetime in London, with those of 1563 and 1603 each eliminating one quarter of the city's population, while often forcing the closure of its theatres for prolonged periods of time, including in 1581–2, 1592–3, 1603–4, 1608–9, 1609–10, 1625, 1630, 1636–7 and 1640 (Gurr 1992: 78). *Hamlet* was written sometime between 1599 and 1601, so it is highly possible that Shakespeare was reckoning with plague's real impact as well as its metaphoric force.

We can say, then, that *Hamlet* has been steeped in plague since its origins – absorbing and emitting it in historical and metaphorical ways. Elsinore, like Thebes before it, is a sick city, and almost everyone is affected while Hamlet strives to locate its source. According to Derek A. Traversi, *Hamlet* is fundamentally about the diseased state, and the play hurtles towards this revelation (1956: 94). Eric S. Mallin takes the idea further by claiming that plague is internalized within the play's dramatic structure as a crisis of form that produces unstructuring. The 'language of bodily corruption metastasises', Mallin maintains, resulting in 'a progressive dispersal of weakness, delusion, passion, and violent physical decomposition among a growing number of susceptible bodies' (1995: 65).

Audiences are also implicated in these dramaturgies of contagion. Some spectators of Shakespeare's theatre did know of the plague's very real threat, and the dangers of its acquisition in crowded public spaces, but we can only speculate that for some it was risk worth taking. But audiences are unlikely to have paid much heed to the difference between medical and cultural contagion due in part to a less distinct sense of where the body stopped and the world began. We can see this play out in Hamlet's own braided references to contagion, which simultaneously signal the stench of decaying bodies, the open border between death and life, and the fuel for vengeance: contagion is real and symbolic, but it is also a theatrical trigger. Similarly, but in very different context, at the initial outbreak of the AIDS crisis in Western urban centres, some audiences and performers believed they were putting themselves at risk by attending or making theatre due to confusion and misinformation around the acquisition of HIV/AIDS. In some theatres, particularly those with openly gay performers, fears circulated that AIDS could be acquired via all bodily fluids, including from saliva and sweat passed around in make-up, costumes, wigs and as a result of close bodily contact (Shnayerson 2013). These ideas did not necessarily colour most audiences' experience of watching Charleson's Hamlet, as he did not actively foreground his personal life, though he was degenerating before their eyes. Nonetheless, as his friends have disclosed, Charleson deliberately channelled his experience into his portrayal and even requested that his condition be made known to the public after his death in a bid to raise awareness of HIV and AIDS (McKellen 1990).

Beau's *Re-Member Me* is deeply rooted in this complex production history of *Hamlet*, and it absorbs the viral into its dramaturgy through strategies of imitation, cross-fertilization and transmission. Although the production emerges more directly from the shadow of AIDS, it offers itself as a sort of cultural antidote, redressing biological death with cultural retrieval, renewal and reinvention. While in a psychoanalytic sense it functions as a work of mourning that strives to find form for grieving the great unmourned, it is more fundamentally invested in the material reorganization of queer, UK, even Western theatrical history. Beau's dramaturgy draws together displaced or unlikely combinations of gossip, ephemera and objects, and the unanticipated intersecting of voices, bodies, places, times, feelings and images. Illness is dramaturgically rerouted as a *dis-ease* with hierarchical and sanitized formulations of history and culture.

While the common medical understanding of contagion is a transmissible disease, less sinisterly the word draws on the Latin *con* (with, together) and *tangere* (to touch).[12] Embedded within this etymology we can detect the relational and affective possibilities of contagious thought and practice – the touching together as well as the tearing apart it denotes. This layered conceptualization permits us to understand a contagious dramaturgy as one invested in the proliferative cross-contamination and circulation of matter and emotion via structuring techniques, representational media and affective technologies on stage as well as amongst audiences. In the case of *Re-Member Me*, we witness Charleson's prematurely halted life and career revived via dramaturgical strategies which allow their impact and legacy to ignite the present. If, for Aristotle, tragedy purges the emotions, especially pity and fear (Aristotle c.335 BCE [2013]), *Re-Member Me*'s queer dramaturgy unleashes a flow of voices, images and ghosts that refuse to be stopped by aesthetic or historical closure.

The live production is not only haunted by absent bodies but visual scratches and auditory scrambles across digital media. In playing with machinic spectres like this, the production also nods to the Wooster Group's *Hamlet* (2007), which is haunted by intrusions of Richard Burton's lauded film portrayal of the prince. More can be found in Icke's *Hamlet* in which Elsinore is surrounded by CCTV footage and televised news that variously relay mysterious apparitions and short circuits. In one sense, these devices and effects give weight to Simon Critchley and Jamieson Webster's claim that '*Hamlet* is arguably the drama of surveillance in a police state' (2013: 48), but on the other they create a sense of Beau's world trying to break through – especially if you had seen his production first, as originally scheduled. That which has been untransmissable due to AIDS, and cultural hostility towards homosexuality, becomes transmitted in Beau's production, with histories and bodies passed around and pieced together in new and often extraordinary ways.

This dramaturgy not only derives inspiration from AIDS's viral form but from regulations enacted by the law. The Sexual Offence Act 1967 did not fully legalize male homosexuality but rather decriminalized it under certain conditions. In fact, some reports claimed that gay people were policed more aggressively in its wake. According to research conducted by Peter Tatchell, 420 men were convicted of gross indecency in 1966, and by 1974 this figure had increased to over 1,700. This continued into the 1980s and 1990s, in no small part owing to the anxiety and paranoia generated by the AIDS crisis. Over 15,000 gay men are estimated to have been convicted in the decades that followed the 1967 Act (Tatchell 2017).

The fact that the Act did not herald clean progress is evidenced by the introduction of Section 28 in 1988 to the Local Government Act 1986, which affected England, Scotland and Wales. The clause compounded the homophobia of the time, which was heightened due to the anxieties around the transmission of HIV/AIDS, and extended to an antipathy towards queer culture. Enacted on 24 May 1988, the amendment stated that a local authority should not

(a) intentionally promote homosexuality or publish material with the intention of promoting homosexuality;
(b) promote the teaching in any maintained school of the acceptability of homosexuality as a pretended family relationship. (Local Government Act 1988: 27)

While the clause continues to state that these conditions 'shall be taken to prohibit the doing of anything for the purpose of treating or preventing the spread of disease' (Local Government Act 1988: 27), it is itself clearly invested in inoculating against the (presumed) transmissibility of homosexuality and queer culture.

Discussing the effect of Section 28 on queer theatre of the time, Catherine Silverstone suggests that while it did not have significant direct legal impact, it had a number of implicit consequences. Silverstone maintains that the clause offered a legal basis for homophobia in local authority contexts and encouraged self-censorship: 'it had the potential to minimize gay or lesbian visibility as constituted by various groups, particularly in the arts where "fringe" theatre groups are often dependent on local authority funding' (2011: 96). Additionally, Silverstone argues that the wording also 'links homosexuality with the spread of disease and works to reinforce negative perceptions of homosexuality, especially in relation to gay men, compounded by the HIV/AIDS crisis' (2011: 96). Despite these damaging effects, Silverstone claims it had the unexpected outcome of galvanizing queer culture against its own containment, spurring on the birth of Stonewall and queer theatre, including path-breaking work by Gay Sweatshop.

If we were to describe the dramaturgy of law, and Section 28 in particular, we might perceive its structure to be hierarchical and divisive, directed at the separation and containment of people, culture and values. But this is not all the law is. For Roy Cohen in *Angels in America*, speaking from the inside as an attorney, 'the Law's a pliable, breathing, sweating ... *organ*' (Kushner 1992: 66). Beau's production shares a sense of the law's porosity and physicality, its capacity to be intercepted by culture as well as to regulate it. As an intervention in commemorating the Sexual Offences Act, *Re-Member Me* endeavours to rewrite the law's punishing effects by becoming a conduit for recording otherwise ignored or vilified subjects and stories. The production does not so much as un-closet queer Hamlets as it allows for now widely known aspects of performers' sexuality and queer cultural history, including AIDS, to filter into our understanding of the role and its legacy, and the impact of queer performers in the UK. While Charleson's final performance is central, we also hear McKellen recall how gay actors were reluctant to come out in the 1980s as the word 'gay was thought to be the worst thing you could say about a young person, or any man'. Gielgud was charged for cottaging in 1953, which gravely affected him personally, as well as damaging his career.[13] And while Beau is not directly affected by these laws, he believes he may be perceived as being too gay to play Hamlet for contemporary sensibilities. But as the production unfolds, homosexuality and Hamlet are recurring bedfellows. Despite the opening conceit, Beau shares a lot in common with Hamlet, as he reckons with the ghosts of his forefathers to reflect on his significance in the scheme of things. But Beau also exceeds Hamlet's dilemma by being the conjurer of the production, who controls the order of bodies and spirits. Around Beau, the stage is scattered with the traces of old productions and frustrated ambitions, which are ultimately channelled into a different theatrical purpose.

Transmitting kinship

Hamlet has been interpreted from innumerable critical perspectives, including being understood as a play that offers insight on desire, mourning, power and family dynamics, amongst others. Certainly traditional family relations have become corrupt, 'more than kin and less than kind' as Hamlet puts it to Claudius (1.2.65). Some critics have discerned queerness in the play's identity gaps and frustrations. For example, Lee Edelman locates queerness in Hamlet's battle with intergenerational succession, torn between the burden of remembering his father and reproducing the paternal line, and his desire to escape this order of expectation. As Edelman posits, '"Remember me" is the fatal text the past inscribes on the Child, preventing the Child from living a life *not* out of joint with time' (2011: 104). In reports claiming Day-Lewis left the National Theatre production having seen his own father, the deceased poet Cecil Day-Lewis, as Hamlet saw his, this intergenerational tension plays out in the most thrilling terms. But part of Hamlet's recurring appeal to successive generations, Edelman suggests, is that 'something keeps him from ever escaping the role of his father's son' (2011: 104). (The same concern permeates his charge to Ophelia, 'Why would'st thou be a breeder of sinners?' [3.1.120–1].) Hamlet's is the anxiety of reproduction which affects us all, according to Edelman, which propels him to murder to escape the otherwise inescapable.

The subject of reproduction plays out in *Re-Member Me* in its meditation on the relationship between queer death and the transmission of queer culture, which finds itself amplified by Hamlet's own preoccupations with lineage. If Beau is our not-Hamlet, Charleson is the ghost summoned to alert us to the crime of the obscuration of queer culture within theatre history. Soon into the performance, a voice asks: 'Do you feel there is an acting tradition that is passed on from one generation to another?' We hear Gielgud respond: 'I think it's a great advantage for one's survival in people's memories if you've played the great classics.' Gielgud's comment acknowledges the status of *Hamlet* in the building of artistic reputation and legacy, but in Beau's production it also alerts us to the impact of AIDS on the death of generations of gay men. In a 1993 issue of *Newsweek*, devoted to discussing the effects of AIDS after the initial outbreak, this point was made forcefully by Gordon Davidson, artistic director of the Mark Taper Forum in Los Angeles, which originally produced Tony Kushner's *Angels in America*. According to Davidson, 'The problem, aside from the horror of the deaths, is that the system by which we encounter art is a system of passing things down, and when you break the circuit the way it is being broken by AIDS, the damage may be irreparable' (Ansen 1993). Flesh may always be heir to 'the heart-ache and the thousand natural shocks', as it is in *Hamlet* (3.1.61), but Beau's production posits intergenerational curiosity and theatre production, sociality and art as important agents of cultural transmission and kinship building capable of countering more difficult circumstances and histories.

In his contentious work on barebacking subcultures, Tim Dean has discussed how the wilful acquisition of HIV via unprotected sex should not so much be understood as an antisocial gesture but one invested in the creation of kinship across bodily and generational divides. This is a form of kinship in which relationships are forged around those who have acquired and transmitted the virus, from one person to another, from one generation to another, such that the 'human immunodeficiency virus may be used to create blood ties, ostensibly permanent forms of bodily and communal affiliation' (Dean 2008: 82). Exchanging viral load instead of wedding rings, Dean proposes, invites us 'to think about barebacking as the basis for not only one's sexual identity but also one's place in a kinship network' (Dean 2008: 82). Dean's reading of barebacking takes seriously how biological or medical contagion breeds social formation in the form of kinship construction. His research responds to a time in the United States just before the advent of PrEP and marriage equality, which have already broadened the way queers might think about sexuality and health, relationships and social participation and recognition. While it may be difficult for some to imagine so-called bug-chasing as affirmative intimacy and not traumatic repetition, particularly given legal and medical changes since Dean's study was published, the project's sense of the need, within some communities, to stay close to the history of HIV in its identity construction is convincing and something which runs through *Re-Member Me* too. However, in *Re-Member Me*, theatre making across boundaries of time, place, form and embodiment becomes a strategy for forging and preserving queer attachments, supplementing, if not supplanting, conventions of legal partnership and structures of theatrical authority and cultural hierarchy.[14]

The enmeshment of kinship in historical attachments more closely resembles what Elizabeth Freeman describes as erotohistoriography. For Freeman, erotohistoriography denotes a mode of historical inquiry that accedes to the persistence of the past in the present and our desirous attachments to this unfinished business, using the body to effect, figure or perform that temporal encounter. 'Erotohistoriography admits that contact with historical materials can be precipitated by particular bodily dispositions,' Freeman posits, 'and that these connections may elicit bodily responses, even pleasurable ones that are themselves a form of understanding. It sees the body as a method, and historical consciousness as something intimately involved with corporeal sensations' (2010: 95–6). Central to Freeman's model is the notion that the body is both a material and historical contact zone, an interface of biological, affective, conscious and unconscious transmissions. Beau's production stages an encounter with the past by positioning his body as a radically open meeting point between other bodies, voices, feelings and histories. Following Freeman and Dean, Beau's performance can be seen to ask us to imagine an erotics as well as a theatrics of contagion, in which attachments to historical and cultural transmissions are central to the sustenance and reproduction of culture. These attachments are not just consciously willed, but the means by which we are already possessed by history. Contagion, in this context, refers not just to a dramaturgical form, but to the ways in which bodies, subjectivities, affects and histories intermingle across time, reminding us of our place within the commune of queer ghosts.

The single isolated artefact which records Charleson's performance as Hamlet is a review by John Peter for the *Sunday Times* whom Beau meets to interview in preparation for the show. It is a glowing account, which focuses on Charleson but spins out to make comment on acting more broadly. The show closes with an audio recording of Peter reading out his original review: 'The way someone like Charleson can transform a production is a reminder that actors are alive and well, that directors can only draw a performance from those who have one in them, and that in the last analysis the voice of drama speaks to us through actors, the abstract chroniclers of the time, and princes not lightly to be dethroned.' The final lines echo Hamlet's own closing lines in which he confirms: 'Fortinbras: he has my dying voice' (5.2.340). That Fortinbras now has Hamlet's voice can be taken to mean he is his ordained surrogate in a way that mirrors Beau's assumed relationship with Charleson and the other queer voices he invokes. If, as in the ACT UP campaigns, silence equals death, for Hamlet death equals silence – 'the rest is silence' being his last utterance (5.2.342). In his lip-synching Beau too is often silent but only to choreograph these equations of silence and death into a different relation so that a chorus of voices representing LGBTQ culture and AIDS activism may enter into dialogue with long-standing existential dilemmas of UK theatre and canonical Western drama more broadly.

Conclusion

At the heart of Beau's *Re-Member Me* is a story about one actor's death due to AIDS at the height of the crisis, a loss compounded by the lack of record of his last performance as Hamlet in the National Theatre and the fading of his career from memory. Beau's dramaturgy finds its form in Charleson's death, against a backdrop of cultural anxiety around the transmission of HIV/AIDS, and gives the man new life by conducting interviews, sourcing others, evoking his life through imitation, memories, moving images, voice recordings, props, materials and reviews. These are interlinked with other theatrical anecdotes, attesting to experiences of playing Hamlet or seeing the role performed. Beau's performance becomes a vehicle of queer cultural transmission, which signposts methods for constructing and sustaining queer histories, while reshaping UK and Western theatre traditions. In practice, it takes the form of a dramaturgy of contagion in which voices are lip-synched and gestures mimicked, and via which histories, bodies and relationships are found, cut, merged, reformed in unexpected and transformative ways. This mode is offered as a way of reanimating those lives affected by social and biological death, infecting the present with the past and offering strategies for cultural cross-fertilization and continuation.

For Carlson, theatre is a 'repository of cultural memory' but is also open to modification and readjustment in new circumstances. 'The present experience is always ghosted by previous experiences and associations,' Carlson tells us, 'while these ghosts are simultaneously shifted and modified by the processes of recycling and recollection' (2001: 2). The queer remembrance of *Re-Member Me*, then, is a gesture of incorporation as well as invention, which frustrates the cheery commemoration of a world believed by many to belong to another time and place, as well as the status of Shakespeare within the canon, and normative readings of *Hamlet*. But it also shows theatre to be a crucial agent of kinship building that does not just represent social relations but produces them in the present, bridging the living and the dead and those to come. This is exemplified by Beau's gesture of offering out-of-joint (and out-of-body) voices a place on his stage and in his throat so that history, memory and culture need not die even if bodies must.

Notes

1 All *Re-Member Me* quotes are taken from the unpublished manuscript provided by the artist.
2 Icke's *Hamlet* played at the Almeida Theatre from February to April 2017 before transferring to the Harold Pinter Theatre in the West End in June. *Re-Member Me* was programmed for a number of nights between March and April of this initial run, taking place on the same set. It has since toured nationally and internationally, including to Under the Radar Festival in New York (2018), Melbourne International Arts Festival (2018) and Perth Festival (2019). Birkbeck's Wellcome Trust Institutional Strategic Support Fund contributed a small financial award towards the development of the project in its early stages, and a version was performed as part of the Theatres of Contagion: Infectious Performance conference hosted at the university in May 2017 from which this publication arose.

3   Eve Kosofsky Sedgwick suggests that in European thought, gossip has been devalued in its association with servants, effeminate and gay men, and all women. Less to do with the 'transmission of necessary news', Sedgwick suggests, gossip can be concerned 'with the refinement of necessary skills for making, testing, and using unrationalized and provisional hypotheses about what *kinds of people* there are to be found in one's world' (1990: 23).
4   The Act decriminalized sex between men over twenty-one in private. It affected England and Wales but did not apply to the Armed Forces or Merchant Navy. Homosexual Acts were decriminalized in Scotland in 1980, taking effect in 1981 (under the Criminal Justice (Scotland) Act 1980) and in Northern Ireland in 1982 (under the Homosexual Offences (Northern Ireland) Order 1982).
5   In 2016 Public Health England reported a 21 per cent decrease in new diagnoses amongst gay and bisexual men, although acquisitions had been rising steadily since 2007.
6   The programme for Eyre's production recognizes this by featuring a three-page overview of actors who have played Hamlet throughout the play's history, from Richard Burbage to Jonathan Pryce.
7   Richard Eyre's *Hamlet* opened on 10 March 1989 and closed on 13 December of the same year. It opened with Day-Lewis in the title role, which was taken over by Northam, then Charleson and then Northam again.
8   This information comes courtesy of the National Theatre Archive. In addition to the absence of photographic record, it was not common practice to record productions until the mid-1990s.
9   McKellen recalls how both he and Charleson were also involved in The Arts Lobby, founded in 1988 to contest Section 28, by arguing it was an attack on culture as well as homosexuals. On 5 June 1988, one month after the law had been enacted, Charleson and McKellen participated in a protest gala at Piccadilly Theatre which provocatively featured work that could be seen to actively 'promote' homosexuality. Two weeks later, McKellen came out as a gay man on Radio 3 at the age of 49. See 'Section 28/The Arts Lobby', available online: http://www.mckellen.com/activism/section28.htm (accessed 21 June 2018).
10 See reviews from *Guardian*, *Standard* and *Financial Times* in National Theatre Archive.
11 Davidson's article includes a detailed analysis of Charleson's performance and quotes from the cast and crew whom he interviewed.
12 See 'contagion' entry in *Oxford English Dictionary* or *Online Etymology Dictionary*.
13 Nicholas de Jongh's play *Plague over England* (2008) explores events surrounding Gielgud's arrest.
14 Legislation to allow for same-sex marriages in England, Wales and Scotland came into effect in 2014.

References

Ansen, D. (1993), 'AIDS and the Arts: A Lost Generation', *Newsweek*, 17 January. Available online: http://europe.newsweek.com/lost-generation-192398?rm=eu (accessed 21 June 2018).

Aristotle ([c. 335 BCE] 2013), *Poetics*, trans. with intro. Anthony Kenny, Oxford: Oxford University Press.

Beau, Dickie (2016a), 'Lost in Trans'. Available online: http://dickiebeau.com/portfolio/lost-in-trans-2/ (accessed 21 June 2018).

Beau, Dickie (2016b), 'Re-Member Me'. Available online: http://dickiebeau.com/portfolio/re-member-me/ (accessed 21 June 2018).

Benedict, D. (1995), 'Good Night, Sweet Prince', *Independent*, 6 January. Available online: https://www.independent.co.uk/arts-entertainment/theatre-good-night-sweet-prince-1566786.html (accessed 21 June 2018).

Carlson, M. (2001), *The Haunted Stage: The Theatre as Memory Machine*, Ann Arbor: The University of Michigan Press.

Critchley, S. and J. Webster (2013), *The Hamlet Doctrine*, London: Verso.

Davidson, R. A. (1999), 'The Readiness Was All: Ian Charleson and Richard Eyre's *Hamlet*', in Lois Potter and Arthur F. Kinney (eds), *Shakespeare: Text and Theater*, 170–82, New Jersey: Associated University Presses.

Dean, T. (2008), 'Breeding Culture: Barebacking, Bugchasing, Giftgiving', *Massachusetts Review*, 49 (1&2): 80–94.

Edelman, L. (2011), 'Hamlet's Wounded Name', in M. Menon (ed.), *Shakesqueer: A Queer Companion to the Complete Works of Shakespeare*, Durham: Duke University Press.

Eyre, R. (2003), *National Service: Diary of a Decade at the National Theatre*, London: Bloomsbury Publishing.

Freeman, E. (2010), *Time Binds: Queer Temporalities, Queer Histories*, Durham: Duke University Press.

Gurr, Andrew (1992), *The Shakespearean Stage 1574–1642: Third Edition*, Cambridge: Cambridge University Press.

Harker, R. (2010), 'HIV and AIDS Statistics'. Available online: http://www.nhshistory.net/aidsdata.pdf (accessed 21 June 2018).

Kosofsky Sedgwick, E. (1990), *Epistemology of the Closet*, Berkeley: University of California Press.

Kushner, T. (1992), *Angels in America, Part One: Millennium Approaches*, New York: Theater Communications Group.

Local Government Act 1988. Available online: https://www.legislation.gov.uk/ukpga/1988/9/pdfs/ukpga_19880009_en.pdf (accessed 21 June 2018).

Mallin, E. S. (1995), *Shakespeare and the End of Elizabethan England*, Los Angeles: University of California Press.

McKellen, I. (1990), 'Ian Charleson: Tribute', *Ian McKellen Writings*. Available online: http://www.mckellen.com/writings/90charleson.htm (accessed 21 June 2018).

Public Health England (2017), 'HIV in the United Kingdom: Decline in New HIV Diagnoses in Gay and Bisexual Men in London'. Available online: https://www.gov.uk/government/uploads/system/uploads/attachment_data/file/648913/hpr3517_HIV_AA.pdf (accessed 21 June 2018).

Ravenhill, M. (2011), *'Ten Plagues' and 'The Coronation of Poppea'*, London: Methuen Drama.

Sexual Offences Act 1967. Available online: http://www.legislation.gov.uk/ukpga/1967/60/pdfs/ukpga_19670060_en.pdf (accessed 21 June 2018).

Shakespeare, W. (2006), *Hamlet*, eds Ann Thompson and Neil Taylor, London: The Arden Shakespeare.

Shnayerson, M. (2013), 'One by One', *Vanity Fair*, 21 August. Available online: http://www.vanityfair.com/culture/1987/03/devastation-of-aids-1980s (accessed 21 June 2018).

Silverstone, C. (2011), *Shakespeare, Trauma and Contemporary Performance*, London and New York: Routledge.

Tatchell, P. (2017), 'Sexual Offences Act 1967: Reform and Repression'. Available online: http://www.petertatchellfoundation.org/sexual-offences-act-1967-reform-and-repression/ (accessed 21 June 2018).

Traversi, D. A. (1956), *An Approach to Shakespeare*, 2nd edn, New York: Doubleday.

3

'A plague o' both your houses': Auditory Contagion and Affective Frequencies in Musical and Intercultural Theatres

Marcus Cheng Chye Tan

Contagion, affect and sound

In Shakespeare's *Romeo and Juliet* (1595), Mercutio's infamous curse, 'A plague o' both your houses!' (3.1.92), exemplifies the potency of affective frequencies. In the play, the pronounced utterance thrice repeated becomes a contagious sonic vibration that initiates the missteps and miscommunications that lead to the eventual tragedy that befalls the star-crossed lovers. It is an 'infectious pestilence' (5.2.10) that delays Friar Lawrence's messenger which then leads to Romeo never receiving the notice; this results in a chain of events that culminates in the tragic end. Whether these events are a consequence of Mercutio's impassioned exclamation is inconclusive but for the early modern audience, curses were potent contagions that when enunciated reverberated with affective frequencies which manipulated reality; it is not merely in the semantics in which curses possess power but the sonicity and sonority – the sounds – that enact change to both the metaphysical and physical planes. As sound, curses move bodies, human and non-human, physical and metaphysical through affective energy.

Music scholars agree that sound as music, its expressive qualities and capacity to move listeners physically, psychologically and emotionally, is its distinct characteristic. Contagion, understood as 'one emotional state, appearance, or condition [...] transmitted to a person (or creature) who comes to undergo the same emotion' (Davies 2011: 138), occurs when one 'catches' the affective state of another outside awareness (Hatfield et al. 1994: 5). As Davies argues, music's expressiveness 'can induce an emotional reaction and [...] the listener is moved to feel the emotion that the music expresses' (2013: 169). This 'mirroring' response and the communication of emotion from music to listener is emotional contagion or infection (2013: 169). Genres, styles and forms of music are used to create mood and atmosphere in various conditions, given its capacities to shift mental states and dictate emotional response: dance music, for example, affects bodies as synchronous motions and can induce trance-like states. It excites bodies to the established rhythms and acts as 'affective glue' (Thompson and Biddle 2013: 11) that adjoins remote bodies.

In considering the implications of sound and music's affective capacities in performance, this chapter will examine the ways in which music operates via affective frequencies that infect spectating and listening bodies with change. The chapter will examine how music is used in intercultural and musical theatres to stimulate and *affect* expressions of vitality (Priest 2013: 45). It will focus primarily on rhythm and ritual, their sonicity, as affect and affective. These considerations will be framed by Susanne Langer's understanding of affect as a symbolic and speculative event, of what it feels like to feel oneself affecting and being affected as an occasion of experience, understood as the experience of 'a qualitative-relational order in their mode of being felt as thought' (Priest 2013: 46). Critically comparing a musical adaptation of Shakespeare's *Romeo and Juliet* – Jerome Robins's *West Side Story* (2017) – and an intercultural variation – the National Changgeuk Company of Korea's *Romyo and Juri* (2009) – the chapter will explore the interpersonal/inter-bodily relations between spectating and performing bodies affected by music's rhythmic affect as potentiality of/in finger-snapping and dance movement, as well as in traditional Korean shaman rituals, employed in the respective productions. It will further explore the movement from affect to effect – of how affective frequencies move receiving bodies and effect an experiential disruption of signification vis-à-vis an interpretation of Shakespeare's *Romeo and Juliet*.

Sound and music indubitably induce, activate and arouse feelings and emotions but sound is also affect. While they are intimately associated, affect is distinct from and other to emotion. Affect is an 'oscillating difference, an intensity that moves bodies, a vibration physically pushing and pulling their material fabric' (Gallagher 2016: 43). It is not emotion for affect is the 'fluctuations of "feeling" that shape the experiential in ways that may impact upon but nevertheless evade conscious knowing' (Thompson and Biddle 2013: 6). It is found in the infectious intensities that move between bodies, body to body, human, non-human, part-body, and otherwise (Seigworth and Gregg 2010: 1) and therefore always interpersonal through circulation and transfer. Affect drives bodies towards potential movement and is also that potentiality itself, the 'not yet' or 'yet-ness' as Spinoza propounds in *Ethics* (1959: 87). Massumi calls this affective in-between state, 'the excluded middle' (Massumi 1995: 85), a third state between activity and passivity, occupying the gap between content and effect (Thompson and Biddle 2013: 6).

It is a condition of 'in-betweenness: in the capacities to act and be acted upon [...] an impingement or extrusion of a momentary or sometimes more sustained state of relations, as well as the passage (and the duration of the passage) of forces or intensities' (Seigworth and Gregg 2010: 1).

In musical theatre, and intercultural theatre that employs traditional or premodern performance styles, music (and sound) is a necessary actant in the mise-en-scène for it not merely defines the genre (as is the case of musical theatre) but becomes the locus of dramatic action and focus of spectatorial attention. As Millie Taylor notes of musical theatre, song and music are central to musical theatre even as it is a combination alongside visual spectacle and the verbal text (2012: 1). Elsewhere, I have posited how music, sound and song are 'integral performative texts' that assist to construct the 'culturally kaleidoscopic mise-en-scène' (Tan 2012: 22). In the case of musical theatres and Asian intercultural performances, whose dramaturgies are defined by musical and choreographic events, the power to shape audiences' response affectively is necessarily beyond the semiotic or semantic given that spectating bodies are immersed in a sonic continuum that inevitably influences and dictates physical, emotive and imaginative qualities. In such sonic dramaturgies, bodily affects are consequently driven by the immediate configuration and interplay (intensities/dynamics/frequencies) of this continuum. Such 'vibrational affects' (Goodman 2010: 46) determine a politics of frequency in which the circulation and modulation of sound, as affective vibrational force, can shape perception, reception, agency and non-agency of the conscious, pre-conscious and post-conscious (Thompson and Biddle 2013: 16).

Snapping, rhythm and groove in *West Side Story*

Sound as affective vibrational force, an auditory contagion, that moves and modulates bodies, reception and meaning is evident in the music of *West Side Story*. Its most recent reincarnation (2016–17 international tour) sees the musical restaged with an identical mise-en-scène as the 1957 original Broadway classic. Touted as the 'No. 1 Greatest Musical of All Time' by the *Times* ('West Side Story' 2017b) and canonized in the genre as one of the ten best musicals of all time by *Rolling Stone* (Spanos 2016), *West Side Story* redefined the musical genre and in many ways heralded the modern musical particularly with its timeless tunes, composed by Leonard Bernstein and Stephen Sondheim, and stylistically hybrid dance sequences choreographed by Jerome Robbins. As Elizabeth Wells explains, *West Side Story* is significant in the history of Broadway musicals because it 'pioneered new methodologies or varied the usual pattern for Broadway productions' by allowing dance to mediate where song or book would previously have carried the dramatic action (2010: 15).

Apart from Bernstein's memorable love ballads such as 'Maria' and 'Somewhere', and fugal jazz infusions alongside complex cross-currenting instrumental work (in 'Cool'), the musical is remembered for its energetic and explosive dance sequences, at times curiously accompanied by finger-snapping (or clicking) such as in the musical numbers 'Prologue' and 'Cool'. In these two pieces, the affective potential is engendered by the 'groove', a propulsive rhythmic sense or feel repeated in form and pulse such that it infects the community of listeners, felt also in the body, here both actors and spectators, with *potential*. Affect is felt as a phenomenological (im)pulse and as a physical desire to snap along or 'move' to the contagious and cyclical rhythm. In the friction and sliding of finger-snapping, the sonicity, resulting from the contact between the thumb and another finger, the 'pop'/'snap' sound consequential from the rapid compression and decompression of air, engenders an affective vibration that moves listeners to partake. The regularity and rhythmicity of the snapping further augments the sound as affect. Tiger Roholt (2014) describes such an experience of rhythmic and sonic affect as 'groove' (as in the phrase 'moving to the groove'). According to Roholt, groove is understood through an active, bodily engagement with a rhythm – it is a 'bodily feeling' (2014: 135) and requires an embodied comprehension. Embedded in Roholt's definition is a phenomenological understanding of affect in which the resonances of pulsating rhythms produced by a body (or bodies) advent a feeling expressed as embodied movement or expression. Groove (and more broadly music) entails some form of somatic comportment (Priest 2013: 47) in which a body is acting and being acted on, and 'the body moved to dance (to/with music) is acting and reacting' (Priest 2013: 47); Roholt terms this comprehension of being 'affected' or reacting through/with the body as motor-intentional affect (2014: 137). This motor-intentional affect, the sense of groove, is not identical to the listening of resonance, depth and 'punch' of drum beats, for in finger-snapping, the familiarity and affinity of the bodily percussion engender a phenomenological affect – of human bodies to/between human bodies, through a sonic body; the body's movement is the creation of the sound as affect.

In experiencing and sensing this sonicity, a body is not affected as emotion but as movement. The impulse to snap along either physically, as material manifestation of (being) affect(ed), or mentally, as an internal pulsation in consciousness, is indication of affect as *affectus* and *affectio*. Massumi explains *affectus* as a potential, the body's varied capacity to affect and be affected (2004: xvi), a 'pre-personal intensity' (2004: xvii) that augments or diminishes the body's capacity to act (2004: xvi). *Affectio*, or affection, on the other hand, is the affective encounter of a body with other bodies, the state of the body as it affects and is affected (Thompson and Biddle 2013: 8). The focus of *affectio*, then, is the body and the ensemble of relations that is defined by its affective capacity (Thompson and Biddle 2013: 9). Experiencing the sonicities (frequency and rhythm) of finger-snapping, the listening body experiences first the potential to be affected and consequently the affection of the body snapping and the snapping as bodily.

In the recent production of *West Side Story*, performed in Singapore between 13 and 24 September, this vibrational affect of distinctive clicks created a sonic continuum in the soundscape that infected actors and audiences; it permeated the fourth wall of the fictional New York to the real spaces of the present. In the musical number 'Cool', finger-snapping is used by Riff (played by Lance Hayes) to regulate the irritability felt by the Jets who are craving to start a brawl with the Sharks before the agreed rumble. After Doc attempts to alleviate the situation and persuade the Jets not to get involved in a street fight, Action and A-Rabb lose their 'cool' and enact their vexations. As Riff sings to the fugal contrapuntal jazz fusion music, telling Action to 'Get cool, boy! [...] Keep coolly cool, boy!', he interjects the spoken with measured finger-snapping that 'grooves' to the established rhythm of the musical accompaniment. Subsequently, all other Jets snap along except for Action who attempts but allows his anger to overwhelm him as he slams his arms on a table.[1] Distinctly, Action does not yet experience *affectio*(n). As the finger-snapping continues, other characters such as Baby John break away from the felt rhythms to perform distinct movements accompanied by the vocalization 'pow'. These interjections, however, are momentary for the dominant sonic continuum of the groove is affective. Even as the characters stop their snapping and break into the energetic and explosive ensemble movement sequences now iconic of *West Side Story*, in the climax of the musical number, the affective contagion of snapping lingers and infects yet again at the end of the number with the Jets clicking in 'cool' synchronicity. While such disruptions may have been choreographed intentionally, one can posit that the vibrational affect of snapping and its rhythm determine a performative politics that unconsciously compels synchronicity and harmony. As a dramaturgical device to advance the narrative, the finger-snapping serves to calm the tension. Metadramatically, it is the affective contagion of the clicks that renders this musical sequence the dramatic meaning: the actors become bodily bound both as a dance ensemble and as 'the Jets' because it is through this sonic affect that they become both affected and affective bodies. Their differences in personality, beliefs and status become dissolved by this percussive affect.

The now iconic body percussive movement that characterizes the revolutionary musical style of *West Side Story* is first introduced in the opening scene. In the 'Prologue', the performance begins with the Jets striding across the stage, snapping their fingers. For the first three minutes of the show, only movement, music and the finger-snaps narrate the plot with these employed dramaturgically to introduce the players and the conflict between the houses. The established sonicity of the Jets' simultaneous clicking becomes a means of claiming identity and territory. Sound is choreographed to affectively declare ownership and kinship as the Jet boys snap their fingers in synchrony – beginning with one, joined in by another, a third and then the rest of the tribe. Accompanied by broad sweeping movements, high leaps and long spacious swings of the extremities, the finger-snapping establishes, as Deborah Jowitt explains of this opening sequence in *West Side Story*, a contained yet expanding sense of territoriality (2011: 0:01:25). This territorial sense that consequently claims material-physical space is produced by the sonorous clicks and snaps that become an 'affective glue' to establish firmly the Jets' spatial identity and group identity through acoustic space. In addition to the unique dance movements that characterize the Jets, the expansive sounds of the clicking infuse neutral space with the specific frequencies of their snapping; this vibrational affect of hypnotic clicking infects all who listen.

When the audience is introduced to Bernado and the Sharks, they likewise begin with finger-snapping, though distinctly their dance movements are smoother and more contained within the body. Dramatically, the competitive clicking is used as a means of rhythmic contest, a 'tit for tat' response to establish presence and territoriality through acoustic occupation. The disruptive tension is contained in the intensities occasioned by the interplay of clicking frequencies but such a sonic performative underscores the affective potential of the common pulse created by the clicks that can be said to unite rather than divide. Visually, the gesture of finger-snapping while not identical is similar; affectively, the pulses and rhythms of the click impact bodies equally and do not distinguish Jet from Shark. The affective dimension thus provokes a unique interpretive response not found in Shakespeare's *Romeo and Juliet*: through affect, the finger-snapping underscores the parallels between the Jets and the Sharks – as affective bodies rhythmitized – despite their espoused differences. More significantly, the mesmerizing clicks advent a moment of affective communion where spectators feel this vibration alongside the performers and in turn the *affection*. Through these vibrational affects, audiences are brought into a communion with the characters in a larger community of affected bodies. As Roholt posits, groove is a feel that informs body movements, experienced and established phenomenologically as one copes with a rhythm and its elements (2014: 111). It is often preconscious and non-cognitive, and movement to the pulse may not always be a conscious deliberate action.

While bodies may differ in ethnicity, culture or movement, as is the case with the Jets and Sharks, music's affectivity dissipates these differences, and its contagion is felt by all.

Feeling, affect and ritual in *Romyo and Juri*

In *West Side Story*, the affective frequencies shift the conflict in Shakespeare's text to prescribe a new political dynamic between seeming foes. The affective experience of music through bodily engagement performs a contradistinction to intent found in the dramatic work and in experiential ways radically alters the understanding of the play. It demonstrates how affect as rhythm (and music) disrupt analytical comprehensions and are abstractions and cannot be reduced to signification. This understanding is congruent with Susanne Langer's explication of abstractions as 'a mode of feeling continuous with the vital activities that course across and through the organism' (Priest 2013: 46). They are experienced as complexities and intensities to be felt abstractly, and feeling marks a continuity between material powers and conceptual force (Priest 2013: 46).

In Susanne Langer's philosophy of feeling, affect is not to be understood simply as a symbolic or speculative event but rather as abstraction that gives expression to the flux of experience. The human organism is able to abstract a qualitative-relational value from sensory particulars and is able to, through these abstractions, constitute vital experience (Priest 2013: 45). Music is an exemplary form of the abstract for it is 'apprehensible if not comprehensible' (Langer 1967: 105); it is an experience of the mode of being felt as thought (Priest 2013: 46). The experience of music requires a bodily, nervous response that implicates itself into the matrix of abstractions or symbolic assembly through which the organism experiences its vitality (Priest 2013: 47). In that vitality is an affective 'bind' even if experienced only in the mind. Unsurprisingly, the abstract foundation of all rituals, premodern or modern, is music and/or rhythm. It is through music in/as ritual that one experiences sound being *felt as thought*, here understood to be the activity of 'nascent acts or suspended impulses initiated by vibratory impressions that one feels as "thinking"' (Priest 2013: 48), with thinking comprehended as a physiological process that terminates not in overt behaviour but in the sheer expression of ideas, the virtual, imaginary experience of music (Priest 2013: 48). Through music, movement, vibration and tempo, ritual creates communities *felt* as shared affective experiences, of feeling as thought, with feelings explained as 'sensory stimulus or inward tension, pain, emotion or intent' (Langer 1967: 4).

In *Romyo and Juri* (2009),[2] director Park Sun-Whan incorporates distinct traditional, premodern Korean rituals to not only 'localize' Shakespeare's *Romeo and Juliet* but also, intended or otherwise, create overt feelings of communality through ritual rhythms. *Romyo and Juri* is an intercultural re-vision that employs both common and lesser-known traditional Korean ritual dance forms as part of its unique dramaturgy. Produced and performed by the prestigious National Changgeuk Company of Korea, the production is performed in the Korean dramatic tradition of *changgeuk*, a form of opera/music theatre that employs *p'ansori*, a traditional form of vocal musical storytelling dating as far back as the mid-nineteenth century. In addition to employing this well-known folk style, the production underscores its historicity by including Korean shamanistic rituals known as *Gut*. The plot remains identical to Shakespeare's but the romantic tragedy is transposed from fair Verona to Palyangchi, a hill located between Cheolla and Gyungsang provinces. There the destiny of Romyo, son of Mun Taegyu, and Juri, daughter of Choi Bullip, unfolds as song, dance and ritual that affectively (and effectively) re-shape spectators' conception and reception of a globally familiar tale. The prevalent ritual qualities of *Romyo and Juri* engender local(ized) communities of experience effected through feeling as thought, the shared potential of affect, and in so doing bind actors and spectators in an act(ion) that modulates the polarized divide between the Montagues and Capulets.

The spectacle that opens the first scene, in which the conflict between the two households is introduced, is performed as a folk ritual and while *changgeuk* remains the primary performance mode, Park introduces a collection of various folk dances including a mask dance, *talchum* (specifically that of a *sanye* or lion mask dance). Immediately following the prologue that is performed as *p'ansori* by the *sorikkun* (singer), *talchum* establishes the rhythms of the scene as all characters dance in a circle around the lion, stepping in time to the resonances of the instruments used in *samul nori* and *pungmul nori* traditions – Korean folk dance-music forms used in harvest rituals.[3] Even as characters from both households (and Romyo and Juri are present in the rhythmic ritual fray) sing to lines that speak about the fracture of the land caused by the persistent hostilities, the melody and movement affectively bind them as a chorus. The *talchum* dance is then replaced by *kkoktu kaksi* – traditional puppet theatre – as the music continues. This shamanistic dance is, contained by the conventions of the traditional dance movement and the upbeat rhythms of the accompanying music, oddly jubilant with the threat of conflict underscored only by the verbal insults each family throws at the other. At the climax of the dance sequence, characters from both houses rhythmically move towards each other and hop, stride and twirl synchronously as a single body to the established sounds. Members from each family dance on different sides of the stage where bodies perform the conflict despite being affectively bound by the same rhythm and melody. This affective potential becomes realized when an 'interlude' interjects with a different rhythm and the *danso*, a traditional end-blown vertical flute, replaces the sonorities of *samul nori*. Moving to new sounds, characters from both households come together to dance in synchrony, as an ensemble. Even as actors continue to hurl insults at the opposing household, their bodies move in identical steps. Like *West Side Story*'s affective finger-snapping, the vibrational affect of rhythm is experienced as *affectio*/affection in which felt bodies embody rhythm as concurring motions.

The ritualistic dance (ritual in dance, ritual as dance) becomes an affective event that interpellates communal identity. The liminal state of the ritual dance is marked by sounds' contagious affect through which a sense of commonality and communality is engendered. This feeling extends beyond the stage for in the stage(d) ritual, spectators are infected with vibrational affect, of feeling as thought, the bourgeoning impulses felt in the 'thinking' of movement and participation. These affective frequencies infect the preconscious and urge one's body to move in/as pulse with other bodies. In *Romyo and Juri*, a brewing dissonance that threatens the order of Palyangchi becomes an affective harmony driven by the contagious cadence of ritual dances.

The effects of sonic affect are also evident in the first meeting of Romyo and Juri. While Shakespeare employs visual imagery of ecclesiastical piety, such as Romeo's self-comparison to a pilgrim 'profan(ing) with [his] unworthiest hand' (1.5.92) the saintly palm that belongs to Juliet, and light and darkness (where Romeo declares how Juliet 'doth teach the torches to burn bright!' (1.5.33) as she stands out against the darkness like 'a rich jewel in an Ethiope's ear' (1.4.45)) to portray the lovers' mutual adoration, Park renovates these to become a harvest ritual feast and in so doing retains the textual elements of devotion and worship but creates an opportunity for enchantment through ritual music and movement. In this scene, a performance of *ganggasullae* becomes the highlight of Choi Bullip's celebratory proceedings.

Ganggangsullae is a 5,000-year-old ritual dance that is performed under the full moon as part of *chuseok* (Autumn Eve), a celebratory harvest festival held around the autumn equinox. *Ganggangsullae* is performed only by women as it is also considered to be a fertility ritual and, at times, a celebration of young newly-weds. The ritual dance involves different phases including a section called *notdari bapchi* (commonly translated as 'treading on roof tiles') where women line themselves in a straight line and, with backs bent, allow the lead singer to walk across their arched backs while chanting 'ganggangsullae' in response to her leading verses. At Choi Bullip's feast, Juri assumes the role of the lead singer as she treads on the 'roof tiles' and chants. Rhythmically and with poise, she strides forward across each 'tile' to meet Romyo who stands at the front of the man-made bridge.

Ganggangsullae, in *Romyo and Juri*, is a public spectacle and its performance includes all characters from both households; Romyo and Juri, unlike Romeo and Juliet, do not meet in the shadows and their romantic encounter, intentional or otherwise, becomes a communal celebration sanctioned through ritual dance. This 'play-within-play' sequence that features the harvest ritual exemplifies the affective capacities of ritual and ritualistic music. While one may use the term 'ritualistic' to describe the structural, possibly repetitive and cyclical sequence in many forms and styles of music, music employed in ritual amplifies its affectivity as a 'double' performative. The condition of ritual is ontologically affective for it occasions the state of 'in-betweenness' in its liminality; rituals are affective states that infect bodies and where potential occasions change – spiritual, mental, emotional or otherwise – in the post-liminal state (the material effect of affect). Music in ritual is contagious for it invites listening and participation and in so doing incorporates one into the sonorous body of recurring articulations, pauses and cadences that yield a sonic continuum dislocated from temporality, a suspended performative time that possesses the 'yet-ness' to affect other bodies, metaphysical or physical.

This suspended performative moment, in which the ritual dance seems to supersede the dramatic narrative, is evident as actors step out of character to dance to the rhythmic clangs established by the *kkwaenggwari* – a small flat brass gong. At this point, the *kkokdoosue* (lead player of a traditional vagabond play troupe called *namsadangpae*) and other actors invite audience members on stage to partake of the ritual dance by forming the 'roof tiles'. As spectators step onto the stage and into the ritual space, they begin moving in tempo to the rhythms without being told. When *ganggangsullae* begins and Juri walks on the tiles, the chorus of actors and spectators sing to the cyclical refrain, 'ganggangsullae'. The ritual's measured metrical development from *gin* (slow) to *jung* (middle) and *jajeun* (quick), as felt in the increasing tempo, becomes embodied by the actors and spectators on stage who, after Juri completes her tile-treading, dance and hop in a circle that encloses Juri in a performance of *Wolwoli Cheong Cheong* ('Moon, moon, radiant moon') – the opening sequence of the *ganggangsullae* where dancers join hands to form a circle and dance in a round, mimicking the circularity of the full moon – thereby underscoring the performative ritual, its suspended liminality and affectivity.

In using *ganggangsullae*, Park turns Romeo and Juliet's secret rendezvous into a public event of affective frequencies in/as ritual that is effected by actors/characters and spectators and witnessed by the heavens. The use of *ganggangsullae* transfigures the meeting of the lovers into a sacral consequence born from social ritual effected through affect. While Romeo and Juliet's exchange of love's vows enacts individual will that defies the stars, the ritual of *ganggangsullae* transmutes Romyo and Juri's encounter into a communal event sanctioned by the gods and endorsed by affect-ed audiences whose participation, felt as action or as thought, affirms their (fatal) union.

Framed in Langer's expression of affect as feeling (of the abstract), ritual music is felt and received as abstraction and comprehended as symbolic thought, here specifically as ritual and community. This feeling of community is the 'imaginary experience of music' (Priest 2013: 48) where shared symbols of the musical and physical movements create and bind – an occasion that 'make(s) things conceivable' (Langer 1942: 244). What such musical semblances and symbolizations make specifically conceivable or imaginable is our affectivity. This affectivity or vitality of affects invites thought on how a world may be felt rather than how it is or how it must be experienced. In employing music in/as/and ritual, Park refigures the relationship between the warring households and Romeo and Juliet's clandestine, forbidden romance. The affective frequencies in ritual 're-sound' with a different narrative for characters and audiences in Park's intercultural adaptation, one whose polarized opposites are unified by felt rhythms, and commonality and communality remain the bedrock of Korean society, or at least it expresses that desire and posits a world that should be felt as opposed to how it is narratively presented.

A politics of affective frequencies

In *Romyo and Juri*, the intercultural mise-en-scène is composed of affective frequencies that communicate a popular Western story to a Korean audience. In many ways, the sounds of *Romyo and Juri* are the dominant actant by which Shakespeare's play is appropriated and 'nationalised' for the affectivity of these ritual sonicities creates community acoustically even as these sounds have themselves been politically appropriated as national sounds – *samul nori* and *p'ansori* are the musical styles that the South Korean government actively promotes as 'Korean' with the latter claiming status as a Masterpiece of the Oral and Intangible Heritage of Humanity. Yet the affectivity of these frequencies, their quality of contagion, renders this performance equally global: with sufficient familiarity of Shakespeare's romantic tragedy, one does not need to comprehend *hanggul* or identify the ritual practices employed to 'feel' and be moved by Park's production for one will be affected by the cyclical, rhythmic frequencies on the stage, and these communicate meaning without words. New meaning is engendered because these 'local' sounds made global through affect rewrite *Romeo and Juliet* through a rescripting of the relationships between characters and households: affective union modulates the age-old strife that forms the context for Romeo and Juliet's inability to be together. One can posit, therefore, that the contagion of ritual sounds manipulates a politics of reception. Sound and its affective potential bestow intercultural theatres that employ premodern performance dance and dramatic forms a contagious power that can dictate revised receptions and spectatorial experiences. In many ways, attending to the effects of affective frequencies in the soundscapes of intercultural theatre enables new dialogues on issues of cultural and identity politics. While sounds, and music, their timbre, tonality, structure and other formal characteristics can be attributed to distinct cultural and national styles, the affective qualities of music lend new sensibilities on the movement and transculturality of these sounds that can possibly break the binaries of self-other, West-East, colonial-postcolonial which have haunted intercultural theatre scholarship for the last two decades.

While such affective frequencies can move bodies to unity and community, this sonic power can also be considered 'tyrannical'. As *West Side Story* demonstrates, this 'tyranny' of musical affect, the capacities to direct feeling, thought, and feeling as thought, engenders a politics of sonic power which dictates (emotional and affective) reception. While there are considerations of how music is used as means of sociopolitical resistance or as instruments of control or propaganda,[4] less has been said about how music can dictate conformist emotions in absolute terms. Music is persuasive not only because it is able to emote listeners and that the musical expression of particular human emotions is an essential and common dimension of musical meaning and experience (Elliot 2010: 86); where contemporary musicals are concerned emotions are frequently elicited by lyrical ballads which frequently adhere to established success formulas common in pop music (repetitive refrains and predictable melodic progressions are some examples),[5] but music is also suasive since it generates affective intensities intercorporeally, between bodies, precognitively. One can conjecture that the timeless appeal of *West Side Story* lies not only in the musicality or musical expression of the melodies but in the radiation and circulation of affect consequent of the palpitating and explosive dance sequences and infectious finger-snapping – the rhythms created by bodies and music and bodies to music. *West Side Story*'s interpersonal, inter-bodily intensities exemplify how rhythm, movement and music in interplay possess the capacities to (re)shape receptions beyond cognitive comprehension.

Conclusion: 'All are punish'd'

In an ironic twist of how Prince Escalus claims, in the final scene of *Romeo and Juliet*, 'All are punish'd' (5.3.294), both *West Side Story* and *Romyo and Juri* demonstrate how despite (superficial) divisions, all are bodies of affect, and bodies affected. If sonic affect dictates how a spectator-listener *feels* or should feel in its phenomenological reception, and where affect is always precognitive and pre-reflexive, one wonders about a possibility of resistance in such an 'oppressive' politics of sound. As Massumi reminds, affect is a real condition, is everywhere, is in effect and is transversal (1995: 106–7); 'This fact about affect – this matter-of-factness of affect – needs to be taken seriously into account in cultural and political theory. Don't forget' (1995: 107).

Notes

1. See the video excerpt of the production here: https://www.youtube.com/watch?v=Sg3h-qqAUfI, specifically 1:09.
2. The production can be viewed in its entirety at 'Asian Shakespeare Intercultural Archive', http://a-s-i-a-web.org/index.php.
3. *Pungmul nori* and *Samul nori* are Korean folk music traditions that involve drumming, singing and dancing. They are considered as a form of farmers' music (*nong ak*) and are played at harvest rituals or community events. *Samul nori* is a modern development from the older *pungmul nori* tradition that came about with greater urbanization and modernization.
4. See Morgan and Reish (2018).
5. A recent scientific study proves why simplicity and predictability are the key factors in popular music's commercial success. See Percino et al. (2014).

References

Davies, S. (2011), 'Infectious Music: Music-Listener Emotional Contagion', in P. Goldie and A. Coplan (eds), *Empathy: Philosophical and Psychological Perspectives*, 134–48, Oxford: Oxford University Press.

Davies, S. (2013), 'Music-to-Listener Emotional Contagion', in T. Cochrane, B. Fantini and K. R. Scherer (eds), *The Emotional Power of Music*, 169–76, Oxford: Oxford University Press.
Elliot, D. J. (2010), 'Music and Affect: The Praxial View', *Philosophy of Music Education Review*, 8 (2): 79–88.
Gallagher, M. (2016), 'Sound as Affect: Difference, Power and Spatiality', *Emotion, Space and Society*, 20: 42–8.
Goodman, S. (2010), *Sonic Warfare: Sound, Affect and the Ecology of Fear*, Cambridge, MA: The MIT Press.
Hatfield, E., J. T. Cacioppo and R. L. Rapson (1994), *Emotional Contagion*, Cambridge: Cambridge University Press.
Jowitt, D. (2011), 'West Side Story: Pow! The Dances of West Side Story', *West Side Story*, 50th Anniversary Edition, [Film] Dir. Jerome Robbins. USA: Metro Goldwyn Mayer (MGM) Studios.
Langer, S. (1942), *Philosophy in a New Key: A Study in the Symbolism of Reason, Rite and Art*, Cambridge, MA: Harvard University Press.
Langer, S. (1967), *Mind: An Essay on Human Feeling*, vol. 1, Baltimore, NJ: Johns Hopkins University Press.
Massumi, B. (1995), 'The Autonomy of Affect', *Cultural Critique* 31: 83–109.
Massumi, B. (2004), 'Notes of the Translation and Acknowledgements', in G. Deleuze and F. Guattari (eds), *A Thousand Plateaus*. London and New York: Continuum.
Morgan, J. E. and G. N. Reish (2018), *Tyranny and Music*, Lanham, MD: Lexington Books.
Percino, G., P. Klimek and S. Thurner (2014), 'Instrumental Complexity of Music Genres and Why Simplicity Sells', *PLOS One*, 9 (12): e115255.
Priest, E. (2013), 'Felt as Thought (or, Musical Abstraction and the Semblance of Affect)', in M. Thompson and I. Biddle (eds), *Sound, Music, Affect: Theorizing Sonic Experience*, 45–64, London: Bloomsbury.
Roholt, T. C. (2014), *Groove: A Phenomenology of Rhythmic Nuance*, New York: Bloomsbury.
Romyo and Juri (2009), Director, Park Sun-Whan. The National Changgeuk Company of Korea, Daehangno Arts Theatre, Seoul.
Seigworth, G. J. and M. Gregg (2010), 'An Inventory of Shimmers', in G. J. Seigworth and M. Gregg (eds), *The Affect Theory Reader*, 1–28, Durham and London: Duke University Press.
Shakespeare, W. (2012), *Romeo and Juliet*, ed. René Weis, London: Arden Shakespeare.
Spanos, B. (2016), 'Readers' Poll: The 10 Best Musicals of All Time', *Rolling Stone*, 15 June. Available online: http://www.rollingstone.com/music/pictures/readers-poll-the-10-best-musicals-of-all-time-20160615 (accessed 10 December 2017).
Spinoza, B. (1959), *Ethics; and, on the Correction of Understanding*, trans. Andrew Boyle, London: Everyman's Library.

Tan, M. C. C. (2012), *Acoustic Interculturalism: Listening to Performance*, Houndsmill, Basingstoke: Palgrave Macmillan.

Taylor, M. (2012), *Musical Theatre, Realism and Entertainment*, Surrey, England: Ashgate Publishing Limited.

Thompson, M. and I. Biddle (2013), 'Introduction: Somewhere between the Signifying and the Sublime', in M. Thompson and I. Biddle (eds), *Sound, Music, Affect: Theorizing Sonic Experience*, 1–24, London: Bloomsbury.

Wells, E. (2010), *West Side Story: Cultural Perspectives on an American Musical*, Lanham, MD, Toronto, and Plymouth, UK: Scarecrow Press.

'West Side Story' (2017a), [Theatre] Dir. Jerome Robbins, Joey McKneely, Singapore: Esplanade Theatre. [Date experienced 27 August].

'West Side Story' (2017b), Available online: http://en.westsidestory.de/ (accessed 3 January 2018).

4

'Look not upon me, for thine eyes are wounding': Infectious Sights in Shakespeare's Theatre of Contagion

Shani Bans

This essay examines Shakespeare's ocular metaphors of transmission, infection and contagion, particularly focusing on how a medical conception of vision would turn the theatre into a site of contagion. By examining the paradoxical nature of how the eye operates as both poisonous pathogen and vulnerable entry point to contagious passions, I trace the ways in which Shakespeare's work dramatizes contention between different theories of vision. In doing so, I argue that the act of seeing in Shakespeare's drama is not an exclusively pleasurable experience but, rather, a painfully infectious one. Beginning with *King Henry VI Part 2* (1591) and the lethal exchange of looks between Henry and Suffolk, I then turn to Phoebe and Silvius in *As You Like It* (1599) in order to argue that eyes in Shakespeare's drama – emitting and receiving the infectious gaze of desire – are sometimes not powerful agents which cause harm but frail organs susceptible to contagions which alter not only *what* characters see but *how* they see. Taking a loosely chronological approach, I move from these specific moments of infectious sights in *King Henry VI Part 2* and *As You Like It* in order to examine how Shakespeare's language of contagion evolves in *Twelfth Night* (1601), a play that not only comments on the infectious nature of lovers' sights but offers a meta-theatrical commentary on theatre as a site of contagion.

'Theatre', derived from the Greek verb 'θεάομαι' (to see or behold) and the Latin noun '*theātrum*' (a place to view from), creates multiple and conflicting viewpoints from which vision takes place. By examining anti-theatrical treatises, such as Anthony Munday's *A Second and Third Blast of Retreat from Plays and Theatres*, which held the 'vnchaste aspects the eies' of the actors to be responsible for breeding 'filithie cogitations [in] the mind' (1580: 1–2) of their spectators, this essay argues that in the early modern theatre spectators were not passive observers but both actors and spectators were actively participating in the creation of a theatre of visual contagion. Throughout this essay, I examine Shakespeare's drama in relation to early modern discourses on the theories of vision and ocular anatomy, the plague, and early modern architecture. Such an approach not only enables us to situate Shakespeare's theatre within a wider discourse on early modern sights/sites of contagion but, in doing so, allows us to interrogate theatre's role in the transmission of contagious emotions.[1]

Wounding and wounded eyes: Visual theory in *King Henry VI Part 2* and *As You Like It*

The second act of *King Henry VI Part 2* begins with a miraculous healing: a blind man, Simpcox, seems to have been cured by Saint Albans's shrine and is able to see again. Only after Gloucester insists that they examine his eyes more carefully, 'Let me see thine eye ... / In my opinion yet thou seest not well' (2.1.104–5), does Simpcox grudgingly confess that he had never been blind. This scene is indicative of two central and overlapping concerns of the play: characters' inability to see clearly, and the corruption and fallaciousness at the core of Henry's court. For example, Henry's 'dimmed eyes' (3.1.218) may literally be obstructed by the 'unhelpful tears' caused by Gloucester's abdication but they are further dimmed by the feigned and fraudulent passions of his courtiers. Ironically, Margaret and Suffolk – Henry's most trustworthy advisors, who warn him not to fall for 'the mournful crocodile / [and thereby become] With sorrow snared relenting passengers' (3.1.226–7) – are responsible for feigning sorrow in order to beguile Henry, diverting him from seeing clearly. Where once he was Henry's 'guide, and lantern' (2.3.25), Margaret and Suffolk's defamation of Gloucester contaminates Henry's opinion of him and thereby makes the king blind to his councillor's sincere petitions. It is only after the honest man's death that the gullible king sees past Suffolk's feigned sorrow:

> **King Henry**   Thou baleful messenger, out of my sight!
> Upon thy eyeballs murderous tyranny
> Sits in grim majesty to fright the world.
> Look not upon me, for thine eyes are wounding;
> Yet do not go away; come, basilisk,
> And kill the innocent gazer with thy sight. (3.2.48–53)

Vulnerable to Suffolk's feigned friendship, Henry wavers between a suicidal inclination to be killed by Suffolk's basilisk-like gaze and a desperate desire for visual immunity from his murderous eyeballs. Through this lethal exchange of looks Shakespeare illustrates two opposing, and yet correlative, models of vision: Suffolk's tyrannous eye that, like the gaze of the basilisk, can 'kill the innocent gazer with [his] sight' and Henry's fragile, innocent and wounded eye susceptible to Suffolk's infectious sight.

The two opposing theories of sight that circulated in the medical discourse of early modern England, as Marcus Nordlund describes, were extramission and intromission. The extramission theory, which was more prevalent of the two, argued that the eye emitted *pneuma* (fiery beams) which coalesced (*sunancheia*) with the visual species (*eidola*) that were thought to radiate out of the object and into the surrounding medium (usually the air). The coalescent stream that formed between the fiery beams from the eye and the visual species from the object were believed to penetrate through the pupil and into the soul. The intromission theory of sight, initially proposed by the medieval Arab oculist, Alhazen, and developed by the sixteenth-century scientist, Johannes Kepler, however, argued that the eye was not a powerful agent that projected fiery beams but a passive receptor of light from external objects which entered *into* the eye.[2] While the two theories differ in their understanding of the direction of the beams, projecting from or entering into the eye, both held the eye to be the primary *portal* of visual transmission. In *Essaies upon the Five Senses*, the poet Richard Brathwait describes 'the eye of all other Sences is most needful, so of all others it is most hurtfull ... there is no passage more easie for entry of vice than by the cranie of the eye' (1620: 3). Eyes were thought to be 'most hurtfull' precisely because of this 'cranie of the eye', that is to say, 'a small narrow opening or hole; a chink, crevice, crack, [or] frissure' (Oxford English Dictionary: 1a) in the eye, which being so small made the unwitting entry or expulsion of contagion easy.

Here therefore, Henry plays the vulnerable victim of extramissive egress – 'the innocent gazer' – and accuses Suffolk's eyes to be full of 'murderous tyranny' that are capable of not only 'wounding' but able to 'kill ... with thy sight' (3.2.40–54). This analogy to the basilisk originates in Pliny who described the mythical reptilian beast, the basilisk or the 'cockatrice', as one who is able to kill via direct eye contact. In *Discourses of the Preservation of the Sight*, a treatise concerning ocular maladies and remedies, the French physician Andreas Laurentius describes how 'the Basiliske by his sight poyseneth all them who look vpon him' (1599: 38). Shakespeare employs this proverbial motif throughout his drama: while in *Richard III* (1592), Anne berates Richard's wooing of her and complains that the sight of him 'dost infect [her] eyes', and moments later she wishes her own eyes 'were basilisks to strike [Richard] dead' (1.2.148–50), in *Cymbeline* (1610), Posthumous complains that the ring Iachimo shows him as proof of his wife's infidelity 'is a basilisk unto [his] eye, / [And] Kills [him] to look on't' (2.4.107–8). Both Anne and Posthumous use the basilisk metaphor to convey a deep-rooted anxiety about the dangers of seeing and being exposed to the poisonous sight of others. In Henry's indecision over whether he desires visual immunity from Suffolk's basilisk-like gaze or whether he would rather be killed by it, Shakespeare illustrates how the contagious nature of vision in the play is symptomatic of a wider underlying disease of political instability and corruption in the play. Moreover, by associating Suffolk's vision to the 'chiefest prospect murd'ring basilisks' (3.2.328), Shakespeare highlights Henry's compulsive desire to stigmatize sight as a contagious sense.

However, Henry's suicidal plea to be killed by Suffolk's infectious sight is not met with a lethal beam but, instead, with Suffolk's refusal to wear 'murder's crimson badge' insisting, 'we ... are no murderers' (3.2.181). Although Suffolk was involved in Gloucester's murder, by refusing to be associated with the basilisk's murderous eyes, Suffolk avoids participating in 'the eye-emitted ray paradigm' (Langley 2006: 343). Shakespeare returns to this dismissal of the myth of the basilisk in *The Winter's Tale* (1611) when Camillo falsely accuses Polixenes for spreading 'a sickness / Which puts some of us in distemper' (1.2.379–80), Polixenes denies his accusation of contamination by refusing to participate in the basilisk metaphor, 'make me not sighted like the basilisk', he says, because despite having 'looked on thousands' he insists he has 'killed none' (1.2.383–5). 'For the Basilisk, and the inflamed eye do not infect us by the bright beams which come from them', concurs the physician Laurentius, 'but by a naturall substances, which is very subtile ... which infecting the ayre, is by it transported to us' (1599: 43). Although including the basilisk in their medical discourses, early modern physicians, like Laurentius, dismissed the notion of extramissive infection to argue, instead, that diseases were transmitted via a contagious atmosphere into the eyes (intromission). It is not the eye but the *medium* through which the eye sees that is responsible for infectious activity. Suddenly, 'the fatal balls of murdering basilisks: / The venom of such looks ... / Have lost their quality' (*Henry V*, 5.2.17–18). If the basilisk's ability to infect through its eyes is, as Sergei Lobanov-Rostovsky argues, 'a fantasy of the eye's power ... that killed ... both by seeing and *being* seen' (1997: 198, original emphasis), then by dispelling the myth of the basilisk-like eye, oculists, such as Laurentius, pried open the eye in order to dismiss such fantasies.

Under the anatomist's scalpel, the eye was no longer a powerful agent of infection, but, as Lobanov-Rostovsky observes, 'the eye become ... a frail organ, a proper object of anatomy' (1997: 196). As the English oculist Philip Barrough notes in *The Method of Phisick*:

> But the eye which is wont with curious inspection to pry into all other things, and to find out the nature and order of them, hath bin *unable to unfold his owne wonderfull constitution*, and hath bene alway[s] blind in judging of it selfe. (1583: 49, my emphasis)

As the oculist's living eye looks into the secrets of the dead eye upon his dissection table, ocular anatomy made the eye subject of its own gaze and, in doing so, revealed its intricate composition and inherent fragility. As object, the passive eye is 'blind in judging of it selfe'; as subject, it seeks to scrutinize itself in a desperate attempt for self-knowledge. Barrough's 'little round subject' (1583: 49), with its constitution folded and hidden from sight, is cut open to reveal its 'secret and wonderful notions' to the gaze of all. If 'the Latines', as the physician Laurentius notes, 'call [eyes] *Oculi*, because they are as it were hidden and inclosed within a hollow valley', then, cutting open the eye and exposing its 'hidden and inclosed' interiority (1599: 22), early modern oculists revealed that 'the substance of the eye [to be] altogether soft, bright, and shining, cleere, thick and waterish; soft, that so it may readily admit and receiue the forme of things' (Laurentius 1599: 24). By dissecting the eye to reveal the optic nerve's connection to the brain, Laurentius admitted that 'I was enforced to chaunge mine opinion' about the extramission theory (1599: 23–4). Dissection reduced the eye to a bundle of 'fleshy strings', held together by 'certaine little filmes or skins (which are called of some tunicles or coates) which vntie and fasten together the whole eye' (Laurentius 1599: 26–9).Plucked out of the head, pinned down by the oculist's scalpel and pried open to reveal layer upon layer of fragile flesh, the eye is no longer a powerful basilisk emitting poisonous beams but a powerless organ made of a 'waterish; soft' material (Laurentius 1599: 24). Extinguishing the eyebeam metaphor, oculists revealed the eye to be weak and permeable, a conduit to contagions. Where in *King Henry VI Part 2*, Shakespeare conveys an unnerving anxiety about the eye's ability to infect and be infected, in *As You Like It* he dismisses 'the fantasy of the eye's power' (Lobanov-Rostovsky 1997: 196) and joins the oculists' debate about the material fragility of the eye.

Of all the love pursuits in *As You Like It*, the shepherd Silvius's quest of the shepherdess Phoebe is most self-aware of the 'eye-emitted ray paradigm' (Langley 2006: 343). While the play follows the Elizabethan love-lyrics convention of the mistress's eyes carrying lethal eyebeams that hurt her lover,[3] for example when Orlando's complains about how Rosalind's 'frown might kill' him and his heart is 'wounded … with the eyes of a lady' (4.1.188; 5.2.19), in the exchange between Phoebe and Silvius, Shakespeare not only challenges such love-lyric conventions by giving the female mistress,

Phoebe, a voice to defy and overcome the lyrical tropes that are inflicted on her by Silvius, but, in doing so, the playwright highlights a cultural shift in representations of the eye as powerful agents of infection to vulnerable victims susceptible to contagion. Fed up of Silvius's pursuit, Phoebe disdains his use of the extramissive eyebeam to woo her:

> **Phoebe** Thou tell'st me there is murder in mine eye.
> 'Tis pretty sure, and very probable,
> That eyes, that are the frail'st and softest things,
> Who shut their coward gates on atomies,
> Should be called tyrants, butchers, murderers....
> But now mine eyes,
> Which I have darted at thee, hurt thee not;
> Nor I am sure there is no force in eyes
> That can do hurt. (3.5.10–27)

Phoebe argues that the female eyes are not 'tyrants, butchers, [or] murderers' but 'the frail'st and softest things'; curiously, her description of the function of the eyelids as 'coward[ly] gates' that 'shut … on atomies' demonstrates accurate knowledge of the anatomy of the eye and resembles the physician Laurentius's description of the '[eye]lid, which openeth and shutteth … for feare that the eye should bee corrupted' (1599: 23–4). While Silvius clutches on to 'a fantasy of the eye's power' (Lobanov-Rostovsky 1997: 196) to hurt, Phoebe shames him – 'O, for shame, for shame / Lie not, to say mine eyes are murderers' (3.5.18–19) – for holding women accountable for infectious sights, accusing him of counterfeiting swoons and poetic hyperbole. Like the sceptical anatomist probing into the body to discovery its diseases, Phoebe demands that Silvius 'show the wound [her] eye hath made' only for him to claim that 'the wounds [are] invisible' (3.5.20, 31); turning her eyes upon Silvius and deliberately darting them in his direction, Phoebe proves she is not a basilisk and that 'there is no force in the eyes / That can do hurt'. It is not the other's eyes that are wounding (as both Henry and Silvius assume) but their own eyes which, because of their inherent fragility ('eyes … are the frail'st and softest things'), make their sight susceptible to contagions.

Loving looks: Plagued vision in *Twelfth Night*

Twelfth Night is arguably Shakespeare's most plague-ridden play. Within the opening lines of the play, Orsino describes his first sight of Olivia:

Orsino   O, when mine eyes did see Olivia first,
Methought she purged the air of pestilence. (1.1.18–19)

Following the Paracelsian theory of contagion, which held that the pathogen entered from the outside (usually from the air), infiltrated and contaminated the body, Orsino's description of Olivia as an antidote that purges the foul air of its pestilence alludes to the early modern belief that one could remove infectious miasmas in the air by wearing aromatic perfumes near the nose. Writing in response to the 1603 plague epidemic, the writer and physician, Thomas Lodge, describes how 'the plague proceedeth from the venomous corruption of the humours and spirits of the body, *infected by the attraction* of corrupted aire ... which have the propertie to alter mans bodie, and poison his spirits' (1603: E3r, emphasis added). Central to both Lodge's and Shakespeare's notion of contagion is the process of being 'infected by the attraction' to corrupt spirits. By opening the play with 'the air of pestilence' contaminating Illyria, Shakespeare foregrounds the infection of love that pervades throughout the play. Whereas in *King Henry VI Part 2* and *As You Like It*, Shakespeare exploited the metaphor of the basilisk's gaze in order to dispel the extramission theory of sight and expose the eye to be a fragile organ susceptible to infections, in *Twelfth Night* he complicates the effects of contagious sight further by using the language of love as contagion to articulate an uneasiness about the influence – or rather, in-*flow*-ence – of the language of love which contaminates and alters the beloved's identity.

Mourning the death of her brother, Olivia keeps herself isolated from and guarded against visitors for, as her maid Maria describes her, she is 'addicted to ... melancholy' (2.5.165). Already infected with melancholy – a physical and psychological malady which, according to Galen, was caused by an imbalance of the four humours (black and yellow bile, phlegm, and blood) – Olivia seeks to protect herself from contaminative risk. For example, Orsino's gentleman, Valentine, describes how 'like a cloistress she will veiled walk / And water once a day her chamber round with eye-offending brine' (1.1.27–9) as if to disinfect her room from infectious sights. In the next scene, the Captain tells Viola, a castaway separated from her twin brother, Sebastian, in a shipwreck, that Olivia 'hath abjured the sight / And company of men' (1.2.37–8). Her face covered in a veil, her eyes able to see but hidden from the sight of others, Olivia neurotically controls her sight and others' ability to see her, repeatedly refuting Orsino's declarations of love by insisting that she 'cannot love him' (1.5.210, 215, 234). Olivia's caution against love is not unwarranted, since drawing her veil to show Cesario (Viola disguised as one of Orsino's gentlemen) her face without obstructions proves to be most harmful:

Olivia   How now?
Even so quickly may one catch the plague?
Methinks I feel this youth's perfections,
With an invisible and subtle stealth,
To creep in at mine eyes. (1.5.248–52)

In her private confession, Olivia compares falling in love with Cesario to catching the plague. Despite her cautious attempts to insulate herself from infectious sights, this one moment of careless unveiled exposure leaves Olivia plagued with love. We know from Orsino that the 'spirit of love [is] quick and fresh' (1.1.9); however, Olivia is still surprised by how 'quickly' Cesario's 'perfections' infect her. Shakespeare's contemporary, the French physician, Jacques Ferrand, describes 'love [a]s a kind of poison that is generated within the body itself [or] that slips in through the eyes ... [which are] the true conduits by which [love] flows and glides into our bowels ... where it generates malign ulcers and venomous bile' (1610: 230; 242). If, for Olivia, love infects 'quickly', Ferrand describes how love 'flows and glides'. Curiously, both Shakespeare and Ferrand evoke love to be an accidental contamination: it 'creeps in at [the] eye' or 'slips in through the eyes' with the victim unaware. As a contagion, love is dangerous precisely because it 'creeps' and 'slips' into the eyes unseen with 'an invisible and subtle stealth'. It is, therefore, unsurprising that Olivia compares her lovesickness to catching the plague since both diseases were believed to penetrate the body, through the naked eye, from external, alien, and invisible pathogens.

Indeed, lovers in Shakespeare are constantly suffering from visual plague: when advising Romeo to find another lover, Benvolio prescribes him to 'take ... some new infection to thy eye, / And the rank poison of the old will die' (*Romeo and Juliet*, 1.2.46–7); describing how the lords are infected by their ladies, Biron complains in *Love's Labours Lost* (1597), 'They are infected ... / They have caught the plague, and caught it of your eyes' (5.2.423–4). Whereas extramissive eyebeams, as Langley argues, 'in the love-lyric assumes an erotic charge, an implicit sense of proto-sexual mingling' (2006: 343), in his romantic dramas Shakespeare increasingly emphasizes the intromissive theory of sight, making the lover's eye the recipient of infections but, in doing so, conveys an awareness of the eyes as the portals for sexually transmitted diseases. Shakespeare's metaphor of love as a contagious and pathogenic emotion that is transmitted into the eyes is rooted in early modern medical treatises. The body of a lover, writes the scientist and polymath Francis Bacon, 'emitteth some Maligne and Poysonous Spirit, which taketh hold of the Spirit of Another. Such infection from Spirit to Spirit [occurs] most Forcibly by the Eye' (1627: 251). Eye to eye, spirit to spirit, each loving exchange breeds contamination, causing lovesickness to be more than just an emotion but a fatal physical ailment. If, as Alison Bashford and Claire Hooker put it, 'quite literally, according to its etymology ("con": together; "tangere": touch), contagion can put us in touch' (2001: 1), then lovesickness, like the plague, was intimate infection and, as such, dependent upon communal tactility; just as the plague relied on proximity to its victim in order to transmit parasites from host to host, the exchange of loving looks carries 'maligne and poisonous spirit[s]' from one person to another and, in doing so, infected and altered the observer. In his portrayal of infectious sights passing between lovers in *Twelfth Night*, Shakespeare offers insight into the contaminating effects of theatre on spectators. In what follows, I turn to the architecture of early modern playhouses in order to examine its effect on the sight lines between spectators and actors and how, in turn, the structure of theatres facilitated contagious sights, before returning to *Twelfth Night* to investigate how the Malvolio plot offers a meta-theatrical commentary on theatre as a site of contagion.

Architecture, antitheatricalists and theatre as a site of contagion

Gathering his group of actors in the woods to prepare for their play, 'The Most Lamentable Comedy / And Most Cruel Death of Pyramus and Thisbe' (1.2.10–11) to be performed for the Duke, Peter Quince opens Act 3 of *A Midsummer Night's Dream* (1596) by stumbling upon a 'marvellous / Convenient place for [their] rehearsal' (3.1.2–3):

> **Quince** This green plot shall be our stage, this hawthorn brake our tiring house, and we will do it in action as we will do it before the Duke. (3.1.4–5)

For Quince and his 'rude mechanicals' (3.2.9), theatre does not require a building, nor a raised platform, but simply a 'green plot'. Prior to the building of formal playhouses in Elizabethan England, 'a theatre', writes Stephen Orgel, 'was not a building, [but] a group of actors and an audience; the theatre was any place in which they chose to perform' (1991: 2). Yet the publication of Sebastio Serlio's *Architettura* in 1545 (translated into English by Robert Peake in 1611) heavily influenced the English construction of public buildings, especially the early modern playhouse. Ben Jonson's collaborator and famous architect, Inigo Jones, for example, used the Serlian amphitheatre models as inspiration for both his construction of the new barber-surgeon's theatre in London and his Cockpit Theatre in Drury Lane (Laoutaris 2008: 15). Serlio's designs taught English architects about the importance of the 'subtill and ingenious Arte of Perspectiue' (1611: fol.1v), particularly in the construction of 'scenes of th[e] Theatre' which require one to adjust the building in accordance to the sight lines of the spectator who must see 'standing aboue ground, [so] that a man may perceaue how the Scene' unfolds (1611: fol.24v). In the first English treatise on architecture, *The First and Chief Groundes of Architecture*, John Shute emphasizes the impact of 'Sebastianus Serlius, a meruclous conning artificier in our time' (1563: A3r) and argues for the importance of mathematical precision and a 'good sight in Geometrie, consequently in Opticke' (1563: B2v) for the structure of buildings. Advancements in the art or science of 'Optica ... properly called perspetiue' (Shute 1563: F2r) extended to influence not only skilled painters[4] but also playhouse architects. 'Optics', as Keir Elam notes,

> was built into the very structure of the public theatre, with its strategic attention to the crucial question of sightlines, guaranteeing the visibility of the players from every point in the architectonic arc ... The early playhouses were explicitly dedicated to favouring and facilitating spectatorship. (2014: 100)

Unlike the venues for court masques, Elizabethan amphitheatres were three-dimensional with no fixed front-facing focal point; instead, as Elam observes elsewhere, there were 'multiple points of view along a 270-degree axis' (2017: 301) from which to view the stage.

The architecture of the playhouse helped facilitate spectatorship by opening up the visual space of the theatre. The place and seat from which the playgoer watched a performance was determined by the social and financial status with the highest-ranking members being sat closest to the stage. During the reign of King James I, however, new perspective settings were put in place in the court playhouses where the monarch sat at the centre to not only see the play but be seen to see it (Orgel 1991: 16). With the King sat at the centre and playgoers assembled around him, 'the monarch', writes Orgel, 'became the centre of the theatrical experience ... and the audience around him at once became a living emblem of the structure of the court' (1991: 10–11). Thus, there were not only multiple sight lines from which to view a play but a hierarchy of perspectives which participated in either reciprocal and non-reciprocal viewing between the player and the playgoer. Such a hierarchy simultaneously controlled how and what the playgoer saw, and yet, because the playgoer had no fixed focal point, their visual experience could be easily manipulated, distorted, or obstructed either by the playgoers themselves or through theatrical illusion onstage.

For the antitheatricalists – Puritans who believed theatre to be a place of debauchery and who were writing during the closure of the playhouses caused by the plagues of 1593 and 1603 – such manipulation of the playgoers' sight was potentially dangerous precisely because, they argued, theatre could infect its audience through contagious sights. Just before the 1593 plague epidemic, the antitheatricalist Stephen Gosson instructed his readers that 'playes are the inuentions of the deuil … detest them. Players are masters of vice … loath them' (1582: G8v). The polemicists took it upon themselves not only to warn spectators of the dangers of going to the theatre but also to cure them of their addiction. Developing the arguments of Gosson, Anthony Munday emphasizes the role of the spectators' sight in actively participating in theatre's contamination:

> Onlie the filthiness of plaies, and spectacles is such, as maketh both the actors & beholders giltie alike. For while they saie nought, but gladlie looke on, they al by sight and assent be actors. (1580: 3)

The 'spectacles' infect the 'beholders' with 'filthiness of plaies' precisely because of the pleasure obtained from looking; as they 'gladlie looke on', argues Munday, player and playgoer participate in mutually destructive contamination, both 'giltie alike'. Curiously, Munday describes how the sight lines between 'actors & beholders' merge so that 'they al by sight and asset be actors'. The welding together of players' and playgoers' sight, argue the antitheatricalists, is highly dangerous because it makes the playgoer impressionable to theatre's infectious sights. They that 'came honest to a play', argues Gosson, may depart infected (1582: G4r) and return home to re-enact the vices they saw onstage.

In *Twelfth Night*, Shakespeare complicates the relationship between theatre and the antitheatricalists through the subplot of Malvolio's madness. Following from Darryl Chalk's argument that 'Malvolio is constructed as a kind of antitheatricalist in the play' (2010: 187), I argue that Malvolio plays the role of not only the puritanical enemy of theatre but also the plagued lover and infected playgoer. As an antitheatricalist, Malvolio is constantly trying to inhibit the pleasure-seeking members of Olivia's court from taking 'delight in masques and / Revels sometimes altogether' (1.3.93–4), which he calls 'uncivil rule' (2.3.104). As a lover, Malvolio 'take[s] the infection of the device' (3.4.109) – the forged love letter written by Olivia's maid, Maria, and her uncle, Sir Toby – which tricks him into believing that Olivia is 'in love with him' (2.3.139). Just as Olivia's love for Cesario contaminates her, so too Malvolio is infected by the letter and follows the instructions to change his clothes, 'I will be strange, stout, in yellow stockings, and cross-gartered' (2.5.138–9), and alters his disposition to 'please the eye' (3.4.21) of his supposed beloved. Having watched Malvolio fully embody the role of the mad lover which they devised for him, the group gather to analyse their findings:

Sir Toby	Is't possible?
Fabian	If this were played upon a stage, now, I could condemn it as an improbable fiction.
Sir Toby	His very genius hath taken the infection of the device, man.
Maria	Nay, pursue him now, lest the device take air and taint. (3.4.106–10)

Aside from the comic value of this scene, Sir Toby and Maria's response betrays an anxiety about Malvolio's lunacy and the possibility of spreading his infection. While Sir Toby observes how easily Malvolio has 'taken the infection of the device', that is to say, how susceptible Malvolio is to their staged trick, Maria is concerned that his infectious nature may 'take air and taint' others. Like 'the air of pestilence' (1.1.19) described by Orsino in the opening of the play, Maria acknowledges the dangers of infection spread via their imaginations and words. Fabian's meta-theatrical comment about 'if this were played upon a stage' adds another layer to the language of contagion in this scene whereby Shakespeare ironically points out that Malvolio's infectious state is nothing more than 'an improbable fiction'. Therefore, Malvolio transforms from playing the antitheatricalist, as Chalk argues, to adopting the role of plagued lover, before eventually becoming the playgoer who the antitheatricalists (now mockingly played by Sir Toby and Maria) think to be infected and in need of 'physic' (2.3.144).

To cure Malvolio of his lovesick-madness and prevent further contamination, Maria, Sir Toby and Feste, Olivia's jester, confine the lovelorn councillor and keep him 'in a dark room … bound' (3.4.130). Sir Toby dressed as 'Sir Topas the curate' and Feste 'being Master Parson' (4.2.13) 'visit Malvolio the lunatic' (4.2.19) who complains of being 'laid … in hideous darkness' (4.2.26). Despite being imprisoned in a cupboard, Malvolio is convinced by Sir Toby and Feste that 'there is no darkness' but 'bay windows transparent as barricadoes' (4.2.30–1), accusing Malvolio to be infected and 'more puzzled than the Egyptians in the fog' (4.2.35), yet another reference to the plague, this time referring to the ancient plague of Egypt. If, by inclosing Malvolio, the court tricksters act as the antitheatrical physicians who insist on curing him of madness, then, by staging this cure as a meta-theatrical scene, Shakespeare hints at the palliative quality of theatre. In *Twelfth Night*, Shakespeare challenges the antitheatricalists' association of theatre as a site of contagion by both staging Malvolio's infection and curing him of it through theatrical performances within the play itself.

Conclusion

Shakespeare's theatre of contagion offers its own cure. While in *King Henry VI Part 2* and *As You Like It*, Shakespeare adapts the outdated theory of extramission that held the eye to be a powerful agent of visual transmissions, typically used in Elizabethan love lyrics, in order to reveal the fragility of the eye, in *Twelfth Night* he complicates the relationship between the eye's vulnerability to infectious emotions, such as love, and the theatrical space as a site of contagion. While the primary narrative of the lovers offers a commentary on love as a sympathetic contagion that infects through corresponding looks, the Malvolio subplot stages a metatheatrical interpretation of theatre as a cure, albeit a cure that progresses out of an anxiety about contamination. Malvolio's cure at the end of the play must be theatrical precisely because he begins the play by condemning 'delight in masques' (1.3.93); Sir Toby and Maria's cure of Malvolio must occur as a scene 'played upon a stage' – a play-within-a-play – precisely because, as Fabian puts it, it is 'improbable fiction' (3.4.107). If, as Munday argues, theatre merges the sight lines between 'actors & beholders' so that 'they al by sight and assent be actors' (1580: 3), by staging metatheatrical scenes, Shakespeare's theatre creates a safe distance from which spectators can view the theatrical contamination without being directly infected by it.

In doing so, Shakespeare encourages us, as spectators, to actively engage our sight within the metafiction of Malvolio's contamination and – like Feste, who insists that by 'being Master Parson, [I] am Master Parson' (4.2.13) – to merge our sight lines with the actors, to dissolve the distinctions between fictional representation and reality, and from the safety of our seats to cheerfully accept our contamination.

Notes

1 I would like to thank the London Arts and Humanities Partnership (AHRC) for funding my research; I am grateful to Eric Langley for his generous feedback and for his guidance throughout the years which have led to up to this essay.
2 For a history of the theory of vision, see Lindberg (1976); for an account of visual theory in early modern drama, see Nordlund (1999).

3 For an account of the effects of eyebeams in early modern love lyrics, see Langley (2009).
4 For the influence of optics on early modern English painting and poetry, see Gent (1981).

References

Bacon, F. (1627), *Sylva Sylvarum; or, a Naturall Historie in Ten Centuries*, London: John Haviland and Augustine Matthews.
Barrough, P. (1583), *The Method of Phisick: Containing the Causes, Signes and Cures of Inward Diseases in a Mans Body, from the Head to the Foote*, London: Richard Field.
Bashford, A. and C. Hooker, eds (2001), *Contagion: Historical and Cultural Studies*, London: Routledge.
Brathwait, R. (1620), *Essaies upon the Five Senses*, London: E. G.
Chalk, D. (2010), '"To Creep in at Mine Eyes": Theatre and Secret Contagion in Twelfth Night', in M. Neill, D. Chalk and L. Johnson (eds), *Rapt in Secret Studies: Emerging Shakespeare*, 171–193, Newcastle upon Tyne: Cambridge Scholars.
Elam, K. (2014), 'New Directions: "Ready to Distrust Mine Eyes": Optics and Graphics in *Twelfth Night*', in A. Findlay and L. Oakley-Brown (eds), *Twelfth Night: A Critical Reader*, 99–122, London and New York: Bloomsbury Arden Shakespeare.
Elam, K. (2017), *Shakespeare's Pictures: Visual Objects in the Drama*, London, Oxford, New York, New Delhi, and Sydney: Bloomsbury Arden Shakespeare.
Ferrand, J. ([1610] 1990), *Erotomania; or, a Treatise on Lovesickness*, ed. and trans. D. A. Beecher and M. Ciavolella, Syracuse: Syracuse University Press.
Gent, L. (1981), *Picture and Poetry 1560–1620: Relations between Literature and the Visual Art in the English Renaissance*, Leamington Spa: James Hall.
Gosson, S. (1582), *Plays Confuted in Five Actions*, London: Thomas Gosson.
Langley, E. (2006), 'Anatomizing the Early Modern Eye: A Literary Case-study', *Renaissance Studies*, 20 (3): 340–355.
Langley, E. (2009), *Narcissism and Suicide in Shakespeare and His Contemporaries*, Oxford: Oxford University Press.
Laoutaris, C. (2008), *Shakespearean Maternities: Crises of Conception in Early Modern England*, Edinburgh: University of Edinburgh Press.
Laurentius, A. (1599), *A Discourse of the Preservation of the Sight: Of Melancholike Diseases; of Rheumes, and of Old Age*, trans. R. Surphlet, London: Felix Kingston for Ralph Jacson.
Lindberg, D. C. (1976), *Theories of Vision from Alkindi to Kepler*, Chicago and London: University of Chicago Press.
Lodge, T. (1603), *A Treatise of the Plague Containing the Nature, Signes, and Accidents of the Same*, London: Thomas Creed.

Lobanov-Rostovsky, S. (1997), 'Taming the Basilisk', in D. Hillman and C. Mazzio (eds), *The Body in Parts: Fantasies of Corporeality in Early Modern Europe*, 194–217, London: Routledge.

Munday, A. (1580), *A Second and Third Blast of Retreat from Plays and Theaters*, London: Henrie Denham.

Nordlund, M. (1999), *The Dark Lantern: A Historical Study of Sight in Shakespeare, Webster, and Middleton*, Gothenburg: Acta Universitatis Gothoburgensis.

Orgel, S. (1991), *The Illusion of Power: Political Theatre in the English Renaissance*, Berkley: University of California Press.

Oxford English Dictionary. Available online: http://www.oed.com/ (accessed 10 June 2018).

Serlio, S. ([1545] 1611), *The First Booke of Architecture*, trans. R. Peake, London: Simon Stratford.

Shakespeare, W. (1998), *The Arden Shakespeare Complete Works*, eds A. Thompson, D. Kastan and R. Proudfoot, London: Arden Shakespeare.

Shute, J. (1563), *The First and Chief Grovnds of Architectvre*, London: Thomas Marshe.

5

Catching a Feeling: A Practice-based Inquiry into Affective Contagion in Elizabeth Inchbald's *The Massacre*

Rebecca McCutcheon

Introduction

Historically contagion has been characterized with almost entirely negative connotations. From its origins as a term articulating the spread of disease, to its nineteenth-century emergence in the understanding of crowds (as in the work of Le Bon and Tarde, discussed below), contagion is rarely viewed in a positive light. At the same time, contagious affect is a central element of most theatre with the spread of feelings of pleasure, laughter or horror amongst audience members often contributing to the experience of performance. Theatre is a social situation, a shared, live experience, so that a sense of contagiousness is ever-present, whether it be in the exposure to ideas, affect or sometimes disease. Arguably then, both negative and positive contagion have always been part of the theatrical experience. Focusing on my own practice-based research, in this chapter I examine the process of deliberately working with affective contagion. As I will discuss, far from having relatively narrow and simple negative associations, the power and range of possibilities of contagious affect are vast and complex.

In this chapter I focus on my practice-as-research leading to the site-based performances of *A Testimony and a Silence* at Dilston Grove, London, in 2014. This performance-making process worked with Elizabeth Inchbald's rarely performed play, *The Massacre* (1792), as a starting point. Inchbald was a successful actor, editor and writer whose playwrighting output achieved professional success in her lifetime, but despite this, her work has remained neglected since her death. *The Massacre* deals with the sectarian massacres of Huguenots by Catholics in 1572. Within this text a conceptualization of contagion as mob behaviour is a central theme. Through my practice-as-research performances of *A Testimony and a Silence*, contagion became interwoven into almost every aspect of the work, becoming an organizing thematic of the research and production phase, contributing to practices that might be termed 'contagious dramaturgies'.[1] Here I examine contagious affect in performance in light of cultural geography, affect theory and theories of social contagion.

A site-based practice of unperformed texts

As a director my site-specific practice has included directing work with a range of theatre texts and sites, from Christopher Marlowe's *Dido, Queen of Carthage* in a women's refuge in Soho in 2006 to Arthur Schnitzler's *Round Dance* at the Roundhouse, Camden, in 2004. My directing approach assumes a generative relationship between site and text, seeking not a simple mapping of a singular narrative onto space but assuming dissonance and disruption between text and site, with the site offering a creative and discursive frame for the text, so that in the gaps and disjuncture, new interpretations and processes emerge.

My practice-as-research is located within this work and in the exploration of the particular opportunities and openings site-based practice offers to texts that lack performance histories. This is a feminist practice of retrieval and space making, seeking creative and cultural space for the artistic examination of silenced female voices. Site-based performance practice offers non-traditional, non-canonical settings in which to encounter plays as a maker and creates modes of reception for audiences in which greater openness to unknown stories and intensely experienced relationships to the text are foregrounded.

The work at Dilston Grove was informed by a practice that I think of as 'archaeological' (Pearson 2010: 42) with the tracing of the histories of the space generating a set of stimuli, memories and imaginings with which to encounter our text. This characterisation of the site, as a palimpsest layering different uses over time visible through physical traces, I connect with Michel de Certeau's characterisation of 'space' and 'place' – for de Certeau 'place' is the formal, sanctioned use of the site, and 'space' refers to more informal and tactical appropriations (de Certeau 1984: 117). As will be discussed in the following section, formal, sanctioned uses of place at Dilston interweave with evidence of informal appropriations of the space in ways that contribute to a complex set of affective atmospheres. Identifying and working with these atmospheric affects was one of the affective dramaturgies developed in my directing process.

The places and spaces of Dilston Grove

Dilston Grove in Southwark Park, Bermondsey, is an unusual Grade II listed building. Built as a church for Clare College Cambridge's London mission in 1911, it is the first in situ poured concrete building in the UK, designed by Sir John Simpson and Maxwell Ayrton, designers of the Wembley complex. Its proportions are tall and narrow, and its concrete walls are unlined, giving an exceptionally raw feeling and smell to the interior space. In the 1960s the church fell into disrepair until 1999 when Bermondsey Artists' Group established Dilston Grove as an exhibition space.

The site presents two very distinct place identities, after de Certeau: its current place identity, as exhibition space, and its former place identity, as a church. Strictly speaking, the first is its legitimate place identity, but its identity as a church arguably predominates. The interior, although stripped of ecclesiastical apparatus, still contains many strong religious associations. Steps up to a former altar area form one of the few spatial divisions in the room; a side door containing a stairway up to a former organ loft provides the only elevated view of the space available. Church 'props' have been stripped away but the spaces for them remain, like a footprint, evoking recollections of past church experiences.

In addition to this duality of Dilston's place identity, traces of the period of disuse offer hints of a disturbing or disruptive 'spatial practice'. Site as church and site as art space bracket a period without a defined identity. Evidence of this period appears throughout the space in the form of cracks to the walls, scratches on the painted concrete surface, patterns and marks which hint at temporary annexations now long gone and unrecorded. These traces of damage or neglect carry an unsettling quality within the space.

In engaging with Dilston Grove as a site for *The Massacre*, these three traces of past use each played a role at different points in the creative process. The play's status, as a silenced account of atrocity, became a central thread to which Dilston Grove's current identity as an exhibition space provided a frame, as a kind of memorializing space, a thread which was developed in designer Tallulah Mason's scenographic installations in the space and the design/directing concept for elements of the performance. Its past identity, as a religious place, resonated with the play's subject matter, which centres on the persecution of a group of Protestant Christians, and informed some costume and character choices. The play's tension around the representation of the violence it recounts and its suppression found a spatial metaphor in the traces of abandonment and disuse visible in the space. This constellation of place identities and spatial practices offered a rich starting point from which to approach and explore the text in the space.

The Massacre and negative contagion

Inchbald adapted *The Massacre* from an anonymous English translation of a play entitled *Jean Hennuyer, the Bishop of Lizieux or the Massacre of St Bartholomew*, which recounts the history of the Catholic Bishop of Lizieux during the 1572 St Bartholomew's Day massacres. These were sectarian killings of affluent Huguenot Protestants by Catholics in France during 1572, which began in Paris and subsequently spread across several French provinces (Diefendorf 2009, Sutherland 1973). The original text claims that the violent events it describes are based on eyewitness accounts, claims that Inchbald retains in her footnotes. Inchbald's interest in, and mistrust of, the suggestibility of humans is a recurrent theme in her writing; in the farce, *Animal Magnetism* of 1788, Inchbald had sent up the popular pseudo-medical theories of Dr Fransz Mesmer and his use of hypnosis. Her treatment of the forces of affect in *The Massacre* takes a much more urgent view of the dangers present where such invisible forces are unleashed.

Inchbald wrote her version of *The Massacre* at the height of the French Revolution in 1792, during The Terror, when rumours in England of extreme violence were rife. The play first circulated to theatre managements for performance, an idea from which Inchbald withdrew. It was subsequently prepared for publication, but again, Inchbald withdrew it. It was published in 1833 after Inchbald's death. In the 'Advertisement' (foreword) to the published play text Inchbald writes:

> From the time that I first undertook the foregoing scenes, I never flattered myself that they [the scenes] would be proper to appear on the stage. The subject is too horrid, that I thought it would shock, rather than give satisfaction. Still, I found it so truly tragic in the essential springs of terror and pity, that I could not resist the impulse of adapting it to the scene. (Inchbald [1833] 2012: 357)

In Inchbald's memoir, editor Boaden hints that advice to suppress the play from Inchbald's friends, Holcroft and Godwin, was driven by 'party and self-interest', as the play might be read as exposing 'republican horrors' (Inchbald [1833] 2012: 304). In the play's repeated suppression, from performance and then from publication at all, what emerges is a play hot with dangerous associations, liable to infect any mind that comes into contact with it.

Though written almost 100 years before nineteenth-century theories of contagion began to emerge, these ideas were arguably anticipated by Inchbald's play. Inchbald appears to be driven by an impassioned sense of bystander guilt and powerlessness, perhaps founded in her position as a distanced observer of atrocities in Paris, a city she had lived in and loved, or perhaps by her experience as a Catholic of the Gordon riots in London (riots against Catholics by Protestants of 1780). Whatever the origin, contagious behaviours surface repeatedly as a disastrous force throughout the play.

Inchbald depicts a fictionalized Huguenot family, the Tricastins, in the intimacy of their home, awaiting the return of their son and husband, Eusebe Tricastin, from a Huguenot wedding in Paris. They learn that terrible events have taken place, the wedding party has been attacked and murdered, and Eusebe a possible victim. When Eusebe arrives he describes in broken, fragmented passages his experience. He depicts in lurid detail violence spreading across societal boundaries as taboos are broken down:

> I saw aged men dragged by their white hairs; a train of children following to prevent their fate, only to rush upon their own. I saw infants, encouraged by the fury of their tutors, stab other infants, sleeping in their cradles. (Inchbald [1833] 2012: 365)

This speech is footnoted with an explanation testifying the image's origin: 'Shocking, even to incredulity, as these murders may appear, the truth of them has been asserted in many of our public prints, during the late massacre at Paris' (Inchbald [1833] 2012: 365).

The taboo-breaking, dehumanizing violence described by Eusebe is viewed as contagious by Mme Tricastin. She compares it to an airborne disease:

> Rather let us fly the danger which threatens us. We know the tendency of the people, even of this place – the infection of the metropolis still spreads – let us leave the city – nay the land – and not breathe its air til the sweet breeze of peace restore its lost tranquillity. (Inchbald [1833] 2012: 370)

Violence is here characterized as an infection – a transmissible sickness the susceptibility to which is a 'tendency' of the people of the town – involuntary and environmental. Escape from this threat will occur when they reach a place where peace reigns – also as an airborne entity, restoring its sweetness after the pestilence of violence.

Fear of contagious violence re-emerges in the second act when the family learn that the mob has reached the town, vividly imaged as a quickly spreading conflagration: 'The rage of the adverse party is not confined to the capital: some from thence are arrived in this city, and have increased that flame, which has long since been kindled amongst our populace' (Inchbald

[1833] 2012: 372). The character of contagion has shifted: from airborne, it is now a fire, catching hold of those around it. Eusebe seeks to confront the mob, a move his father opposes – appealing to him to resist a reflexive response to violence through imitation: 'I can feel for the various passions which transport you, my child, to this excess of despair – but do not imitate your foes' (Inchbald [1833] 2012: 372). This depiction of the townsfolk anticipates the depictions of crowds more than a century later in Gustav Le Bon's *The Crowd* – a mass of people involuntarily held in the sway of regression and violence. The violence here is viewed as potentially spreading through the function of imitation – for Le Bon et al., as for Inchbald, the role of imitation is characterized as wholly negative, relating to 'lower' functions, to violence, to loss of control and negative behaviours.

In the third act, the forces of contagion are brought climactically onto the stage. Dugas, the leader of the town's mob, is seen fomenting increasing violence in a crowd outside the court. The family are put to trial and unexpectedly released by a humanist Catholic judge, Glandeve. The family are jubilant when they are confronted by the death at the mob's hands of Mme Tricastin and their small children. The violence has steadily encroached on the action until the stage is filled with the bodies of the women and children who have been brutally murdered while the men create their compact of agreement.

Thus, anxiety over contagion forms a recurring theme within *The Massacre*. Contagious affect is depicted as airborne, spreading violent impulses infectiously, like a disease between people and places. Next, contagious affect is presented as a conflagration, igniting people like so much dry kindling. Finally, Inchbald presents contagious affect as spread via imitation and reflexive response: deeply suspect, regressive and in opposition to both rational thought and social good.

Tracing contagion's historical contexts

The idea of contagion in relation to illness and disease is traceable across a range of cultures and time periods. J. K. Stearns, in *Infectious Ideas: Contagion in Premodern Islamic and Christian Thought*, offers an early account of the spread of plague found in the gospel as evidence of the longevity of the concept: 'I am of the opinion that all the epidemics, like any plague, are spread amongst people by evil spirits who poison the air or exhale pestilential breath, which puts a deadly poison into the flesh' (1 John 3.16; Martin Luther 1527, quoted in Stearns 2011: 21). Here the transmission of disease is understood as a mechanism which operates through a cluster of vectors, some of which are medical (airborne on 'pestilential breath'), others supernatural (evil spirits). This clustered identification of disease with its symptoms, and with a range of causations, prevailed through the early modern period until the shift in medical paradigms of the nineteenth century, towards a causal theory of contagion. Here, according to Andrew Cunningham in *The Laboratory Revolution in Medicine* (2002), a shift in concepts of contagion becomes dominant, as occurring strictly due to microbial infection.

Ideas of behavioural or affective contagion, distinct from medical models, also emerge in the nineteenth century in the social sciences, as concepts through which imitation is theorized. In this view, certain physical behaviours are viewed as contagious, such as yawning and laughing, and in common with the medical spread of disease, involuntary. The physical behaviours transmitted through contagion may then give rise to associated emotions – such as anger, amusement or fear. Discussions of behavioural and affective contagion emerge with force in the writings of Le Bon and Gabriel Tarde on the collective behaviours of the group and the crowd. For Le Bon, writing in 1897: '[U]nder certain given circumstances ... an agglomeration of men presents new characteristics very different from those of the individuals composing it. A collective mind is formed' (Le Bon 1994: 25).

The key characteristics of this newly formed 'collective' mind amongst crowds include a sense of invincibility and lack of restraint, due to the sheer force of numbers of people in the crowd; suggestibility and contagion: 'in a crowd every sentiment and act is contagious, and contagious to a degree that an individual readily sacrifices his individual interest to the collective interest' (27). For Le Bon this leads to 'the disappearance of the conscious personality – by the mere fact of joining a crowd a man descends several rungs in the ladder of civilisation ... in a crowd he is a barbarian' (27).

Related to Le Bon's analysis is Gabriel Tarde's *Laws of Imitation*, Tarde posits a notion of collective behaviour driven by imitation in which a powerful level of suggestibility replaces conscious will:

> When we speak of obedience, we mean a conscious and voluntary act. But primitive obedience was far different ... The obedience of crowds and armies to their demagogues is strange. And so is their incredulity. (Tarde 1903: 81)

For Tarde, like Le Bon, and Inchbald before them, affective contagion is an irrational and dehumanizing facet of human social life to be resisted and suspect. Imitation is presented as one of the key mechanisms through which the spread of both emotions and actions occurs and is characterized negatively almost without exception.

In- and out-groups in *A Testimony and a Silence*

At the outset of our practical inquiry's development, the idea of the transmission of affect across groups linked the subject of *The Massacre* (belonging to the Catholic or the Huguenot group), our readings on negative contagion emerging through our research (participation in a crowd as an 'in-group' behaviour) and our experience of performance. Performances set up the 'in'-group – audience and performers – as participants in a shared experience. There are conventions around being a 'good' or 'appropriate' audience member. While it felt important not to compel obedience from the audience, and it is important to recognize that participation in groups in performance for most audience members involves an awareness of participating in a set of rules, it still seemed possible to explore some dynamics of the group in performance to approach experiences of contagion and affect in a limited and consciously critical way.

In developing our performance in the space, we staged the first act of the play in the chancel of Dilston Grove. The Tricastins are seen in their domestic environment receiving the news of the massacre and Eusebe's return. By using a relatively contained part of the space and encouraging the actors to include the audience in the domestic setting they were performing, the aim was to transmit feelings of empathy and intimacy with the Tricastins. Audience members were addressed directly by the actors, some seated in chairs in the space as if they were members of the household. Actors made use of accidental physical touch and of eye contact. At the end of the act the audience and performers held hands in a circle, preparing to leave the 'home' together. During this section of performance, audience members reported feelings of inclusion and welcome in the space, which triggered feelings of connection to the family.

The audience were moved down the space by the company to a much more open part of the site, treated by the actors as an external street scene. The actors shifted their relations to the audience. They behaved as 'in-group' mob members, questioning and harassing the audience as they searched for Tricastin's father. The actors moved through the audience, herding them with aggressive body language and accusing each of them of being the person they hunted. Here, audience members reported feeling unnerved and uneasy at being exposed in an open space and protective towards the Tricastin family. '[It was] moving, engaging – at times uncomfortable. Allowing me to connect to the individuals to whom the history happened (if that makes sense). Feelings of horrible and unnerving crowd dynamics' (audience response to post-performance questionnaire) (Figure 5.1).

Figure 5.1 The performance space at Dilston Grove. Photo courtesy of photographer Jamie Smith.

In the final part of the performance the audience were marched by the company to stand by the chancel steps for the mock court. In this transition, the cast came the closest to coercive behaviour towards the audience, tying white armbands on some (the in-group sign of the Roman Catholics in the St Bartholomew's Day massacres). In this 'court-room' formation, the audience were instructed to line up opposite each other. Here audiences reported feeling resistance and anger, a desire to move away from the event, but equally powerless to stop things from happening.

In these distinct group dynamics our aim was to explore how treatment of the audience as complicit group members, on the side of both the Tricastins and the mob, led to experiences of negative contagion. This is not to make claims that audiences were unaware of their real role as an audience. However, through deploying affective strategies of connection and intimacy – treating audience members as part of the 'family', using eye contact and accidental touch to guide them in the space – and through activating the pliable obedience that is the 'good' audience members' tacit contract with the performers, we explored something of the experiences of group participation that are central themes in the play.

No audience members felt unaware of their surroundings, but many reported feeling empathy, fear and compassion for the Tricastins, and anger, hostility and fear of speaking out to the mob. Audiences reported an intensity of involvement in the story almost always grounded in an emotional response to an actor's non-verbal cues. The act of placing audience members strongly in or out of a given group within the process appears to have contributed an intensity of involvement in the story and attachment to the characters. While audiences in traditional theatre contexts relate to characters and narrative, in site-based and participatory forms, a qualitatively more intense sense of experiential engagement is often apparent. These explorations of in-group behaviour and negative contagion seem to indicate that at least part of this qualitative difference relates to affective (and contagious) responses. Significantly contagion was not restricted to negative affect but felt as positive by the audience, such as through the intimacy and empathy felt for the Tricastins, as became evident in audience feedback responses, which we gathered after each performance: 'Space and atmosphere contributed a lot – you could feel more than just hearing and understanding the character's words' (audience response to post-performance questionnaire).

The affective turn and site-specific perspectives

In 'Understanding the Affective Spaces of Political Performance', cultural geographer Nigel Thrift argues that ideas of affective contagion, such as those of Tarde, Le Bon and Inchbald, fell out of favour in the twentieth century due to their appropriation and negative characterization by the intellectual right. In recent years however, contagion has been reconsidered in the turn to affect, this time with more positive associations. The role of imitation, Thrift argues, is not 'just' an animal drive leading to negative mob behaviours but as an expression of positive empathic mimicry, widely present in social encounters, and as a means through which processes of sympathetic induction occur throughout social life. Thrift argues that an understanding of the role of imitation draws a helpful focus on the 'delicate separation between one's own mental life and that of another' (Thrift 2009: 88).

This contemporary theorization of affect arguably originates in the philosophy of Baruch Spinoza and his radical concept of bodies. In *The Ethics*, Spinoza lays out axioms on the nature of bodies. Bodies are not defined by their organic form, or by their substance, he argues, but 'bodies are distinguished from one another by reason of motion and rest, speed and slowness, and not by reason of substance' (Spinoza 1994: 126). What a body is must be considered as equivalent to what a body can do, and the capacity to do is defined along two axes: kinetic and dynamic. On the kinetic axis, for Spinoza, 'all bodies either move or are at rest' (Spinoza 1994: 126). The dynamic axis refers to the capacity a body has to affect and be affected by other bodies. Spinoza also argues that bodies are not restricted to individuals, but 'when a number of bodies, whether of the same or of different size, are so constrained by other bodies that they lie upon one another ... we shall say that those bodies are united with one another' (Spinoza 1994: 126).

Spinoza's expanded idea of the body, as both possibly collective and not limited to the human, creates space to consider encounters between individuals and groups, and between other, non-human bodies. Spinoza's focus on the significance of the capacity to influence (the 'dynamic' axis) is similarly expansive. It creates space in which to consider a range of behaviours, which may be non-verbal, perhaps not always conscious. The significance of environment, connected with porousness through the capacity to influence other bodies, frames site-specific and immersive theatre as perhaps pre-eminently affective encounters.

This revaluing of processes of affective contagion connects with a number of the concerns of contemporary theatre practice in which environment, interaction and participation between audience and performer play a role. Awareness of the porous boundaries between performers, spectators and their shared environment is a formal concern of practitioners working across diverse fields, from site-based practitioners such as dreamthinkspeak, immersive theatre practices such as Punchdrunk and Shunt collective, or the practice of intimate theatre such as in the work of the late Adrian Howells.

At Dilston Grove, we became interested in exploring the possibilities of this more expansive notion of affect proposed by Thrift. We wanted to examine to what extent we could invite audiences into spheres of affect to share in the feeling as well as the narrative of particular characters. A concept that facilitated this exploration is Gernot Bohme's view of 'atmospheres' in 'Atmosphere as the Fundamental Concept of a New Aesthetics' (Bohme 1993: 113). As a site-based practitioner 'atmosphere' is something I have habitually engaged with but found to be a nebulous term for something that was very difficult to pin down. There is a paucity of analytical or descriptive terms but, more than this, a sense of difficulty in localizing atmospheres. Is it in the space itself, or is it something that is purely to do with subjective experience? Both of these possibilities seem to miss something important. Bohme places atmosphere in an in-between space that conceptually appears to bear a relationship to the working of affect. For Bohme, the perception of atmospheres needs to be conceived as:

> Neither objective, that is, qualities possessed by things, yet they are something thing like, belonging to the thing in that things articulate their presence through qualities ... Nor are atmospheres something

subjective, for example, determinations of a psychic state. And yet they are subject like, belong to subjects in that they are sensed in bodily presence by human beings. (Bohme 1993: 122)

For Bohme an atmosphere is both/and: both object like, and subject like. This quality of in-betweenness places atmospheres as in process, as an exchange between perceiving subject and the environment that is both of the perceiver and of the space.

Contagious atmospheres and 'micro-environments'

We interrogated the idea of affective atmospheres in the individual character devising work in which each actor was engaged. Each performer developed interactive encounters based on the idea of their character occupying a 'micro-environment' in the space. Each micro-environment had its origins in the coming together of a strand of text, usually a key moment in each character's trajectory, with a feature of the site. The selected feature could be a particular area, a texture or an atmosphere, anything that triggered for that actor a particular feeling or association. The drawing together of text and site occurred through the creative interaction of each actor with the site, and within the group there were a range of performance practices. Thus a dance practitioner responded to the site principally through movement; performers with acting training responded through improvising text and actions. What evolved was a series of individual environments inhabited by a different actor/character. The evolution our engagement with affective contagion introduced was that each inhabitation was underpinned by an emotional state drawn from their character's narrative, expressed in a wordless invitation to audience members to participate in an action. For example, actor Alex Appleby played the character of Colonel Rochelle, a soldier who is scarred by being unable to save the lives of the Tricastin children. Appleby selected a fragment of text in which Rochelle recounts attempting and failing to save Madame Tricastin and her children, imagining that this memory is one that haunts Rochelle. Appleby created a performance vignette in which his character lays out and then collects stones as memorials for the dead. His exchange with audience members was to invite them into his memorial space and to participate with him in placing a stone.

Actor Kate Russell-Smith worked in the chancel, suggesting a nursery environment, with a cradle and children's clothing as supporting objects. Russell-Smith's costume included a pregnancy bump, and the cradle and children's clothing all emphasized her role as mother. Her exchanges with audience members involved her inviting them into her children's bedroom and encouraging them to rock the cradle and to sing a lullaby with her. Russell-Smith's actions became more stylized as she worked with the clothes hung on the wall, as if tucking a row of children into bed. Her performance as an attentive, loving mother in the nursery existed in disconnection with the frame of the chancel so that her actions, though naturalistic, were not literally presented as a nursery environment. Rather what seemed to be experienced by audience members was a response to her maternal warmth, a willingness to attend to and share her loving care, while at the same time implicitly understanding that this representation is a ghosting, imagined enactment of Mme Tricastin.

The rest of the acting company developed interactions that were also inspired by a response to an element of the physical site and combined with a fragment of their character's text. In performance, they would invite audience members to join with them in their 'environment' – to share a drink, to make an origami flower, to open a door, to flee. Audience members moved around the space and would hover with a particular actor. Audience responses to these encounters expressed high levels of emotional engagement and sometimes a sense of confusion about why they felt such an intensity for a character they know little about: 'the space was very sparse and cell like. By contrast, my interactions with the characters were highly human and emotional – they warmed up the space for me' (audience feedback). And also: 'With the mother character I felt a real sense of empathy. She was very … not enticing, but you wanted to go and comfort her' (audience response to post-performance questionnaire).

As each encounter involved an invitation to participate, driven by the underlying emotional need of a character, the mechanism of engagement here is emotionally and affectively led. Audiences were not directly told how to respond, and the text of the invitation deliberately did not explicitly refer to any emotional state, yet audience members asked to describe their experiences reported distinct shifts in response to different actors at different points in the space. Therefore, we might surmise that the emotional or affective connection reported by most audience members was at least in part enabled by the contagious aesthetic structures we sought to cultivate. This is not to say that the nature of each response was identical or identically interpreted. However, I was struck as a maker by the quality of engagement, which was palpable in the space and in the feedback. The use of affective contagion had proved powerful as a means of engaging audiences in a surprisingly deeply felt way with our text and performance. Some audience members reported experiencing discomfort, an anxiety about 'not knowing what is wanted' by performers, a tension which arguably acknowledges the way the performance was actively exploring and playing with the usual confines of audience/performer dynamic. However such discomfort was also reflected upon as productive, recognized or appreciated as part of an encounter that involved them in the performance.

> At first it was quite disorienting – I didn't know who to engage with – it gave the sense of rewinding/replaying memory ... as the piece went on those fragments began to make sense and slot into a whole. I liked the way they set the scene, an atmosphere and some of the play. (Audience response to post-performance questionnaire)

For many audience members, the willingness to engage with the feeling transmitted by a character appeared to support them to feel at ease in an environment that they didn't immediately understand. The use of ideas of contagion as a means of exploring and developing 'micro-environments' and underpinning audience interactions proved powerful in the possibilities they presented for connecting audiences with new narratives. Equally they provided us as makers with conceptual tools through which to generate these connections, supporting us to identify clearly what we wanted to transmit in our interactions and strategies through which to achieve this. I would argue that affective ideas offer valuable conceptual and processual tools to any practice in which the interplay of site, environment and audience is an aesthetic concern. Equally ideas of contagious affect provide a lens through which to articulate subtle, often intangible and unquantifiable aspects of performance and process, such as the role of atmosphere, or the nuance of group dynamics.

Conclusion

As a concept contagion has carried with it strong sets of negative associations, from its origin in the transmission of disease to accounts of contagious behaviours, especially imitative contagion found in Inchbald and later in Le Bon and Tarde. The practice-based inquiry I led as a director working with the text of *The Massacre* certainly confirmed that the play's themes – of in-group and out-group behaviours – evoked powerful responses in contemporary audiences that testify that the concerns that drove Inchbald to write her play focused on events of the sixteenth century retain an enduring relevance and power. Our audiences displayed an ongoing discomfort with our vulnerability to crowd behaviours and a perception of them as involuntary. Yet if contagion can be retrieved from these negative associations then it is possible to reveal a richness in this cluster of concepts that supports greater understanding of and creativity in relation to audience/performer relations. One might even argue that a more positive model of this is particularly evident in the growing fields of site-based and immersive theatres but perhaps equally in more traditional forms.

The more expansive view of affect, as advanced by geographer Nigel Thrift, developing the ideas of philosopher Spinoza, advances a broader view of contagion which appears to diffuse through much of social life – imitation as key to parent/infant bonding, empathy as essential to social cohesion. Conscious recognition of this porousness between one another and things arguably offers us 'a pedagogic nudge aimed towards a body's becoming an ever more worldly sensitive interface, towards a style of being present to the struggles of our time' (Gregg and Seigworth 2010: 12).

In the case of theatre, and this site-based practice-as-research process of unperformed texts, our creative engagement with affective contagion underpinned our development of processes in which audience responses to both site and performance held a compelling quality of intensity and empathy. As a strategy for connecting audiences with texts that are unknown to them, this enabled us to draw a direct, non-cerebral connection directly with the emotions of our audiences, although there are clear limits to understanding the degree or quality of this engagement. However, as a means for generating ways of working articulately with atmospheres, and finding ourselves able to transmit those atmospheres to our audiences, affective contagion helped us identify a new way of thinking about atmosphere as like both subject and object. As a way of thinking through and understanding issues which have characterized audience behaviours and the reception of site-based and immersive works, affective contagion's capacity to connect beyond language, to activate powerful emotions, places it at the forefront of theorizing these relatively new aesthetic forms. As processes and performances of site-based and immersive theatre take root firmly in the mainstream of subsidized and commercial theatre alike, the turn to affect and, within that, affective contagion invites a new set of vocabularies and concepts for creating and understanding the new world of performer/audience and site relations.

Note

1 This project formed part of a practice-as-research PhD process. It was directed by Rebecca McCutcheon and performed by Damian Quinn and Kate Russell-Smith at Dilston Grove, London, 13–14 May 2014.

References

A Testimony and a Silence – Post Performance Questionnaire Responses (2014), Directed by Rebecca McCutcheon, London: Dilston Grove, 13 and 14 May.

Anonymous ([1773] 2010), *Jean Hennuyer, Bishop of Lizieux: Or, the Massacre of St. Bartholomew: A Dramatic Entertainment, in Three Acts. Translated from the French*, London: Gale ECCO Print Editions.

Boaden, J., ed. ([1833] 2012) *Inchbald, Mrs., 1753–1821. Memoirs of Mrs. I. Including Her Familiar Correspondence with the Most Distinguished Persons of Her Time*, London: Forgotten Books.

Bohme, G. (1993), 'Atmosphere as the Fundamental Concept of a New Aesthetics', *Thesis Eleven*, 36: 113–126.

Cunningham, A. and P. Williams (2002), *The Laboratory Revolution in Medicine*, Cambridge: Cambridge University Press.

de Certeau, M. (1984), *The Practice of Everyday Life*, Berkeley: University of California Press.

Dido, Queen of Carthage by Christopher Marlowe (2006), Directed by Rebecca McCutcheon, London: The House of St Barnabas, May–June.

Diefendorf, Barbara B. (2009), *The St. Bartholomew's Day Massacre: A Brief History with Documents*, Boston, MA: Bedford/St Martin's.

Gregg, M. and G. J. Seigworth (2010), *The Affect Theory Reader*, Durham: Duke University Press.

Inchbald, E. ([1833] 2012), 'The Massacre, Taken from the French, A Tragedy in Three Acts, London', in J. Boaden (ed.), *Inchbald, Mrs., 1753–1821. Memoirs of Mrs. I. Including Her Familiar Correspondence with the Most Distinguished Persons of Her Time*, London: Forgotten Books.

Le Bon, G. ([1895]1994), *The Crowd: A Study of the Popular Mind*, Greenville, SC: The Traders Press.

Pearson, M. (2010), *Site-specific Performance*, New York: Palgrave Macmillan.

Spinoza, B. de (1994), *A Spinoza Reader: The Ethics and Other Works*, ed. and trans. Edwin Curley, Princeton, NJ: Princeton University Press.

Stearns, J. K. (2011), *Infectious Ideas – Contagion in Premodern Islamic and Christian Thought*, Baltimore: Johns Hopkins University Press.

Sutherland, N. M. (1973), *The Massacre of St Bartholomew and the European Conflict, 1559–1572*, London: Macmillan.

Tarde, G. ([1890] 1903), *The Laws of Imitation*, trans. Elsie Clews Parsons. New York: Henry Holt & Company.

The Round Dance by Arthur Schnitzler (2004), Directed by Rebecca McCutcheon, London: The Roundhouse Undercroft, October–November.

Thrift, N. (2009), 'Understanding the Affective Spaces of Political Performance', in M. Smith, J. Davidson, L. Cameron and L. Bondi (eds), *Emotion, Place, and Culture*, 76–95, Farnham: Ashgate.

Part Two

Sites of Contamination and Containment

6

Plague Inc.: Theatre's Engagement with Mechanisms of Contagion and Containment

Kirsten E. Shepherd-Barr

This chapter explores the semantic versatility of the term 'contagion' as refracted through the extraordinary diversity of theatre and performance from the nineteenth century to the present. First, I look at representative nineteenth-century theatrical engagements with evolution, biology and other related sciences to show theatre's preoccupation with mechanisms of transmission broadly conceived. This part of the chapter also investigates how and when the line began to blur between a strictly medical definition of contagion and a fuzzier 'social disease' usage, onto which theatre cottoned very early on. Second, I trace the powerful legacy of these theatrical engagements with contagion in two instances: Antonin Artaud's immersive, experiential 'plague as performance' idea and the invention of digital games that allow users to create and 'perform' plagues and pandemics. The line of questioning underpinning these transhistorical examples is how contagion relates to definitions of culture founded, paradoxically, on containment and control, a discussion that forms the third section of my chapter. I conclude by drawing all of these strands together in light of the pressure to forge productive disciplinary cross-contaminations in a professional environment that increasingly regulates, directs and controls interdisciplinarity.

Theatre and contagion have had a long and fascinating interconnection, both on stage and in performance theory. Plague hangs in the air of Sophocles's *Oedipus Rex*; Elizabethan theatre constantly invokes the 'pox'; Ibsen, Chekhov, Brieux and other late-nineteenth-century playwrights boldly discuss diseases like syphilis and tuberculosis; Tony Kushner puts AIDS on stage in *Angels in America*. Contagion is both real and metaphorical and is a powerful tool for the playwright. Equally so for the theorist and critic: Artaud made contagion not just a theme but a central metaphor and the platform of his thought (as I discuss below), while Jonas Barish articulated the age-old 'anti-theatrical prejudice' whose very basis is a fear of contagion, mainly emotional and moral but also physical – the catching of bad things at the playhouse (1985). Religious bodies are often most condemning of theatre's dangerous contagiousness (from medieval links with plague right through to attempts to close down productions such as *Angels in America* across the United States or *Behzti* in Birmingham) yet sanction the inherent danger of contagion within their own sacramental rituals and practices.

Theatre has, however, been strangely absent from studies of contagion as a cultural phenomenon. The recent book *Endemic: Essays in Contagion Theory*, edited by Kari Nixon and Lorenzo Servitje, does not address the interrelationship of contagion and performance, although Jennifer Cooke, in *Legacies of Plague in Literature, Theory and Film* (2009), includes a chapter on theatre. For the editors of *Endemic*, contagion is both a looming threat and a principle of cohesion (Nixon and Servitje 2016: vii). This principle of cohesion 'threatens not by virtue of its menace from without, or even by the ever-present possibility of eruption, but by its very nature as a precarious necessity' (Nixon and Servitje 2016: vii). I am interested in expanding on this idea and testing it out in light of the material that follows with examples drawn from across genres and periods. Although I do focus primarily on the nineteenth century, I take a transhistorical approach in the spirit of Rita Felski's work (Felski 2008, 2011), accentuating how easily the term 'contagion' itself slips out of my grasp and refuses to be contained, like Susan Stanford Friedman's 'definitional excursions' in trying to pin down Modernism (Friedman 2009). My discussion is thus more broadly about mechanisms of transmission than just 'contagion'.

Jill Dolan has said that 'theatre studies hasn't yet claimed new metaphors through which to visualize its work' (Dolan 1993). Theatre *itself*, though, has always mined metaphors, particularly from the realms of science and medicine. While many of the dominant metaphors for recent theatre come from sciences of disorder, chaos and transformation such as quantum physics and mathematics (Vanden Heuvel 2000: 136), nineteenth-century theatre favoured biological and medical metaphors when it turned to science – chief amongst these contagion, often only loosely understood but all the more imaginatively rendered on stage. Far more was happening in the complex interactions of literature, culture and biology than 'the habitual reference to Darwin would have us believe' (Zwierlein 2005: 7). Writers and scientists drew on a common store of language, ideas and subjects; the natural sciences enjoyed 'cultural dominance' during this period and so did theatre, fiction and other forms, and both domains benefited from the rise of newer, bigger and more receptive publics eager to receive them (Zwierlein 2005: 1–6).

Performance and the mind-body continuum

Theatre is particularly well suited for thinking about all kinds of transmission because of its reliance on the body, the presence of actors and audience experiencing a live encounter in shared space – not just bodily but mind-to-mind infection. This makes it especially good at breaking down any real or imagined boundary between mind and body, as the following excerpt from Lucy Kirkwood's *Mosquitoes* (produced in 2017 at the National Theatre) illustrates. The play revolves around a female scientist based at CERN who is helping direct the Higgs-Boson tests. Years before the play starts she had a son, now teenaged, with an elusive scientist who has long disappeared from her life but who apparently reappears in the play as The Boson and interacts only with the audience, not the other characters (though he watches them). He reveals that his disappearance from science and from family and social life was due to a mental breakdown. In an extended monologue, he recalls the moment when he recognized his own mental disorder and the damage it could do to his family. Cooking soup for his eight-year-old son one day, the Boson notices how

> as it starts to bubble you become aware your blood has been replaced by battery acid and this is, yeah it's a disturbing thought but it's a familiar one, you've had this thought before, many times actually but you've always been able to receive it with a kind of like a healthy skepticism ... [now] you realise somehow the seal of your body has *broken* and this acid this acid is no longer contained by your skin veins arteries flesh it's leaching through the pads of your fingers it's in your saliva the moisture in your eyes sweat on your back a wetness a taste in your burning corroding contaminating everything you black smears on the spoon on the bowl you've put on a tray to take to your son who is eight who is upstairs in bed with a cold with a temperature with a fever caused by a rot and suddenly you understand you are the rot you are the disease and then there is a sound like a click like the click of a catch of suitcase and there is relief there is relief because there is order now, whatever else, there is order and so you turn off the gas ... [and] you walk out of the *Sudden black*. (Kirkwood 2017: 68–9)

Extended metaphors of disease and contagion highlight the mind-body continuum to suggest that there is no membrane between them, and furthermore that mental illness rapidly spreads to one's offspring and infects them and their surroundings. The idea was popularized in fiction by the bestselling *Zen and the Art of Motorcycle Maintenance* (1974), which explores the impact of the narrator's mental disorder on his young son, who displays physical manifestations (vomiting, lethargy and other disturbing symptoms) in response to his father's state of mind as if he too has 'caught' the disorder. Kirkwood's metaphor of the battery acid leaching into the soup powerfully expresses this same idea, but it too is entirely narrative; the Boson speaks it, without props, without action, just standing alone on stage in a white lab coat talking to the audience. The difference is that he is present, in bodily form, for his listeners, thus enacting the very threat of contagion that he so powerfully describes.

Kirkwood melds two dominant, competing ideas about transmission (hereditary and contagious), suggesting that maybe the son will become ill like the father both by inheriting the illness *and* by 'catching' it. These ideas were also at play in Alice Birch's *Anatomy of a Suicide* that same year (2017). Both plays show twenty-first-century versions of the nineteenth-century fear and fascination with the blending of these ideas that I discuss below. Kirkwood shows that it is still with us today, persistent and infectious. Performance, I argue, is at the heart of this irresistible pull of contra-medical/scientific ideas of contagion that we know intuitively can't possibly be viable but that still hold a power over us. What if they were true? What if mental disorder really could manifest itself bodily in this way and could be spread like physical illnesses? Such questions underscore the continued status of 'contagion' as unresolved and undefined, subject to multiple interpretations and functioning more as a question than a given.

Deploying disease: Deadly games

In my studies of theatrical engagements with science, particularly evolution (Shepherd-Barr 2006, 2015), I've become especially interested in those moments when science is unresolved and sometimes even contradictory, as with nineteenth-century understandings of how heredity works (pre-genetics), with the early twentieth-century infatuation with eugenics, and with explanations of evolution before the Modern Synthesis. These periods seem to me to coincide with, indeed promote, an openness, an imaginative looseness and creative thinking that finds expression in many art forms. Eugenics, for instance, was one of the most contagious ideas, based on heredity but more about social contagion than actual spreading of germs and disease, and the spectrum of soft to hard eugenics encompasses both genetics and the concept of contagion. Controlling the nature of the population is the ultimate eugenic fantasy.

Although it might not be the same type of theatre, now we have contagion-based gaming. *Plague Inc.* is a game that allows you to unleash a 'sentient, mutagenic pathogen' and 'consume humanity'.[1] The main blurb reads: 'Can you infect the world? Plague Inc. is a unique mix of high strategy and terrifyingly realistic simulation' (Ndemic Creations n.d.). The game allows the user to stage worldwide pandemics and rack up millions of deaths, and the best bit is that she or he does this by choosing the type of plague (a real or a fake one such as a nasty little bug that burrows into the brain). You also choose the method of transmission, the symptoms, etc. (Intriguingly, the game's home page proclaims 'BREXIT events now added into the simulation'.) The site boasts 'over 100 million infected!' – its record number of users – as of 2018. This is the consummate performance of contagion. It's theatre and it's control, just like with that earlier eugenic fantasy.

Similarly, there is a game called *Bio Inc – Biomedical Plague*, 'a biomedical strategy simulator in which you determine the ultimate fate of a victim by developing the most lethal illness possible' (DryGin Studios n.d.). You are in complete control as you 'create your own plague by upgrading diseases, boosting risk factors and slowing down your victim's recovery before a team of highly motivated doctors find a cure and save him' (DryGin Studios n.d.). Such contagion-based gaming has implicit links to performance, as it allows for immersion in the kinds of extreme situations that theatre can represent but not facilitate (because of material limitations and ethical boundaries) and film, for all its digital and material possibilities, can only visualize.

I like to imagine Artaud playing *Bio Inc.* on his phone or putting in a few hours of feverish fun with *Plague Inc.* on his XBox. He likened theatre to plague because both affect 'important collectivities and upset them in an identical way' and hailed the 'spontaneous conflagration which the plague lights wherever it passes ... [it is] an immense liquidization. ... The plague takes images that are dormant, a latent disorder, and suddenly extends them into the most extreme gestures; the theatre also takes gestures and pushes them as far as they will go' (Artaud 1958: 27). Yet Artaud's ideas already had precursors and roots in the nineteenth century. Mary Shelley's 1826 novel *The Last Man* powerfully imagined a future in which all of humankind is obliterated by a deadly plague. The terms she uses to describe it are uncannily like those of Artaud a century later; his innovation is to imagine the contagion in terms of a totalizing, overpowering performance. Another prescient example is the press's outrage over the 1891 London premiere of Ibsen's *Ghosts*, calling it:

Disgusting ... infecting the modern theatre with poison ... An open drain: a loathsome sore unbandaged; a dirty act done publicly; a lazar-house with all its doors and windows open ... Candid foulness ... Absolutely loathsome and fetid ... Gross, almost putrid indecorum ... Crapulous stuff. (Archer 1891: 3)

These are just a few of the choice comments compiled by Ibsen's translator and champion William Archer in his 'Ghosts and Gibberings', published in the *Pall Mall Gazette*, a stream of abuse amounting to a 'theatre of cruelty' in theatrical criticism (Archer 1891: 3). Yet the play itself contains hardly an indecorous line or act, as even the most hostile critics had, with some embarrassment, to admit: the reaction was out of all proportion to the deed itself. It also made people overlook Ibsen's mistakes: *Ghosts* gets its medical facts about the transmission of syphilis wrong as it suggests that the disease has been passed on to the son by the father when its actual mechanism of transmission is maternal – and Mrs Alving is in rude health.

Stanton B. Garner, Jr. argues in his compelling analysis of Artaud in relation to Louis Pasteur that for all his resistance to modern medical culture and medicalized language, Artaud's writing actually *depends* on them. Even while he seeks to transcend the body by employing purification metaphors, Artaud is always brought back to the 'medicalized body produced by modern science' and presented in the medical and scientific discourses that shaped his own experience (Garner 2006: 14). Artaud is more in dialogue with the nineteenth century and its ideas about contagion than he perhaps acknowledges.

Decades before Artaud's manifesto of theatre as plague, the great Italian *fin de siècle* actress Eleanora Duse wrote to Arthur Symons (in words that directly inspired Edward Gordon Craig's seminal essay 'The Actor and the Über-Marionette') that 'to save the Theatre, the Theatre must be destroyed, the actors and actresses must all die of the plague [because] ... they poison the air, they make art impossible' (Duse quoted in Craig 1911: 79). Nevertheless, Artaud is credited with this idea and his influence has been immense and not confined to theatre and performance; there was a vogue for Artaud-like groups in the 1970s, for example, earnestly embracing his Theatre of Cruelty and his denunciation of 'masterpieces' and making Artaud 'a theoretical reference for anti-literary theatre and experiments with rituals of the body and performance' (Milne 2000: 180). It is therefore salutary to remind ourselves how deeply rooted his ideas are in the nineteenth-century theatre and its lively engagement with medical discourse.

How to get infected on the nineteenth-century stage

Theatre participated directly in the widespread speculation about processes of transmission that were much debated in the nineteenth century, a period when mechanisms of heredity were not yet known, so there was often a blurring of the line between heredity and contagion. All sorts of theories abounded as to how things got passed on, usually encompassing either heredity or contagion or a bit of both. As Marvin Carlson points out in his discussion of Ibsen, Strindberg and telegony (or psychic heredity), this was the period of widespread scientific speculation yet little secure knowledge as to 'the process by which new organisms acquired their characteristics' – still largely a mystery, 'although all major biologists of the century advanced theories about it' (Carlson 1985: 774). Some speculated that it was a combination of internal and external mechanisms, heredity and acquired characters. This makes contagion a close relative of evolution, in this respect at least, in this period. Indeed, Weismann coined the term 'telegony' in 1892 for this (in his view spurious) idea of 'offspring at a distance'. Ibsen's *The Lady from the Sea* expresses this idea. Ellida is convinced that she saw the Stranger's eyes in the child she had with her husband, which later died. The dialogue suggests obliquely that that is why she caused the death of their next baby, by throwing herself down the stairs while pregnant. In his exploration of this motif of telegony in the play, Carlson points out that although Ibsen has Ellida's doctor husband reject this 'whimsical concept', the playwright himself 'does not allow the possibility of psychic influence to be so easily dismissed ... [and] the question remains calculatedly open throughout the play' (Carlson 1985: 776).

It is true that a lot was unknown about mechanisms of transmission from the point of view of heredity, but certainly causes of contagion were becoming much better understood in the second half of the nineteenth century via Koch's postulates in the 1880s and the work of Mechnikoff, Pasteur, Lister and others. Lister achieved almost mythical status as a surgeon through his pioneering use of antisepsis techniques and by 1900 had almost single-handedly raised the profile of the profession. Also by 1900 microbiologists had identified the microbial agents responsible for typhoid fever, diphtheria, tetanus, dysentery and other major diseases, though other epidemic diseases like cholera, smallpox and influenza continued to cause devastation. Germ theory (stating that many diseases can be traced to the presence of specific microorganisms within the body) had a major impact on social and political theories and influenced culture more widely; as Garner writes, 'tropes of contagion, pathology, inoculation, and immunity received new currency' in the theatre especially (Garner 2006: 2).

Social and political attempts to contain contagion abounded in legislation like the Contagious Diseases Acts passed by Parliament in 1864 (with subsequent editions in 1866 and 1869) which, in an attempt to control 'vice' (the euphemism for venereal diseases which were then reaching epidemic proportions), gave the police the authority to arrest women suspected of being prostitutes in certain areas and subject them to mandatory physical examination. If found to be infected with a VD, the woman would be confined to a so-called 'lock hospital' until she was given a clean bill of health. This approach punished women instead of the men who were infecting them in the first place.[2]

The French playwright Eugène Brieux directly addressed the sexual double standard in several of his plays. Although his works are rarely staged now, Brieux married medicine and social problems and was quite a hit in his day (around 1900). He dramatized with a new frankness how syphilis really gets passed on, in his play *Damaged Goods* (1901); in particular he became interested in breastfeeding as a mechanism of disease transmission, putting a scene into *Damaged Goods* that focuses on dissuading a mother from nursing for fear of passing on syphilis. He also wrote an entire play about wet-nursing, called *Les Remplaçantes* (1901), which exposes the corrupt wet-nursing system in France that exposes both nurses and babies to disease. The emphasis on breast milk as a source of contagion contrasts sharply with the idea of its life-giving qualities as well as with its time-honoured literary and cultural status as a source of moral virtues and as the epitome of maternal love – captured by James A. Herne in *Margaret Fleming* (1890), when the heroine, suddenly rendered blind by the traumatic revelation that the servant at whose deathbed she is sitting was in fact seduced by Margaret's philandering husband, gropes her way towards the crying newborn whose mother has just died, takes it in her arms, and in full view of the audience gives it her breast. It is not just the breastfeeding on stage that is remarkable but the intriguing and popular misconception that a latent physical tendency, in this case towards blindness, could be triggered by a single event, and so suddenly; again, mechanisms of transmission are at issue and the medical facts are vague (Shepherd-Barr 2012, 2015).

Similarly, the play *Man and His Makers* (1899) by Wilson Barrett and Louis N. Parker reflects nineteenth-century fears about how addiction to alcohol and drugs might be passed around. The hero at first recoils from the implication that he is doomed to inherit and pass on his family's addictive tendencies but then defiantly bounces back from his self-imposed social exile and gets married, has healthy children and lives happily ever after. Henry Arthur Jones explores similar ideas about the physical and moral contagion of alcoholism in *The Physician* (1897), a precursor to Shaw's *The Doctor's*

Dilemma (1907) in its exposure of the unregulated medical profession, and Elizabeth Robins boldly explores female alcoholism in her unpublished play *The Silver Lotus* (1895–6). Each play captures not just ideas of transmission but the way mind and body interact within disease; the plays recognize their complex interdependence (Shepherd-Barr 2015).

Almost the poster child for such dramatic speculation as to mechanisms of transmission is of course Ibsen, who makes poetic use of contagion: the baths becoming contaminated with 'infusoria' in *An Enemy of the People* (1882), the fever being passed through breast milk in *The Master Builder* (1892). Ibsen begins with a medical idea and moves quickly away from its medical context to focus on wider social implications; he instantly transmutes medicine into metaphor by omitting most of the medical facts. *A Doll's House* (1879) does this too; looking at the drafts of the play shows how he gradually tones down and almost sheds the medicine. Most strikingly, Dr Rank originally had a lot more to say about his mysterious fatal illness and expresses overt eugenic ideas in relation to it, which don't make it into the final version. In that play Ibsen also has Helmer, the upright husband, opine that women who commit a crime must be kept away from their children forever for fear of tainting them morally. The line between heredity and contagion is again erased, indicative of much thinking at the time until in the 1890s Weismann showed through his famous experiments with cutting off the tails of mice that the Lamarckian idea of inheritance of acquired characters was not viable and that there was a different, hereditary/genetic mechanism of transmission at work; this would be revealed through the rediscovery of Mendel's work a few years later.

Shaw's play *Too True to Be Good* (1932, a date that belies the fact that Shaw, born in 1856, was a true child of the nineteenth century) entertainingly tries to show how infection *actually* works. The stage directions call for a Patient lying in bed in a tightly enclosed sickroom – obviously trying to keep germs out. Next to her sits a 'Monster', which resembles in shape and size a human being; '*but in substance it seems to be made of a luminous jelly with a visible skeleton of short black rods. It droops forward in the chair with its head in its hands, and seems in the last degree wretched.*' The first line the Monster speaks indicates the typical Shavian paradox: the microbe has become ill from the patient, not the other way around. 'Oh, I wish I were dead,' it exclaims:

> Why doesn't she die and release me from my sufferings? What right has she to get ill and make me ill like this? Measles: that's what she's got. Measles! German measles! And she's given them to me, a poor innocent microbe that never did her any harm. And she says that I gave them to her. Oh, is this justice? (Shaw [1932] 1934: 1132)

The Monster spies the thermometer the doctor has left on the bedside table and sees that the patient's temperature is 103; 'It's all over,' it says and promptly collapses.

Shaw also gets in his customary dig at vaccination (he was scarred for life by a botched smallpox vaccination as a child) and public misconceptions about it; when the Patient's elderly mother begs the doctor to inoculate her daughter, the doctor, at the end of his patience, explains that 'it is no use inoculating when the patient is already fully infected'. The mother replies: 'But I have found it so necessary myself. I was inoculated against influenza three years ago; and I have had it only four times since' (Shaw 1932: 1133).

Too True to be Good gets at the issue of containment that is central to so many plays dealing with contagion: the basic problem of how to control the spread of disease, especially when people fundamentally misunderstand its mechanisms of transmission. It is hardly surprising that the notion of immunity holds an almost magical power over us; 'few concepts possess as much multivocal resonance across different realms of thought and practice' (De Cauwer and Hendrickx 2017: 265). Immunity means containment as well as resistance: regaining the control that was lost to the forces of contagion. This idea of containment relates to the broader notion of 'culture' in ways that I'll turn to now. But it's worth noting a further connection with Artaud here: the preface to his book *The Theatre and Its Double* is called 'The Theatre and Culture', and it opens with the line 'Never before, when it is life itself that is in question, has there been so much talk of civilization and culture.' He bemoans 'a culture which has never been coincident with life, which in fact has been devised to tyrannize over life' (Artaud 1958: 7).

Culture as containment: 'A system of constraints'

Stephen Greenblatt asks: how can we get the rather vague concept of culture to 'do more work for us'? Drawing on a range of thinkers from Bakhtin and Foucault to Benjamin, Geertz and Williams, he says that to begin with, the term 'culture' gestures towards 'what appear to be opposite things: *constraint* and *mobility*. The ensemble of beliefs and practices that form a given culture function as a pervasive technology of control, a set of limits within which social behavior must be contained, a repertoire of models to which individuals must conform' (Greenblatt 1995: 225). There are punishments for straying beyond the limits of a given culture – not extremes like the death penalty or enforced exile, but social ostracism, condescension, slights. Greenblatt sees Western literature as 'one of the great institutions for the enforcement of cultural boundaries through praise and blame' (Greenblatt 1995: 226). Certain genres do this overtly, like satire and panegyric, and of course Greenblatt's work is focused primarily on the early modern period, but nonetheless, he makes a persuasive point: art not only plays a key role in the transmission of culture, it sets up models that help us pattern our lives and that get passed on from one generation to another. Heredity and contagion intertwine. Art thus plays a regulatory and containing role. Being structurally public and exposed, however, theatre consistently falls outside this containment model, despite centuries of theatrical censorship in Britain and similar restrictions on theatre in other parts of the world – manifestations of a tenacious 'anti-theatrical prejudice'.

The paradox arises that 'if culture functions as a structure of limits, it also functions as the regulator and guarantor of movement' (Greenblatt 1995: 227). Boundaries are good insofar as they prompt the artist to test them, to try to move beyond imposed limits or redefine them; and the means to that end are artistic experimentation, improvisation and exchange. Indeed, works of art 'do not merely passively reflect the prevailing ratio of mobility and constraint; they help to shape, articulate, and reproduce it through their own improvisatory intelligence' (Greenblatt 1995: 228–229). Yet the ratio itself remains; the dynamic interplay between mobility and constraint still to a large extent defines 'culture'.

Artaud too expresses this idea, mediated through metaphors of the body. In that same preface to *The Theatre and Its Double*, Artaud goes on to talk of the need for an organic kind of culture akin to hunger – a bodily culture, 'the idea of culture-in-action, of culture growing within us like a new organ' (Artaud 1958: 8). He accuses humans of lacking 'constant magic' in their lives because they are out of touch with the force of their acts: 'it is this infection of the human which contaminates ideas that should have remained divine' (Artaud 1958: 8). His ideal of a liberating, purifying quality of mental and physical extremes of plague-induced experience can be mapped on to the experience of watching performance – the ultimate theatrical contagion yet whose precise mechanisms of transmission still elude us. A powerful example of this mapping can be found not in embodied performance (theatre) but in a performance embedded within a narrative, in the short story 'A White Night' by Charlotte Mew. In a church in rural Spain in the dead of night, a British traveller secretly witnesses the ritual sacrifice of a mysterious white-clad woman by a group of monks. As she is lowered into a chamber beneath the stone floor, he becomes transfixed by her performance and by her unconscious, 'magnetic' power over him. She seems to transform into a spirit or shade, and he notes that it's like a dream: 'the senses seize, the mind, or what remains of it, accepts mechanically the natural or unnatural sequence of events' (Mew in Byatt 1998: 150). Through a kind of mesmerism he is paralysed, unable to intervene in this death drama, able only to watch helplessly and yet with wonder and fascination.

Here of course is the age-old connection between theatre and ritual which has received much critical attention over the past few decades (see for example Schechner 1993, Schechner and Schuman 1976, and Turner 1982). It is a connection that captivated Brecht and Artaud as well. And it relates of course to the *fin de siècle* fascination with the Gothic, the occult, with séances, and with a revival of mesmerism (Willis 2006). Indeed, it seems to express Mesmer's idea of animal magnetism (even to Mew's use of the word 'magnetic'). As Nixon and Servitje observe, the idea of contagiousness has a mysticism about it; it encapsulates 'the mystical bonds of community', revolves around a 'mystically informed tactility' and touches 'the mystical force of the sacred' (Nixon and Servitje 2016: vii). Mew's short story has all of this but goes even further into something startlingly prescient, namely attempting to capture, even simulate, the inner consciousness and precise emotional states of the onlooker – to convey a sense of how the brain is working under the presence of an actor and the watching of a performance. The story seems to me an early account of what we now might call mirror neurons, the 'embodied simulation' (ES) that Ammaniti, Gallese and others have argued for, presenting a new model of intersubjectivity (Ammaniti and Gallese 2013; Gallese and Sinigaglia 2011) that is highly applicable to theatrical performance. Broadly speaking, the proponents of ES identify behaviour by neurons that is stimulated specifically by the activity of observing someone doing something, which prompts a mimicking action in the observer – although this may not play out in completed physical activity. So, for instance, you watch a football match and find yourself mimicking the actions of the players as you get more engrossed in the action: making kicking gestures, punching the air when the players do, taking brief running steps. The same thing happens when we watch a performance, though through powerful social conditioning we unconsciously constrain and control the physical actions our brains want us to carry out.

ES applies particularly to the experience of watching emotion (Cook 2011). Through ES we feel what the other person is emoting, and in Mew's story, it is intense. The minds of the onlooker and of the woman he is watching are locked together, as if his brain is responding directly to stimuli from hers. This is what Kirkwood articulates as well in that monologue from *Mosquitoes* – a dangerous mental state materialized as battery acid leaching along the arm and through the skin and infecting the minds of others.

Interdisciplinarity and intertheatricality as productive contagions

This leads to yet another meaning of 'contagion' that I want to conclude with – the idea of contact with another discipline, a kind of positive contamination, exchange, or contagion of ideas. Oddly, we're right back to the game *Plague Inc*. I'm interested in how the idea of recapturing the danger of contagion (unmanipulated) implicit in Artaud sits alongside the formalization of interdisciplinarity that has happened over the past decade or so within the academy.

Here again issues of mobility and control arise. For instance, there are quite a few funding opportunities that incentivize us to hook up with the most alien, remote discipline we can find; Felicity Callard and Des Fitzgerald discuss this development critically in their book *Rethinking Interdisciplinarity* (2015). One consequence of this mandate is that we are discouraged from collaborations with 'proximate' disciplines, as if they don't 'count', and so we lose out on the productive synergies such interactions often throw up. My example of the Mew story is drawn from just such a 'proximate discipline', and so is my discussion of Greenblatt. Two of my main examples for this discussion of theatre and contagion thus come from realms other than theatre; nor do they come from any scientific or medical disciplines. Yet they have a direct connection to all of these areas. Another consequence of such formalized, mandated and often artificially imposed cross-disciplinary ventures is the loss of serendipity. The more we try to dictate the terms by which disciplinary cross-fertilization occurs, the more we risk losing the surprising, unfettered, grass-roots, organic, spontaneous discovery and enrichment that should come with the meeting of disciplines when that meeting is natural and unforced. It seems necessary to rethink which disciplines, or knowledge domains, or fields, or whatever we want to call them, really can illuminate one another, regardless of intellectually or institutionally dictated notions of proximity or alienness. The reason this is important, indeed urgent, is that it is not just about intellectual endeavour but about who are the main stakeholders in funding opportunities and who gets to dictate the terms of mutual 'contagion' across disciplines (Barry and Born 2014).

The burgeoning field of digital humanities may well hold out some hope for those wary of the pitfalls of mandated interdisciplinarity. I will therefore conclude with an example that comes from this domain. I started with a digital example so it seems fitting to conclude with one, though they are vastly different. The book *A Global Doll's House* by Julie Holledge, Jonathan Bollen, Frode Helland and Joanne Tompkins uses the concept of body-to-body transmission to illustrate the dissemination of acting techniques and traditions in playing the role of Nora. The authors chart the 'bodily transmissions' involved in the dissemination of the collective, cross-generational knowledge of how the role has been portrayed on stage since 1880, a corpus of performance knowledge that has rarely been written down but mostly orally transmitted, and more importantly, 'from body to body through the use of images, gestures, actions, and the representation of emotional states' (Holledge et al. 2016: 91–2). The authors realized that there was 'an extraordinary degree of interconnection … within the production history of a single play … All the major Nordic touring productions of the post-war period were interconnected through a chain of artists that reached right back through the blending years of the play's early history to the original Norwegian production [of 1880]' (Holledge et al. 2016: 79). The authors' methodology is based on Franco Moretti's distant reading, looking for forces behind larger patterns that emerge across broad periods of time (Moretti 2013). On collecting the data from dozens of interviews with a wide circle of actors who had played Nora, they discovered that certain physical tropes were passed down from actor to actor, perhaps via directors as well. Essentially, the role of Nora has been constructed by a rich intertheatrical network of actors and their histories.

From body-to-body transmission and mind-to-mind contagion to cultural dominance and containment is a mind-boggling journey. My aim has been to signal how this journey maps on to larger questions about control that lurk around the edges of all the works discussed and that infiltrate seemingly every instance of contagion, showing how resistant the term still is to conclusive definition and pinning down. If there is 'positive' and productive contagion, theatre is where to find it, though this in no way makes theatre a 'safe space' for the testing out of contagious ideas in the way that playing *Bio Inc.* on your phone might be. Therein lies the key distinction I have been emphasizing all along: the liveness and corporeality of performance necessarily entails an encounter with other minds and bodies that will always have contagious possibilities that cannot be contained. We just need to make sure that our theatrical and academic contagion is not too regulated; as scholars we must recapture spontaneity and serendipity, or else we'll find ourselves playing 'Interdisciplinarity Inc.'

Notes

1 According to its home page, *Plague Inc.* was developed by Ndemic Creations (Bristol, UK), a company founded in 2012. The game has over 85 million users (http://www.ndemiccreations.com/en/22-plague-inc).
2 For a thorough discussion of theatre's relationship to the Contagious Diseases Acts see Eltis (2013).

References

Ammaniti, M. and V. Gallese (2013), *The Birth of Intersubjectivity: Psychodynamics, Neurobiology, and the Self*, New York: W. W. Norton.

Archer, W. (1891), 'Ghosts and Gibberings', *Pall Mall Gazette*, 8 April: 3.

Artaud, A. (1958), *The Theatre and Its Double*, trans. M. C. Richards, New York: Grove Press.

Barish, J. A. (1985), *The Anti-theatrical Prejudice*, Los Angeles: University of California Press.

Barry, A. and G. Born (2014), *Interdisciplinarity*, London: Routledge.

Brieux, E. (1901), *Les Remplaçantes*, Paris: L'Illustration.

Brieux, E. (1911), *Damaged Goods*, trans. John Pollock, in *Three Plays by Brieux, with a Preface by Bernard Shaw*, London: A. C. Fifield.

Callard, F. and D. Fitzgerald (2015), *Rethinking Interdisciplinarity across the Social Sciences and Neurosciences*, London: Palgrave Macmillan.

Carlson, M. (1985), 'Ibsen, Strindberg, and Telegony', *PMLA*, 100 (5): 774–782.

Cook, A. (2011), 'For Hecuba or for Hamlet: Rethinking Emotion and Empathy in the Theatre', *Journal of Dramatic Theory and Criticism*, 25 (2): 71–88.

Cooke, J. (2009), *Legacies of Plague in Literature, Theory and Film*, London: Palgrave Macmillan.

Craig, E. G. (1908), 'The Actor and the Über-marionette', in *The Mask I*, later incorporated into *On the Art of the Theatre*, London: William Heinemann, 1911.

De Cauwer, S. and K. Hendrickx, eds (2017), *Configurations*, special issue on 'Immunity, Society, and the Arts', 25 (3).

Dolan, J. (1993), 'Geographies of Learning', *Theatre Journal*, 45: 418.

DryGin Studios (n.d.), *Bio Inc – Biomedical Plague* [app]. Available online: https://itunes.apple.com/us/app/bio-inc-biomedical-plague/id932497563?mt=8 (accessed 9 January 2018).

Eltis, S. (2013), *Acts of Desire: Women and Sex on Stage, 1800–1930*, Oxford: Oxford University Press.

Felski, R. (2008), *The Uses of Literature*, London: Bloomsbury.

Felski, R. (2011), 'Context Stinks!' *New Literary History*, 42 (4): 573–591.

Friedman, S. S. (2009), 'Definitional Excursions: The Meanings of Modern/Modernity/Modernism', in P. L. Caughie and S. S. Friedman (eds), *Disciplining Modernism*, Basingstoke: Palgrave Macmillan.

Gallese, V. and C. Sinigaglia (2011), 'What Is So Special about Embodied Simulation?', *Trends in Cognitive Science*, 15 (11): 512–519.

Garner, S. B., Jr. (2006), 'Artaud, Germ Theory, and the Theatre of Contagion', *Theatre Journal*, 58:1–14.

Greenblatt, S. (1995), 'Culture', in F. Lentricchia and T. McLaughlin (eds), *Critical Terms for Literary Study*, 2nd edn, 225–232, Chicago and London: University of Chicago Press.

Herne, J. A. ([1890] 1957), *Margaret Fleming*, in Arthur Hobson Quinn (ed.), *Representative American Plays: From 1767 to the Present Day*, New York: Appleton-Century-Croft.

Holledge, J., J. Bollen, F. Helland, and J. Tompkins (2016), *A Global Doll's House: Ibsen and Distant Visions*, London: Palgrave Macmillan.

Kirkwood, L. (2017), *Mosquitoes*, London: Nick Hern.

Mew, C. (1998), 'A White Knight', in A. S. Byatt (ed.), *The Oxford Book of English Short Stories*, 139–54, Oxford: Oxford University Press.

Milne, D. (2000), 'Drama in the Culture Industry: British Theatre after 1945', in Alistair Davies and Alan Sinfield (eds), *British Culture of the Postwar: An Introduction to Literature and Society 1945–1999*, 169–189, Abingdon: Routledge.

Moretti, F. (2013), *Distant Reading*, London: Verso.

Ndemic Creations (n.d.), *Plague Inc.* [Computer game]. Available online: http://www.ndemiccreations.com/en/22-plague-inc (accessed 9 January 2018).

Nixon, K. and L. Servitje, eds (2016), *Endemic: Essays in Contagion Theory*, London: Palgrave Macmillan.

Pirsig, R. (1974), *Zen and the Art of Motorcycle Maintenance*. New York City, NY: William Morrow.

Schechner, R. (1993), *The Future of Ritual: Writings on Culture and Performance*, New York: Routledge.

Schechner, R. and M. Schuman, eds (1976), *Ritual, Play and Performance*, New York: Seabury Press.

Shaw, G. B. ([1932] 1934), '*Too True to Be Good*, in *The Complete Plays of Bernard Shaw*, London: Odhams Press.

Shepherd-Barr, K. E. (2006), *Science on Stage: From Doctor Faustus to Copenhagen*, Princeton, NJ: Princeton University Press.

Shepherd-Barr, K. E. (2012), '"It Was Ugly": Maternal Instinct on Stage at the Fin de Siècle', *Women: A Cultural Review*, 23 (2): 216–234.

Shepherd-Barr, K. E. (2015), *Theatre and Evolution from Ibsen to Beckett*, New York: Columbia University Press.

Turner, V. (1982), *From Ritual to Theatre: The Human Seriousness of Play*, New York: PAJ.

Vanden Heuvel, M. (2000), '"Mais je dis le chaos positif": Leaky Texts, Parasited Performances, and Maxwellian Academons', in M. James (ed.), *Harding Contours of the Theatrical Avant-Garde: Performance and Textuality*, Ann Arbor: University of Michigan Press.

Willis, M. (2006), *Mesmerists, Monsters, and Machines: Science Fiction and the Cultures of Science in the Nineteenth Century*, Kent, OH: The Kent State University Press.

Zwierlein, A., ed. (2005), *Unmapped Countries: Biological Visions in Nineteenth Century Literature and Culture*, London: Anthem.

7

'Is there a doctor in the house?': The Myth and Reality of Audience Psychogenic and Neurological Responses to the Theatre of Horror

Julius Green

This chapter examines purportedly fear-induced responses amongst theatre audiences, and specifically the phenomenon of fainting as a contagious reaction to shocking events portrayed on stage. The first widely reported instances of audience members fainting in response to horror theatre occurred at the Parisian Théâtre du Grand-Guignol (1897–1962), whose programmes of legendarily gory playlets were considered so terrifying that the success of each performance was measured by the number of spectators who passed out (Gordon and Pierron 2000); the management even publicized the fact that a doctor was on standby to treat the casualties (Hand and Wilson 2002: 12). More recently, *The Independent* reported that 'more than 100 people either fainted or left the theatre' during the run of Lucy Bailey's 2014 production of Shakespeare's notoriously bloody *Titus Andronicus* at Shakespeare's Globe (Clark 2014), one of a number of contemporary theatre productions whose publicity has embraced the Guignolesque tradition of heralding 'droppers' as a novel form of product endorsement.

Although actors and directors are inevitably gratified by what appears to be an extreme physical manifestation of the audience's emotional engagement with their work, I will argue that the explanation for spectators passing out during horror theatre is in all likelihood more prosaic, with instances of vasovagal syncope (fainting) most probably being triggered by a straightforward haemophobic response to the sight of fake blood, albeit enhanced in some cases by the power of suggestion and specific aspects of physical location. I will therefore focus my inquiry on the psychogenic, neurological and environmental factors which contribute to the phenomenon, rather than on matters of creative interpretation and performance.

Audience responses to Grand-Guignol

Our knowledge of the work of the Théâtre du Grand-Guignol is based on a very small number of key books, papers and articles – principally the pioneering work of Mel Gordon, Agnès Pierron and, more recently, Richard J. Hand and Michael Wilson. These studies ultimately rely to a large extent on contemporary press reports and extant scripts, as well as a plethora of notoriously graphic monochrome photographs and contrastingly colourful publicity material, much of which is held by the *Bibliothèque nationale de France*. As is often the case with theatre history, however, there is no reference to any extant accounts, contracts or business correspondence, which would anchor all this information firmly in reality. Such is the powerful and self-perpetuating mythology of Grand-Guignol that even today the story we hear is still very much the one that the genre's creators wanted us to hear.

What we do know is that, in 1897, French playwright Oscar Méténier bought a small theatre at the end of a cul-de-sac in the Pigalle district of Paris, as a venue in which to produce his own controversial naturalist plays. Le Théâtre du Grand-Guignol took its name from a popular French puppet character who was notable as a social commentator (Pierron 1996) – the implication being that this was, in effect, the home of plays with a social agenda performed by 'big puppets' in the form of live actors. Méténier's repertoire, which reflected the street life of the area, consisted of works portraying prostitutes, vagrants, criminals and con artists. It was an immediate success.

After two years, Méténier handed over the directorship of the theatre to Max Maurey, who was to pioneer the distinctive brand of theatrical horror show with which Grand-Guignol has become synonymous. His partner in this enterprise was the playwright André de Lorde, known as 'the Prince of Terror', and between them they created a meticulously crafted genre of shock drama that successive managements and a growing pool of writers would maintain and embellish until the theatre's eventual closure in 1962 (Gordon [1998] 2016: 9–42).

Although Maurey retired in 1915, de Lorde would continue to work for the Théâtre du Grand-Guignol until 1926. Several of his scripts were written in collaboration with the experimental psychologist Alfred Binet, and insanity thus became a regular theme of the theatre's ever-changing repertoire along with graphic enactments of shocking scenarios including scalpings, disembowelments, eye gouging, botched surgery, sadism, drug taking, suffocation, torture and executions. Where Méténier's dramatis personae had consisted of colourful Parisian low life, de Lorde's (as well as those of other Grand-Guignol writers) were more likely to feature necrophiliacs, psychopaths and child murderers. Productions exploited the concept of fear in its various forms, with fear of contagion being a particular favourite. Characters were often portrayed as suffering from diseases such as leprosy, rabies and syphilis, with the close proximity of the actors to the tightly packed audience enhancing the imagined prospect of contagion.

An evening's entertainment at the Théâtre du Grand-Guignol would typically consist of a number of short playlets, comprising both these horror dramas and, by way of contrast, a repertoire of specially written comedies (Ruff 2008), thereby ensuring that audiences were subjected to an intense emotional rollercoaster. While budgets were not high, the horror pieces were well-crafted dramas which calculatedly, skilfully and with a great deal of artistry, built tension over a typically twenty-minute period up to a key moment of visual shock. According to Hand and Wilson, 'The plays are exemplary works of one or two-act drama demonstrating a masterful control of dramatic pace and concision; and requiring an innovative use of stage technologies and an ensemble of highly versatile and disciplined performers' (Hand and Wilson 2000: 266).

Skilfully engineered audience response was key to the success of the Grand-Guignol's programme. In a 1957 article in the *New York Times*, P. E. Schneider noted that 'at the Grand-Guignol, grown-ups react to what they see on the stage as violently as children do to the mischief of puppets' (Schneider 1957). Villains would be met with shouts of 'Killer!' and the sight of actors playing horribly scarred accident victims would provoke calls from the audience for a doctor. The regular fans, who were familiar with the genre's conventions, became known as 'Guignoleurs', and it has even been claimed that the management employed 'plants' in the audience to encourage and secure the desired reactions (Deák 1974: 43).

Hand and Wilson note that the study of Grand-Guignol requires an understanding of its 'audience and reception'. It is a form that

> presents an evocative mixture of the horrific and the erotic, the satirical and the realist, the reactionary and the radical, the frightening and the funny, the thrilling and the theoretically determined. No one aspect is clear cut. All these central issues are issues of *response*, relating to the individual psychology and experience of the spectator and the dynamic of the audience. (Hand and Wilson 2002: 78)

Matthew Wilson Smith argues that certain genres of nineteenth-century theatre had effectively engaged in a dialogue with the neurological sciences to create what he refers to as 'theatres of sensation' and that by the time it came to Grand-Guignol, what was being offered was 'a frisson in a new and modern sense; not merely a shiver, tremble or shudder but a current of emotion that spreads through a group' (Smith 2018: 150). He goes on to describe this as 'the *medicalized* frisson of being a neural subject ... Grand-Guignol audiences could convert neurological anxieties – what we might call neuro-neurosis, the condition of being nervous about one's nerves – into neurological ecstasies' (Smith 2018: 150). This 'medicalization' of audience response was noted by an 'eminent physician' in an article appended to a *Daily Express* review of the 1921 London Grand Guignol season:[1] 'Those with heart trouble or neurasthenia might suffer most seriously from the effects of acute fear and excitement such as are said to be aroused by this new piece' (cited in Hand and Wilson 2007: 72).

The psychological and physiological links between fear and pleasure, excitement and sexual arousal were all very much part of the Grand-Guignol's unique attractions. In April 1921, theatre journalist Émile Mas, who was one of the more vocal critics of Grand-Guignol in its heyday, published an article highlighting the dangers of a theatrical genre which he considered to have the effects of an addictive drug on its audiences: 'I consider this kind of theatre to be very dangerous ... (I) do not really see any difference between the absinthe addict, for example, and the fervent enthusiast of these plays which offer nothing but physical excitement! If alcohol corrodes the body, certain displays unhinge the mind and I do not see what distinction can be made between these "products"' (cited in Hand and Wilson 2002: 74).

Fainting at the Théâtre du Grand-Guignol

The most publicized of Grand-Guignol's effects on its spectators was its apparent ability to trigger fainting fits. Vasovagal syncope, the most common form of fainting, results from a sudden chemical imbalance triggered by an emotional or physical stressor, leading to a drop in blood pressure which in turn deprives the brain of oxygen (van Lieshout et al. 1991). An average of two such incidents a night were regularly reported (Gordon [1998] 2016: 29), and the Guignoleurs would gleefully keep tally by counting out loud in chorus as fellow audience members apparently succumbed to the more extreme horrors on stage.

There are a number of possible contributing factors to the Grand-Guignol fainting phenomenon. Even without the efforts of Maurey and de Lorde, theatre buildings, with their often hot and crowded auditoria, are notorious as a physical environment that is likely to induce fainting; the simple physical act of standing up suddenly from a seat can act as a trigger. An 1830 painting by Louis Leopold Boilly, called *The Effect of Melodrama* (reproduced in Davidson 2007: 94), shows a young woman fainting in a theatre box; and with incidents recently reported at Broadway productions as diverse as *A View from the Bridge* (Denham 2016) and *Hello Dolly* (Hinzmann 2017), it is clear that fainting fits amongst theatre audiences are by no means the preserve of the horror genre. What is certain, though, is that the Théâtre du Grand-Guignol was unique in terms of the frequency of the occurrence and that the building itself had a significant role to play in this.

A converted chapel in the back streets of Paris's colourful but slightly threatening red light district, the theatre's location, as well as its distinctively eerie gothic architecture and dim lighting, all made a significant contribution to the sense of foreboding and the build-up of tension that was intrinsic to the structure of the plays it presented (Hand and Wilson 2000). With its compact auditorium and approximately 7 m^2 stage, it was also one of the smallest and most claustrophobic theatres in Paris. Gore has always been a part of public spectacle, from gladiatorial combat to the plays of Webster and re-enactments of the crucifixion. These, however, had all been open-air events; now, for the first time, blood was being spilled close up in the name of entertainment and in an enclosed and intimate space. The most successful British Grand-Guignol seasons were presented at the Little Theatre off the Strand in the early 1920s, and it can be no coincidence that, with its 388 seats, the aptly named Little Theatre was not only amongst the smallest in London but was almost identical in its stage dimensions to its Parisian counterpart. Today's horror films cannot hope to compete with what must have been the extraordinary immediacy of the audience experience.

The Théâtre du Grand-Guignol thus offered much more than an evening of gory spectacle; it was, in effect, an immersive and site-specific event of the sort which many contemporary practitioners aspire to, and, as such, it appears fortuitously to have created the perfect physical and psychological conditions to induce regular fainting fits amongst its spectators. Although there were many attempts to imitate it throughout Paris and the world, and the Pigalle company itself undertook several tours, it is significant that the genre never really thrived outside of its original location.

We should also consider the power of suggestion as a contributing factor to the regular faintings at the Grand-Guignol. Audiences who are told in advance that a performance is likely to make them pass out are arguably more inclined to do so, and in an era when people flocked to see spiritualists, hypnotists, illusionists and mediums, all of whom thrive on group susceptibility, this is even more likely to have been the case. Fainting is known to be a potentially contagious group behaviour and the sight of one person succumbing can itself be a trigger for others to follow. Director Carol

Morley researched this phenomenon for her 2014 film *The Falling*, which deals with an outbreak of fainting amongst schoolgirls. She notes that 'no matter how strange and mysterious mass psychogenic outbreaks appear, or how misunderstood, they remain a powerful group activity ... They are part of the human condition and at their heart lies our overwhelming need for a sense of belonging and connection' (Morley 2015).

A somewhat less likely thesis arises from Pierron's observation that 'women often prepared themselves for adultery by throwing themselves, half-dead with terror, into their neighbours' arms: flirtation, Grand-Guignol-style' (Pierron 1996). Karen Quigley extrapolates this to the extent that she characterizes the outbreaks of fainting amongst audiences as a strategic collusion between the management and their patrons with the specific aim of facilitating licentious behaviour (Quigley 2011). However, while contemporary photographs and illustrations bear out that female patrons would indeed frequently make physical contact with a male partner in response to events on stage, this does not in reality appear to have been directly related either to the theatre's alleged use as a venue for sexual liaisons or to audience members passing out.

Grand-Guignol's exploitation of blood-injury-injection phobia

The actual cause of the Grand-Guignol faintings was in all likelihood much more straightforward. Vasovagal syncope, which is often experienced by medical students when observing their first operation or autopsy, is commonly triggered by haemophobia, usually grouped with two related phobias as blood-injury-injection (BII) phobia (Ayala et al. 2009). There are a number of explanations as to why some people pass out when they see blood, including an instinct to 'play dead' in response to a perceived threat (Murray 2016) or the body reducing blood pressure in order to minimize potential blood loss of its own. With around 3 to 4 per cent of the population suffering from haemophobia (Sanford 2013) there was every likelihood that, in an audience of 285, a number of people would faint in the normal course of events as a direct response to the 'blood' content of a standard Grand-Guignol programme. This is borne out by the context of the two most frequently cited occurrences of the phenomenon. On one occasion six people were reported to have fainted when a character whose eyeball had been gouged out re-entered the stage with a blood-encrusted hole in her skull; and, on another, a record fifteen playgoers lost consciousness during a particularly realistic blood transfusion (Schneider 1957). Unlike some later revivals, fake blood itself was in fact used relatively sparingly in order to ensure maximum impact when it did appear, and according to Pierron the build-up was just as important; 'Horror was produced by lighting, atmosphere, and a magician's technique (misdirection of attention prior to shock)' (Gordon and Pierron 2000). In the words of legendary Grand-Guignol leading lady Maxa, *'l'imagination est toujours supérieure à la réalité'* (cited in Hand and Wilson 2000).

It is particularly interesting to note the proportionately high number of males reportedly affected by blood-injury-injection phobia in this particular context, especially given that, as noted by Buchanan and Coulson (2012: 24), some studies show there to be a higher prevalence of the phobia amongst females (Wani et al. 2014) while others show it to be equally common in both genders (Milosevic and McCabe 2015: 190). Aubrey Hammond's famous promotional artwork for the 1921 London Grand-Guignol season (reproduced in Gordon [1998] 2016: 45) is fascinating in that it focuses on what is going on in the auditorium rather than events on stage, but even more so in that, on close examination, it is only men who appear actually to be being taken ill. When Kenneth Tynan created a Grand-Guignol version of Shakespeare's *Titus Andronicus* for a 1951 London season, his then wife Elaine Dundy noted that 'men fainted at every performance and had to be carried out. Women remained seated and upright until the end' (Dundy 2001: 117). Photographs from 1953 show a young American G. I. at the Parisian theatre fainting in his seat and being revived by his friends with a drink (reproduced in Gordon [1998] 2016: 61), and Schneider observes that at Grand-Guignol performances, 'men faint more easily than women, but this may be due to the fact that women tend to cover their eyes at the crucial moment, while men want to see to the bitter end' (Schneider 1957). It seems unlikely that this was the actual explanation, and more probable that for male spectators during the heyday of Grand-Guignol, many of whom would have fought in at least one of the world wars, the sight of blood may have triggered a traumatic response conditioned by front-line experiences; although there is some indication that the trend prevails amongst theatre audiences even today.

It didn't take Max Maurey long to capitalize on the commercial possibilities of the fainting phenomenon, and he soon began to promote it as an endorsement of the effectiveness of the theatre's work. Various medicinal remedies were advertised as being available in the foyer, but Maurey's masterstroke was the appointment of a 'house doctor' to attend to spectators taken ill during the performance. This news was seized on with alacrity by the press and became a popular subject for cartoonists, with one contemporary drawing (reproduced in Hoggatt 2011) famously depicting Maurey telling a concerned husband that the doctor was not available to attend his fainting wife as he himself had passed out. As is typical of Grand-Guignol mythology, this clearly fanciful incident is often now reported as fact, and it is also questionable whether the 'house doctor' was actually a qualified medic or simply an actor playing a role and thus part of the overarching artifice of the genre.

As well as garnering valuable publicity for the theatre (the gimmick has since been much imitated by both theatre and film producers), the presence of the 'doctor' very cleverly raised the stakes in the ongoing interactive game with the audience by adding yet another trigger that was likely to provoke fainting in those who were susceptible to it. These days, around 3 per cent of people experience anxiety when visiting the doctor (Esposito 2014), although it seems probable that this would have been higher in an era when the popular perception of the medical profession was informed by the literary quartet of doctors Frankenstein, Jekyll, Moreau and Van Helsing (Fiedler 1996) rather than by *Holby City*. Although technically in a different category of phobias, the fear of doctors (iatrophobia) is linked with blood-injury-injection phobia by its association with blood-related medical procedures (Milosevic and McCabe 2015) and, unsurprisingly, the enactment of surgical operations was well known to result in the highest number of casualties amongst Grand-Guignol audiences (Schneider 1957). By positioning the supposed doctor in the foyer in view of the incoming audience, and even having him carry out 'examinations' of some of them, Maurey was cleverly ratcheting up anxiety levels even further and, through the power of suggestion, helping to induce instances of vasovagal syncope amongst haemophobics. Given the sophistication of this strategy, it is tempting to conclude that the influence of Alfred Binet at the Théâtre du Grand-Guignol extended beyond his script collaborations with de Lorde.

The unique theatrical genre which Maurey and de Lorde created survived successive managements, performers and creative contributors as well as, remarkably, the genuine horrors of two world wars, until the Théâtre du Grand-Guignol finally closed its doors in 1962, sixty-five years after its founding. During this period it had entertained a gloriously mixed demographic made up of the Parisian beau monde, tourists, invading and liberating armies and local working-class residents. By the 1960s, cinema had conclusively taken ownership of the horror genre, and thrill seekers simply had so many options available to them that they did not need to venture into the back streets of Pigalle to find them. Audiences fainting at the sight of fake blood, however, is an occurrence which still fascinates theatre makers and which publicists continue to enjoy making the most of.

'Blood is telling a story'

In 2014, Lucy Bailey's production of *Titus Andronicus* at Shakespeare's Globe confirmed that live theatre's ability to create extreme group emotional and physical responses in its audiences remains potent. *The Independent* (whose own critic claims to have fainted on the opening night) reported that 'the "grotesquely violent" Shakespearean tale of revenge has 14 deaths, many violently bloody, as well as rape and mutilation. But that's nothing compared to the audience casualty toll' (Clark 2014), and quotes Bailey herself as saying, 'I find it all rather wonderful. That people can connect so much to the characters and emotion that they have such a visceral effect. I used to get disappointed if only three people passed out.' According to Marina Warner, writing in *The Guardian*, 'Lucy Bailey's explicit production of Shakespeare's most ferocious tragedy has even brought a new word into circulation: "droppers" – members of the audience who faint clean away at the violence taking place all around them ... What we are feeling as we sit there in the Globe – what perhaps the "droppers" are experiencing – is recognition, the ancient principle of storytelling' (Warner 2014).

The scene that was largely responsible for the 'droppers' was, reportedly, the entrance of Lavinia, who has been raped and had her hands cut off and tongue cut out. According to Bailey, 'With Lavinia, it's hugely about her imagined pain and the shock of it all' (Clark 2014). Although a gift to the Globe's publicists in true Grand-Guignol tradition, both Warner and Bailey are at risk of over-intellectualizing the phenomenon, and it seems most likely from the context that the primary trigger for fainting audience members was once again, very straightforwardly, the sight of 'blood'. Theatrical make-up artists have traditionally taken pride in the realism of their stage blood, which in itself is a substantial contributing factor to the audience responses we are considering here; although arguably the haemophobic response itself is to an extent predicated on the quality of the 'storytelling' – whether at the Théâtre du Grand-Guignol or the Globe – being sufficient momentarily to convince audiences that they are witnessing the real thing.

The art of stage blood is a sufficiently serious business to have warranted a 'stage blood round table' in 2006, held, coincidentally, at Shakespeare's Globe. Participants agreed that in Elizabethan times theatre makers would have used animal blood, along with vermilion, vinegar and wine, with varied results. There was, however, disagreement as to the emotive impact of the sight of blood on early modern audiences with some delegates arguing that the daily violence in society, including public executions, meant stage blood was likely to have affected them more, while others believed they would have been desensitized (Bower 2017). The legendarily gory special effects of the

Théâtre du Grand-Guignol itself were originally created by Paul Ratineau, who worked at the theatre in various capacities from 1902 to 1942; his formula for alarmingly realistic fake blood remained a closely guarded secret. According to Gordon:

> Although varieties of stage blood have existed since the time of the classical Roman theatre, the Grand-Guignol made something of a fetish of them. A dark, sticky stage blood signified old wounds; a lighter, dripping fluid showed new ones. The standard formula consisted mostly of a heated mixture of carmine and glycerine. Combined daily in a cauldron, the heated liquid flowed like blood but also coagulated after a few minutes to form scabs. (Gordon [1998] 2016: 56)

American props-maker Eric Hart, who has undertaken a detailed analysis of the making and use of special effects at the Théâtre du Grand-Guignol, notes that in the 1950s ingredients included currant jam (for blood which did not need to flow) and methyl cellulose, which thickens in cold water and gels when heated (Hart 2010). By 1962, according to a report in *Time* magazine, nine different shades of stage blood were being prepared daily ('Outdone by Reality' 1962). Meanwhile, the representation of human intestines and other body parts continued to rely on regular deliveries from local butchers and taxidermists, and creative solutions were found to such intriguing problems as how to make an eyeball bounce. Given the close proximity of the audience, the verisimilitude of all these effects – and in particular of the 'blood' – was critical to the success of the enterprise and specifically to inducing publicity-worthy blood-phobia-related outcomes.

In the 1960s and 1970s the most widely used brand of stage blood in the UK was Kensington Gore, created by chemist John Tinegate, but, in a 2017 interview with Gavin James Bower of *The Stage* newspaper, Royal Shakespeare Company (RSC) make-up artist Fi Keston notes that audiences have since become more demanding 'with an appetite for realism … They want blood, guts, gore and grime' (Bower 2017). According to Bower himself, these days 'two types of blood are used in the theatre. The first is syrup based, sticky, looks wet and never dries. The second is alcohol based – denatured, industrial but non-toxic – and its drying effect means the blood ultimately stays in place'. Keston, who at the time of the interview was applying four pints of fake blood a day to actors in the RSC's production of *Coriolanus* in the company's specially designated 'blood room', adds that a thickener is also used, such as corn flour or a roux. 'Blood is like ice cream,' she says. 'It's colouring, sugar and thickener – and it has to be able to go in the actors' mouths,' and she notes that blood manufacturers are notoriously secretive about exact recipes – 'a bit like chefs'.

'Blood is a serious thing,' concludes Keston, 'Blood is telling a story,' and even Lucy Bailey admits to the importance of the stage blood formula used in her *Titus Andronicus*; 'You instinctively know the blood is fake, but here (at Shakespeare's Globe) you can't see that it is, because it isn't filtered by lighting. So your senses take on a very different perception of it. We were also canny in using dark blood all the time – usually in the theatre it is too bright so people don't believe it' (Shenton 2017). It certainly appears to have been sufficiently realistic to trigger multiple cases of vasovagal syncope amongst haemophobics and, in the spirit of Grand-Guignol, the Globe's publicists went out of their way to reassure their audiences that trained first aiders were on standby (Furness 2014).

Fainting as a marketing tool in contemporary theatre

This collusion between theatrical make-up and publicity departments is a little-considered manifestation of live theatre's long-established game-playing relationship with its audiences and of the multidisciplinary artifice which this entails. Recent productions capitalizing on the publicity potential of 'droppers' include the National Theatre's 2016 production of Sarah Kane's *Cleansed*, featuring the notably Guignolesque spectacle of a man having his tongue cut out; 'If the audience faints, our play is doing its job,' claimed its fight director (Razaq 2016). The following year, when a journalist questioned the veracity of reports of audiences fainting at the sight of the gore in the Broadway production of *1984* (2017) and accused the producers of using them as a marketing tool, the play's publicists responded that 'the production wishes to make perfectly clear that every incident of fainting, vomiting, or bolting from the performance by audience members is completely accurate, and not, in any way, meant to be used to promote the play in the media' (Sherman 2017). The irony intrinsic in issuing a statement to the media to this effect only served to enhance the inherent theatricality of the debate.

A year after the purported incidents of fainting at *Cleansed*, *The Times* reported that the Royal Court, where the play had received its original production in 1998, was issuing 'trigger warnings' in order to 'avoid distressing audience members' who might experience adverse reactions to the content of certain productions (Sanderson 2017). It is interesting to note that the trigger warnings themselves were considered newsworthy, and it is even arguable that the wording of such warnings may in certain cases contribute to provoking the very responses that they are purportedly designed to avoid, just as Maurey's 'house doctor' was patently more likely to heighten anxiety amongst haemophobics than to reduce it – what Smith describes as 'neuro-neurosis' (being nervous about one's nerves).

In 2017 *Titus Andronicus* returned, this time presented by the Royal Shakespeare Company. Prior to the production's opening it was reported that 'the heart rate of some audience members will be monitored by wristbands … to answer the question: does Shakespeare still shock?' (Alberge 2017). The results of this pseudo-scientific exercise were inconclusive, with comedic moments found to provoke a similar increase in heart rate to 'shocking' ones (Morgan 2017), and are in themselves of no more medical significance than the findings of a group of doctors who recently set out to establish whether or not horror films actually make blood 'curdle' (Nemeth et al. 2015). The publicity surrounding the RSC's experiment had, however, succeeded in raising expectations in true Grand-Guignol style. Audiences had been alerted to the fact that they were being monitored by doctors, thereby potentially heightening anxiety amongst BII-phobics, and although vasovagal syncope is caused by a sudden drop in blood pressure rather than an increase in heart rate, 'awareness' of fast heart rate can itself act as an emotional trigger generating the response (Kenny and McNicholas 2016). The (again typically male) 'droppers' were back; as noted by one critic, 'About an hour in, a huge amount of blood is smeared over Titus Andronicus's raped and mutilated daughter Lavinia; hands lopped off, tongue cut out. A bearded man three rows behind me was carried by neighbours from his seat to, one hopes, the onward attentions of St John's Ambulance' (Woodall 2017).

The contagious legacy of Grand-Guignol

Over a hundred years ago, a back-street Parisian showman and his colleagues fortuitously stumbled on a unique theatrical formula that combined a very precise and site-specific locational ambience with exactly the right consistency and quantity of fake blood to trigger a haemophobic response in those who were susceptible to it, along with a consequent psychogenic response amongst a number of those witnessing their dilemma. Much to their delight, the creators of Grand-Guignol, with its famous portrayals of contagion of all sorts, had discovered that they themselves were able to transmit what is effectively a contagious medical condition directly from the stage to the audience. Although it is uncertain whether Maurey himself fully understood the medical causes of the fainting phenomenon, his genius was actively to provoke and promote it as a selling point for his product – a strategy which today's theatre makers continue to embrace.

The fact that my inquiries have focused on the bizarrely marketable interface between the consequences of blood-injury-injection phobia and what today is termed 'immersive theatre' is not intended to negate the undoubted artistry of either the creators of Grand-Guignol or of the many contemporary theatre practitioners whose work echoes elements of the genre. Perhaps, though, it would be fitting for the make-up artists and publicists to take a bow – alongside the writers, directors and actors – for their historically important role in this uniquely contagious brand of storytelling.

Note

1 Per Hand and Wilson (2007: 3), London's 'Grand Guignol' is unhyphenated.

References

Alberge, D. (2017), 'Royal Shakespeare Company to Monitor Our Tolerance for Gore', *Sunday Times*, 2 July. Available online: https://www.thetimes.co.uk/article/royal-shakespeare-company-to-monitor-our-tolerance-for-gore-56gj28xdj (accessed 14 January 2018).

Ayala, E. S., A. E. Meuret and T. Ritz (2009), 'Treatments for Blood-injury-injection Phobia: A Critical Review of Current Evidence', *Journal of Psychiatric Research*, 43 (15): 1235–1242. Available online: http://www.sciencedirect.com/science/article/pii/S0022395609000880 (accessed 14 January 2018).

Bower, G. J. (2017), 'Baying for Stage Blood: Meet Theatre's Gore Merchants', *The Stage*, 20 October. Available online: https://www.thestage.co.uk/features/2017/baying-for-stage-blood-meet-theatres-gore-merchants/ (accessed 14 January 2018).

Buchanan, H. and N. Coulson (2012), *Phobias*, Basingstoke: Palgrave Macmillan.

Clark, N. (2014), 'Globe Theatre Takes Out 100 Audience Members with Its Gory Titus Andronicus', *Independent*, 22 July. Available online: http://www.independent.co.uk/arts-entertainment/theatre-dance/news/globe-theatre-takes-out-100-audience-members-with-its-gory-titus-andronicus-9621763.html (accessed 14 January 2018).

Davidson, D. Z. (2007), *France after Revolution: Urban Life, Gender, and the New Social Order*, Cambridge, MA: Harvard University Press.

Deák, F. (1974), 'The Grand Guignol', *The Drama Review*, 18 (1): 34–43.

Denham, J. (2016), 'A View from the Bridge Halted by Audience Member Fainting', *Independent*, 2 February. Available online: http://www.independent.co.uk/arts-entertainment/theatre-dance/news/a-view-from-the-bridge-halted-by-audience-member-fainting-shortly-after-actor-took-his-top-off-a6849261.html (accessed 14 January 2018).

Dundy, E. (2001), *Life Itself*, London: Virago.

Esposito, L. (2014), 'How to Overcome Extreme Fear of Doctors', *US News and World Report*, 1 July. Available online: https://health.usnews.com/health-news/patient-advice/articles/2014/07/01/how-to-overcome-extreme-fear-of-doctors (accessed 14 January 2018).

Fiedler, L. (1996), *Tyranny of the Normal: Essays on Bioethics, Theology and Myth*, Lincoln, MA: David R. Godine, Publisher, Inc.

Furness, H. (2014), 'Globe Audience Faints at "Grotesquely Violent" Titus Andronicus', *Telegraph*, 30 April. Available online: http://www.telegraph.co.uk/culture/theatre/william-shakespeare/10798599/Globe-audience-faints-at-grotesquely-violent-Titus-Andronicus.html (accessed 14 January 2018).

Gordon, M. ([1988] 2016), *Theatre of Fear and Horror: The Grisly Spectacle of the Grand Guignol of Paris 1897–1962*, Port Townsend: Feral House.

Gordon, M. and Agnès Pierron (2000), 'Transcript of Post-performance Discussion at the Exit Theatre, San Francisco', *Shocktoberfest!!*, 26 October. Available online: http://www.thrillpeddlers.com/talkback.html (accessed 14 January 2018).

Hand, R. J. and M. Wilson (2000), 'The Grand-Guignol: Aspects of Theory and Practice', *Theatre Research International*, 25 (3): 266–275. Available online: http://www.grandguignol.com/tri_1.htm (accessed 14 January 2018).

Hand, R. J. and M. Wilson (2002), *Grand-Guignol: The French Theatre of Horror*, Exeter: University of Exeter Press.

Hand, R. J. and M. Wilson (2007), *London's Grand Guignol and the Theatre of Horror*, Exeter: University of Exeter Press.

Hart, E. (2010), 'The Gore of Grand Guignol', *Eric Hart's Prop Agenda*, 11 October. Available online: http://www.props.eric-hart.com/features/the-gore-of-grand-guignol/ (accessed 14 January 2018).

Hinzmann, D. (2017), 'Audience Member Faints at Bette Midler's "Hello, Dolly!"', *Out Magazine*, 22 March. Available online: https://www.out.com/theater-dance/2017/3/22/audience-member-faints-bette-midlers-hello-dolly-would-rather-die-miss-act-2 (accessed 14 January 2018).

Hoggatt, M. (2011), 'Horrors of the Grand Guignol', *Harvard Houghton Library blog*, 1 November. Available online: https://blogs.harvard.edu/houghton/2011/11/01/horrors-of-the-grand-guignol/ (accessed 14 January 2018).

Kenny, R. A. and T. McNicholas (2016), 'The Management of Vasovagal Syncope', *QJM: An International Journal of Medicine*, 109 (12): 767–773.

Milosevic, Irena and Randi E. McCabe, eds (2015), *Phobias: The Psychology of Irrational Fear*, Santa Barbara: Greenwood.

Morgan, F. (2017), 'Titus Got This Critic's Heart Pumping – and Here's the Proof', *The Stage*, 26 October. Available online: https://www.thestage.co.uk/features/2017/titus-got-critics-heart-pumping-heres-proof/ (accessed 14 January 2018).

Morley, C. (2015), 'Mass Hysteria Is a Powerful Group Activity', *The Guardian*, 29 March. Available online: https://www.theguardian.com/film/2015/

mar/29/carol-morley-the-falling-mass-hysteria-is-a-powerful-group-activity (accessed 14 January 2018).
Murray, C. (2016), 'Fight, Flight or … Faint? Why Some People Pass Out When They See Blood or Feel Pain', *The Conversation*, 27 April. Available online: http://theconversation.com/fight-flight-or-faint-why-some-people-pass-out-when-they-see-blood-or-feel-pain-57348 (accessed 14 January 2018).
Nemeth, B., L. J. J. Scheres, W. M. Lijfering and F. R. Rosendaal (2015), 'Bloodcurdling Movies and Measures of Coagulation: Fear Factor Crossover Trial', *BMJ*, 351: h6367.
'Outdone by Reality' (1962), *Time*, 30 November. Available online: http://www.grandguignol.com/time1962.htm (accessed 14 January 2018).
Pierron, Agnès (1996), 'Theatre of Horrors', *Grand Street*, trans. Deborah Treisman, Summer. Available online: http://www.grandguignol.com/grandstreet.htm (accessed 14 January 2018).
Quigley, K. (2011), 'Theatre on Call: Participatory Fainting and Grand-Guignol Theatre', *Performance Research*, 16 (3): 105–107.
Razaq, R. (2016), 'Cleansed, National Theatre: "If the Audience Faints, Our Play Is Doing Its Job," Says Fight Director of Controversial Play', *Evening Standard*, 24 February. Available online: https://www.standard.co.uk/news/london/cleansed-national-theatre-if-the-audience-faints-our-play-is-doing-its-job-says-fight-director-of-a3187921.html (accessed 14 January 2018).
Ruff, F. J. (2008), 'The Laugh Factory?: Humor and Horror at Le Théâtre du Grand Guignol', *Theatre Symposium*, 16: 65–74.
Sanderson, D. (2017), 'Theatre Introduces Audience "Trigger Warnings" to Avoid Upset', *The Times*, 15 February. Available online: https://www.thetimes.co.uk/article/theatre-introduces-audience-trigger-warnings-to-avoid-upset-cc8lw30m2 (accessed 14 January 2018).
Sanford, J. (2013), 'Blood, Sweat and Fears: A Common Phobia's Odd Pathophysiology', *Stanford Medicine*, Spring. Available online: http://sm.stanford.edu/archive/stanmed/2013spring/article6.html (accessed 14 January 2018).
Schneider, P. E. (1957), 'Fading Horrors of the Grand Guignol', *New York Times Magazine*, 18 March. Available online: http://www.grandguignol.com/nytmag.htm (accessed 14 January 2018).
Shenton, M. (2017), 'Do Theatre Shows Need "Trigger Warnings"?', *The Stage*, 22 February. Available online: https://www.thestage.co.uk/opinion/2017/mark-shenton-theatre-shows-need-trigger-warnings/ (accessed 14 January 2018).
Sherman, H. (2017), 'Is 1984's Bloody Staging Really Leaving Audiences Fainting in the Aisles? I Don't Buy It', *The Stage*, 28 July. Available online: https://www.thestage.co.uk/opinion/2017/howard-sherman-1984s-bloody-staging-really-leaving-audiences-fainting-aisles-dont-buy/ (accessed 14 January 2018).
Smith, M. W. (2018), *The Nervous Stage: Nineteenth-century Neuroscience and the Birth of Modern Theatre*, New York: Oxford University Press.

Van Lieshout, J. J., W. Wieling, J. M. Karemaker and D. L. Ecke (1991), 'The Vasovagal Response', *Clinical Science*, 81: 575–586.

Wani, A. L., A. Ara and S. A. Bhat (2014), 'Blood Injury and Injection Phobia: The Neglected One', *Behavioural Neurology*, 24 June.

Warner, M. (2014), 'There's Method in Theatre's Blood and Gore', *Guardian*, 12 May. Available online: https://www.theguardian.com/commentisfree/2014/may/12/theatre-blood-gore-titus-andronicus (accessed 14 January 2018).

Woodall, J. (2017), 'Titus Andronicus, RSC, Barbican Review – Blood Will Out', *theartsdesk.com*, 20 December. Available online: http://www.theartsdesk.com/theatre/titus-andronicus-rsc-barbican-review-blood-will-out (accessed 14 January 2018).

8

'I don't know why she's crying': Contagion and Criminality in Clean Break's *Dream Pill* and *Little on the inside*

Molly McPhee

A frenzied *spree*; a crushing *wave*; radiation from a *hotspot*: collective nouns for criminal activity often affiliate crime with the uncontainable. As the infection and body count of a crime *epidemic* denotes, what is uncontainable about criminal threat can also be contagious. These idioms portend an erosion of boundaries – civic, physical, environmental and moral. Within this, they implicitly appeal to applications of force, even and perhaps especially extralegal ones, to incapacitate an impending ravage of criminal acts.[1]

In carceral societies such as the United Kingdom and United States, 'contagious crime' transcends the figural. The social sciences position contagious criminal behaviour as an articulation of *social contagion*, a concept first made prominent by sociologist Robert Park (1915). Building on the nineteenth century's innovations in epidemiological modelling, investments in social reform and the formalization of public health frameworks, social contagion adapted bacteriological theories of disease transmission to explain cultural contact and transmission of behaviour (Wald 2008). Today, epidemiological modelling generates all-too-real predictive policing algorithms engendered by extreme social bias, peddled to the public via racist and classist politics of fear and danger (e.g. Skeem and Lowenkamp 2016). Accordingly this chapter approaches 'social contagion' as a metaphor weaponized to discipline, imprison and kill – through police brutality, acts of deportation and the 'letting die' of negligent prison management.

Social contagion, legitimated through policing and policy, leads to conditions of death and social death-in-life for disproportionate numbers of people of colour; people with refugee or immigrant status; people living with complex mental health conditions; addiction; and personal histories of abuse, among many factors (see Prison Reform Trust 2017). In this, I suggest here, social contagion acquires the syntax of Achille Mbembe's concept of necropolitics (2003). Necropolitics describes technologies of governance that implement 'death worlds' for those who threaten the security of white hegemony and heteropatriarchy inherited from colonialism. When contagion, as a necropolitical metaphor, creates conditions of social and physical death for the others of white heteropatriarchy, what capacity does theatre have to intervene? How might performance practice create the conditions for audiences to become aware of both their discursive and their affective investments in the necropolitics of contagion?

Since 1979, UK-based Clean Break Theatre Company's dramaturgy of women and crime aims to redress prejudicial imbalances in the UK legal system. In this chapter, I argue that two recent works by the company, *Dream Pill* (Rebecca Prichard, touring 2010–15) and *Little on the inside* (Alice Birch, touring 2013–14), activate and interrogate pre/conceptions of social contagion via sites of textual infection and emotional contagion. In particular the line 'I don't know why she's crying' (which opens both plays) proliferates, hosting transmissions of character and complicating criminal affects between the plays. This chapter positions the epidemiological modelling of policing and sentencing as a necropolitical tool; mirroring these social practices, a contagious dramaturgy creates carceral objects out of dissident bodies.

In 2013, audiences crowded into one of the dressing rooms at the Almeida Theatre, London, for Clean Break's *Dream Pill* by Rebecca Prichard: the story of Bola and Tunde, two Nigerian girls sex-trafficked to the UK. Audiences then moved to the Almeida foyer for performances by the same actors, now portraying two adult women in prison, in *Little on the inside* by Alice Birch. Despite a lack of narrative continuity between the two plays, echoes of Bola and Tunde's lines in *Dream Pill* provide the formal structure for *Little on the inside*. Two innocent girls have suddenly become criminalized, but implicitly so; in *Little on the inside* the two characters perform a rumour of *Dream Pill*'s Bola and Tunde – or an assumption, even a prejudice. Predicated on physical and cultural contact, this is social contagion at work as a performance aesthetic, working to reveal how the social imaginary of women and crime creates the material conditions for women to enter the criminal justice system.

Contagions of threat and compassion

In the spirit of an expansive metaphor, I suggest that Clean Break's artistic model participates in a contagious assemblage for every production. The company brings women theatre artists (some with lived experience of the criminal justice system and some without) and audiences into aesthetic vectors of imprisonment, subject formation and empowerment at the theatre. One of the ways this is achieved in the productions of *Dream Pill* and *Little on the inside* relies on movement – of both performers and audiences – between imagined carceral zones.

In an Almeida Theatre dressing room, small audiences encountered the story of Bola and Tunde, two young Nigerian girls sex-trafficked to the UK. Rebecca Prichard's *Dream Pill* brings the audience into the immediate space of the two performers, both professional actors, who interact with the audience throughout. Bola and Tunde address the audience sometimes as other girls in captivity with them; sometimes as punters; at times, more implicitly, as theatre-goers. A stripped down, poor theatre aesthetic with minimal lighting and props supports these sudden ruptures of identification. The performers' animation, stories and laughter pull the audience into a wavering awareness of the narrative scenario: the play 'lets you forget they're trafficked children. You just see them as children and then suddenly you remember why they're there' (Director Tessa Walker in Caird 2011). This makes for an emotionally challenging and politicized audience-performer relationship. *Dream Pill* affords no reprieve: neither narratively for the young girls and even less for the audience who by the end of the thirty-minute play have been interpellated into the structure as its co-creators through audience interaction.

Forty-five minutes following *Dream Pill*, the same actors – Susan Wokoma and Simone James – perform Alice Birch's *Little on the inside* in the Almeida Theatre foyer. Where the discretely drawn characters of Bola and Tunde once were, now stand A and B – granular, hyper-lyrical data points striding around the stage and bouncing off the walls of what, it becomes clear, is a prison cell. As with *Dream Pill*, there is minimal lighting, sound and set. *Dream Pill*'s opener 'I don't know why she's crying / She just has days like this. She's just having a bad day / Why are you here?' becomes Alice Birch's opener: 'I don't know why she's crying. / I don't Know why she is crying. / She steps out of the sea with a crown of dolphins I've got eleven brothers and six sisters I love you so much I could die and die and die' (2013). The diffuse, wild A and B crackle like the exposed innards of Bola and Tunde: guts, ectopic rhythms and gleefully mutating stories break down and reform in the viral ravage of Birch's structure.

Where Prichard's *Dream Pill* works as a limit case to interrogate the audience's social and affective participation in the trafficking of young, innocent black bodies, Birch's *Little on the inside* throws audiences into a scenario of implicit criminalization of adult black bodies, this time in state-sanctioned captivity. Both plays provoke and problematize audiences' desire to empathize with performances of black pain and resilience. The variable positioning of innocence and guilt in the two plays reveals what

Saidiya Hartman identifies as 'the need for the *innocent* black subject to be victimized by a racist state in order to *see* the racism of the racist state' (2003: 189, original emphasis) and fiercely challenges audiences to recognize this paradigm. If Bola, Tunde, A and B are performed on a continuity – as they are in the double bill – the audience's own trajectory from witnesses of innocence to quasi-complicit traffickers and jailers becomes an unavoidable performance within the matrix of social contagion.

As part of the 2013 Almeida Festival, the plays each occupied quotidian spaces within the theatre: a dressing room for *Dream Pill* and a foyer for *Little on the inside*. These spatial in-betweens displace the plays' theatricality, an effect that becomes amplified by uncertain temporalities between the plays – they echo each other in words and gesture, but not narrative. Though both narrative environments are carceral, their extreme disparity derives in part from an ambient attribution of guilt. The carceral environment of the trafficked girls of *Dream Pill*, held against their will, functions as an *innocent-carceral* environment (guilt belongs with the captors in degrees of complicity with the audience). The environment of *Little on the inside* signifies, by contrast, a state-sanctioned *guilty-carceral* of adult women in prison. Alongside each other, the plays dilate an aporia fundamental to carceral society: treatment of prisoners simultaneously as slaves and as citizens.

This vacillating perception of guilt and innocence within captivity stems from Enlightenment discourse around applications of the 'social contract' in penal reform. Rousseau's social contract, as adapted by eighteenth-century legal scholars, positioned the modern citizen as infinitely capable of self-reform through the corrective assistance of the state. Yet public imagination of the prisoner/captive was then, as it is indeed now, equally enflamed by the figure of the slave. This dual consciousness – the abjection of the slave, dehumanized and without rights, alongside the rehabilitating rationality of the citizen – continues to regulate and inform contemporary perceptions of carcerality. That the same actors perform first as slaves, then as prisoners, crystallizes this central discord within the carceral state, where prisoners become dehumanized within the prison system, even as they are expected to engage in self-reform and rehabilitation as productive members of society.

In the performance event, *Dream Pill* is literally the immediate past of *Little on the inside*. Yet audiences' sense of temporal progression is complicated by narrative dislocation: while the women in prison are not narratively connected to Bola and Tunde, they *are* textually connected. This helps to displace what the audience may hold in terms of hegemonic constructs of procession of time, agency and life chances for those who are criminalized. The plays enact a ruptured temporality, demonstrating a sentencing protocol of the present that captures rather than adjudicates. There is never a clear sense of why Birch's characters in *Little on the inside* are in prison; instead they exist in a brutalized present that draws into question the teleology of the justice system.

The net effect of these continuities and ruptures – physical, temporal and narrative – is a performance of the remainders of flesh and law. Vibrant storylines become unhinged in the space of *Dream Pill* and *Little on the inside*, and in the space of the performance the black characters become what Alexander Weheylie describes as a 'fleshly surplus' (2014: 2), which both articulates and transcends oppression. Crucial to this interpretation of *Dream Pill* and *Little on the inside*, Weheylie's concept of 'racializing assemblages of subjection' (2014: 2) radically reinvests the perception of black subjectivity on a dynamic spectrum through and beyond pain. The 'freedom dream' of the carceral state is alive in this theatre and is what brings the audience into complicity with the social discourse surrounding the narrative: 'Rather than displacing bare life or civil death, [these assemblages] excavat[e] the social (after)life of these categories ... [and] can never annihilate the lines of flight, freedom dreams, practices of liberation, and possibilities of other worlds' (Weheylie 2014). The audience are drawn into a racializing – and socially contagious – assemblage through what Leticia Sabsay calls 'permeable alliances' in which 'affective investments and shared vulnerability [...] reconfigure social antagonisms, calling into question the hegemonic borders of the body politic' (2016: 297). Such a relational permeability, between and amongst audience and performers, connects audience members' own subjective vulnerability to pathogenic vulnerability experienced by the politically and socially oppressed. Audiences achieve a discursive awareness of how social antagonisms, contagiously dispersed through prejudice and bias, become agents of criminalization. This awareness, fledged and maintained through the affective registers of social contagion, operates via emotions of threat and compassion.

Dream Pill and *Little on the inside* bring audience and performers into scenarios of criminalization that rely on the cultural power of what René Girard terms a 'reciprocal affinity' between disease and social disorder (1974: 834). Underlying this reciprocity, for Girard, is a mimetic violence that animates both concepts. *Dream Pill* and *Little on the inside* germinate a similar reciprocal affinity of mimetic violence: here, between compassion and threat. A painful twist of the affective and social dimensions of the two emotions capitalizes on majority white audiences' 'compassionate' response to black pain, alongside 'threatened' response to black resilience.[2]

Audience and critical response to *Dream Pill* and *Little on the inside* took on markedly different tones when performed together, as at the Almeida Festival, and apart, as each play has its own production history separate from the other.[3] Putting aesthetic differences between the plays for the moment aside, I contend that the audience commentary reveals a strong shift between responses to portrayals of innocent children in contrast to criminal adults – and that these responses vacillate along a scale of threat. For *Dream Pill*, feeling silenced was a common response: 'the two girls address questions to us, the audience, to which, of course, we cannot answer. We are made dumb before them' (Woddis 2010) and 'a devastating directness that leave[s] you feeling lost for words' (Taylor 2010). Even more frequently, people talked of mobility. Of physical mobility: 'Sometimes people couldn't move afterwards' (Walker in Caird 2011); 'At the end, they all got up and ran to the stairs to get out!' (Clean Break 2010). And of emotional mobility: on Twitter, sixteen audience members called *Dream Pill* 'moving' or 'captivating'.[4] In stark contrast, the responses to Birch's *Little on the inside* take on the tenor of an assault. Guts and body parts feature prominently: 'bruising – a bloom wrapped in barbed wire' (Love 2013); 'hard work to stomach' (Bowie-Sell 2014); 'an impactful punch' (Pritchard 2013); 'wallop' (Cox 2014); 'hiss[ing]' or 'sear[ing]' acid (Pringle 2013; Love 2013); 'a blow-torch blasted directly into your face' (Gillinson 2013); 'illusions shatter and blood is spilt as actor and audience are left in tears' (Slater 2014). Following Brian Massumi's assertion that 'the affective reality of threat is contagious' (2015: 195), I suggest that the rehearsal of both threat and compassion in the theatre of Clean Break generates an emotional rupture: a tearjerking.

Tearjerking

> About 20 minutes in, a woman fainted. [...] After the performance a young woman sitting on the floor was crying and would not get up for some minutes. Eventually her friend convinced her that it 'wasn't real, it's only a play' and she felt able to leave.
> *Dream Pill* Show Report 4, 17 November 2010, Soho Theatre

In thinking about emotional rupture, I want to position crying at Clean Break's *Dream Pill* as a contagious affect peculiar to a practice of tearjerking; by this I mean eliciting, conjuring and measuring tears in the encounter with narratives of imprisonment. Tim Etchells writes in 'The crying game of theatre': 'I'm not immune to a crying jag myself but I think weeping is of most interest in an audience when it's held in check or tension with other things ... The best tears come unbidden' (2009). Etchells uses disciplinary terms to discuss crying – *bidding, holding in check, crying jag* – all pointing to the punitive side of tearjerking. In the 1910s the effervescent gestures of soda jerks and beer jerks were appropriated by US journalists to describe a new kind of writing: *tearjerkers* were 'newspaper stories about tragic situations' (Online Etymology Dictionary). Tearjerking modes of artistic production became closely connected to traditions of penal reform and consciousness-raising in social and criminal justice domains.[5] Connections between aesthetic experience and call to action are manifestly present in Clean Break's approach today: 'DON'T JUST GO HOME' read the back of the programme when *Dream Pill* was first performed (2010).

In her essay 'On Affect and Protest', Deborah Gould articulates the connection between emotion and political mobilization as overshadowed by Western scholarship with 'a tendency to render emotion in cognitive and rationalist terms, thereby taming it' (2010: 23). *Dream Pill* and *Little on the inside* overtly work against this trend with the opener 'I don't know why she's crying' and its subsequent mutations. Rationalist awareness is situated as not only fallible but structurally affiliated with the unseen captor's universalist perspective – in other words, the prison-industrial complex in its punishment of bodies who know, or create knowledge, within cultural spaces and methodologies anathema to white, hegemonic subjectivity. Foucault discusses such knowledges as 'subjugated': 'a whole series of knowledges that have been disqualified as nonconceptual knowledges, [...] hierarchically inferior knowledges' (2003: 7). In *Dream Pill* the audience slinks towards an awareness of the fictional Bola and Tunde, and other enslaved and trafficked children, as articulating simultaneously 'the foundation of the national order' and the 'position of unthought' (Hartman 2003: 184–5): blackness and black sentience as the unthinkable other to the audience's rationalist discourse. In *Dream Pill* crying does not allow a 'restitution' of black subjectivity into a carceral freedom narrative of heroism, survival and triumph. Instead it forces recognition of the racialized and material circumstances of children under violent domination. This complication of knowledge construction pulls the audience out of their sense of stability as unquestioned ally.

Crying in an audience demonstrates the generation of a social mechanism that is possibly more politically effective in a social field which has become wary of rationalist or moralist appeals for change (Willett and Willett 2014: 87). A tearjerk play, evoking again the effervescence of the soda jerk, blubs and bubbles over in a flow between audience and performers, moving through a reef of emotion, affect and political mobilization. In this, the tearjerking affect reaches a symbiosis with concepts of emotional contagion. To return again to Etchell's vocabulary, 'I'm not immune': crying can infect as a transmissible event. The arrival of tears – bidden or unbidden – flowing around the audience space allows for a shift in the audience's sensorium. This shift is an affective articulation within a sociopolitical space, relating to an epidemiology of affect: mimetic communication that spreads in the wider community with a role in 'making – and breaking – of social bonds. These [affective modalities] form the basis for a sense of belonging, and, ultimately, of the polis, as what forms the affective bases of political orders' (Gibbs 2010: 191). If any one emotion hovers between the affective and the rational – some emotions pull more on cognitive processing than others (Gould 2010) – then a contagion of emotions as cultural-biological feedback loop brings multiple channels into play, from imitative behaviour (crying because others are, or Bola and Tunde are), to culturally constructed emotions (crying because of the situation of the narrative), to performances of judgement (crying because of a social requirement to respond to unacceptable brutality).

Judgement and contagion form a key nexus of the tearjerking apparatus of *Dream Pill*. 'By an affect', writes Teresa Brennan, 'I mean the physiological shift accompanying a judgment' (2004: 5). A majority white audience watches two black actors perform as sex-trafficked children:

> Just as the master depends on the slave[, f]or the one who is projected upon, the drive becomes an affect, a passionate judgment directed inward, a judgment that constitutes a kind of hook on which the other's negative affect can fix. (2004: 111–12)

Prichard tearjerks the audience with *Dream Pill*; in staging an encounter with sex-trafficked children she demands that the audience acknowledge their social duty to judge the situation, and at the same time, she provides no easy object on which to hook that judgement. Her writing refuses to allow Bola and Tunde to stand as victims in front of the audience; it also refuses the audience their own injurability by splicing the grief and dread that the audience wants to feel with quirky, funny lines and hopeful shouts from the actors. The projection of judgement travels around the space like a bottle rocket – the situation of Bola and Tunde is so unacceptable that there is no adequate landing zone for this impassioned, negative affect. *Dream Pill*'s original staging on Dean Street, with Soho walk-ups all around, brings the audience to the very precipice of recognition. Instead, the girls turn to the audience in the last lines of the play: 'Are we real? Are you?' – keeping open the dialogic address. A play, depicting children subjected to unspeakable acts of violence, has the audacity to question the reality of the audience!

To return to the performance of November 2010: a woman fainted and a woman was on the ground weeping. Here the tearjerk resurfaces, as a yank, a pull downwards. Witnessing Bola and Tunde – as trafficked characters, as black people, as actors, as confident and funny characters, as raped characters, as people coming off the stage to touch the audience – manifested an extreme discomfort at this event of permeable co-constitution. One of the reasons for this discomfort is, finally, recognition that *Dream Pill* is not 'only a play' as the friend of the crying woman says.[6] To be on the floor weeping with abandon following a performance of *Dream Pill* presents a complex set of impulses and affects, arising from witnessing black pain, in combination with a denial of easy empathy. Crying here also encompasses a necropolitical gesture.

Bola and Tunde begin and end *Dream Pill* lying on the floor. The audience member's mimetic body on the ground recalls Sara Ahmed's notion of the 'stickiness' (2014: 4) of emotion – enveloped by contingent pain, she is stuck to the floor in an 'over-representation of the pain of others … significant in that it fixes the other as the one who "has" pain, and who can overcome that pain only when the Western subject feels moved enough to give' (Ahmed 2014: 22). In this context, appropriative crying at black pain supports the necropolitics of the carceral state in which the theatre is made. In many crucial ways, the friend consoles truthfully: this *is* only a play. The girls, not girls, are not being held at the theatre; they have risen from the floor to take a bow and leave the stage. The lights are up and people are filtering back upstairs. Yet the crying woman refuses to rise.[7] Her mirroring, sticky articulation of pain, refuses to let the girls rise, in what becomes a necropolitical entanglement. The world of *Dream Pill* yokes the subjectivity of its characters to the 'triple loss' of slavery, as Mbembe identifies it: 'absolute domination, natal alienation, and social death (expulsion from humanity altogether)' (2003: 21), a form of 'death-in-life'. Yet in Prichard's writing, the girls live, and live at times exuberantly; their vulnerability is agential and never in a state of equivalency with their injurability. The 'permeable alliances' afforded by the play in fact bring the audience's own reality into a differential distribution of vulnerability ('Are we real? Are you?'). Thus the tears that do not allow a rise from the floor, when emerging from the necropolitical instincts of a citizen of a carceral state, become an act of aggressive mourning. The 'omnipotency' (Mbembe 2003) of this instinct both to create and to memorialize the living dead lends it all the powers of tentacular, totalizing ontology, laden with affect – reaching all the way to something so seemingly harmless as crying at theatre.

Guts and algorithms

In Alice Birch's *Little on the inside* A and B leave *Dream Pill*'s expression through direct address to embrace a physically active back-and-forth filled with shouts and jumps and narrative loops that seem to refer to a private world only they can know. As fragments of Prichard's text ricochet through Birch's, A and B regenerate as remainders – both as data points of Bola and Tunde, and social pathogens entirely unmoored from any one subjectivity. A text filled with organic imagery, riddled with guts, yet combines and recombines with algorithmic precision.

Little on the inside operates within a semantic of 'predictive' governance that invests significant public and private capital in converting the metaphor of organic contagion into social necropower via a development of crime mapping software based on epidemiological modelling tools. Crime mapping in the UK draws on a mixture of homegrown and commercially marketed risk assessment algorithms deployed in carceral states worldwide. Rather than indicating crime of the future, policing 'predictions' expand on an indefinite sentencing protocol of the present, stemming from conviction histories – postcode, ethnicity, age, gender, religion and sexuality, among other 'data'. Facilitating what R. Joshua Scannell calls 'deep managerial time' these 'data-driven police practices … conjure new social objects. Not exactly human, but extracted and recombined from the human, these carceral quasi-objects thrive on dilating human life chances and debilitating human bodies' (2016: 248). A and B express this not-exactly-humanness but they also embody a communal resistance through riots of movement and touch, building on and solidifying each other. This is Rizvana Bradley's notion of 'kinaesthetic contagion': 'Black bodies cut movement's law … Black movement, insofar as it is understood to be embedded in a mode of sociality concerned with the irreducible and eruptive potential of black life and labor, *is contagious*' (2018: 23, 24, original emphasis). As Bola and Tunde become A and B in Alice Birch's *Little on the inside*, they resonate as enfleshed remainders of the law, cut free in contagious movement.

In tandem, *Dream Pill* and *Little on the inside* articulate the relationship between slavery, prison and – crucially – theatre in carceral societies today: the shift of register exposes the judging, and policing, algorithms alive in the audience. In his concept *habeas viscus*, Weheliye explores 'the breaks, crevices, movements, languages, and such found in the zones between the flesh and the law':

> The conjoining of flesh and habeas corpus in the compound *habeas viscus* brings into view an articulated assemblage of the human (viscus/flesh) borne of political violence, while at the same time not losing sight of the different ways the law pugnaciously adjudicates who is deserving of personhood and who is not (habeas). (2014: 11)

Predictive algorithms and biased sentencing in courts of law – in their allocation of 'personhood' – make the political promise of *habeas viscus* a vital one. Rational 'knowing' via the surveilling mechanisms of theatre is under siege, as is the traditional dramaturgical model of compassionate middle-class liberalism, that is sending playwrights to the margins to gather messages for the centralized, hegemonic audience. Where in Prichard's *Dream Pill* this model becomes disrupted through the permeable co-construction of audience, performer and social narrative, in Birch's *Little on the inside* the play as a form of cultural hegemony is deconstructed through character and language – leaving a contagious residue from the crevice between flesh and law.

In Birch's play the enactment of behavioural contagion between the plays crystallizes in splits, breakdowns, and reconstitutions of language and knowing. A and B exist in this transmission in a relationship of what Christina Sharpe calls anagrammatical blackness (2016). They are never only who or what they appear to be on stage: prisoners, lovers, women, black. They are scrambled identities – anagrams of Bola, Tunde; guards and theatre-goers. Existing 'in an index of violability and also potentiality' (2016: 75), they are informatic data points. The audience is prevented from allocating a 'personhood' to A and B. Nameless and fluid, and if not interchangeable, verging constantly on rupture, 'they are good at pretending to be other people', writes Birch in her character notes. Essentially, contagiously, every word rolls with the performative remainders of a stranger's tongue in one's own mouth; in this, one or many new legal vocabularies of *habeas viscus* become enunciated.

In her work on outbreak narrative, Priscilla Wald writes of the stratified social body: 'Constituting a threat to [social] borders, the [contagion] carrier, one of "the individual parts," comes dangerously close to being equated with the dissociable diseased organ' (2008: 77). Following this same vein, Birch's play manifests a body of prolifically dissociable organs. 'Over the other side of that wall. Just behind that patch of grass by your foot, the bit that's all burnt and covered in hair and thick dark moss and shoelaces' – A and B place all their organs on this prison boundary wall. Chins, lips, hearts, faces and guts are all proffered as tokens of conciliation, of rejoining the social body: 'I'd cross seas on a raft made of fish guts and the bones from little faces and I'd fight Every Single Thing that I found, just to get to your lip' (Birch 2013).

In a 2007 article, Ian Hacking asks: 'Does anyone ask criminals about to be executed in the United States whether they would care to have their organs recycled? ... [Bills proposing measures to allow for this consistently] fail to pass' (84). Later, Hacking discusses the 'strange family relations' created by organ transplants: '[Recipient] Mr B also feels that he bears some of the soul of young C, not just his energy but also some of C's quirks and fascinations' (Hacking 2007: 94). *Little on the inside* explores just this contagion of character, the parasite that haunts the host or engenders the host to new/old consciousness. There is no resolution to A and B; they rise and die off in many ways, multiple times through the performance.

Little on the inside writhes and contorts with the infection of the legal sentence, bringing it to violent articulation via viral, deliberately enfleshed language of guts and heartbeats. Birch's destratified voices give an embedded framework from within which ethics of precipitating another's tongue can be deeply examined, the ethics required when hearing the voice of a group of people who are, as A petitions, 'consistently threatened with the removal of her tongue in a very real manner, members of the jury, and so on and so forth' (Birch 2013).

Conclusion

In the UK, 22 per cent of all women in prison had no previous convictions or cautions (Prison Reform Trust 2017: 36). Bola, Tunde, A and B are voices, bodies, histories, which in contagious dialogue give a storyline of many women trapped and criminalized as a result of social oppression. As these plays demonstrate, Clean Break's prison theatre is about everything in the world, including prison. They manifest storylines that sustain, and grow, run rampant and lush in carceral environments.

A continued legitimation of state- and culturally-sanctioned police brutality, stigma within legal systems and predictive policing depends upon the contagion metaphor. The weaponization of social contagion instructs the social field to aggressively contain, and 'prevent', epidemic overflows of criminality and violence. As I have investigated here, one way of becoming aware of personal investment in social contagion, and correspondingly its greater or lesser investment in us, is through the conscience-catching permeability of the theatre. *Dream Pill* and *Little on the inside*, in their precipitation of affective response to carceral zones across multiple sites of performance, make the complicity with policing more powerful. They also engender resistance. Within its contagious assemblage, theatre facilitates immense imaginative and material agency to recognize criminalizing bias as it threatens to saturate social life in carceral states.

Notes

1 In the first months of 2018, London 'in the grips of a knife crime epidemic' has been widely reported by British and international press; yet look further, and mentions of crime epidemics in London crop up in 2017, 2016, 2015 and on. In stark contrast, police brutality (in London or elsewhere) remains comparatively rarely discussed in the terms of contagious epidemic.

2 'The Audience Agency's [UK theatre] booking data from 2011/12 to 2014/15 … showed that 90% of bookers in 2014/15 were white. [In London] … 79% of London bookers are white, 12% Asian/Asian British and 4% Black/Black British' (Arts Council England 2016: 53). Black and minority ethnic population in London is 40 per cent (ACE 2016).

3 *Dream Pill* production history, dir. Tessa Walker: Soho Theatre (2010); Metropolitan Police's Human Trafficking Conference (2010); annual London Safeguarding Children Board conference (2011); Edinburgh Festival Fringe (2011); White Ribbon Campaign Scotland tour (2012); Latitude and Greenbelt Festivals (2012); Almeida Festival (2013); National Underground Freedom Center (US, 2015, dir. Eric Vosmeier). *Little on the inside* production history, all dir. Lucy Morrison: Almeida and Latitude Festivals (2013); Edinburgh Festival Fringe (2014).

4 'Moving' x 14: @iAmBayo 9 August 2011; @JoBoaden 20 August 2011; @walkingheads 26 August 2011; @inthewrongcrowd 1 March 2012; @MissRudiBlue 25 August 2012; @knighthallagent 26 July 2013; @soophiaf 25 July 2013; @SKShlomo 28 August 2011; @tamashatheatre 20 August 2011; @NickHernBooks 18 August 2011; @scotrefcouncil 18 August 2011; @yosoyrobcavazos 10 August 2011; @jenclokey 6 August 2011; @EmilyJJenkins 6 August 2011. 'Captivating' x 2: @OpenClasp 14 July 2012; @jenclokey 6 August 2011.

5 Within British criminal justice policy and legislation, a key illustration of tearjerking impact from the period: in reaction to John Galsworthy's 1910 *Justice* audiences' 'many "tear-stained" letters to the then Home Secretary, Winston Churchill, begging him to reconsider the use of solitary confinement' immediately resulted in changes to British legislation (McAvinchey 2011: 43).

6 Prichard's AHRC-funded research for *Dream Pill* involved consultation with the Metropolitan Police's Human Trafficking Team, ECPAT (End Child Prostitution, Child Pornography and the Trafficking of Children for Sexual Purposes), AFRUCA (Africans Unite Against Child Abuse) and the Poppy Project.

7 On not allowing the actor to rise for applause, Frank Wilderson notes: 'not only is the slave's performance (dance, music, etc.) the property of white enjoyment, but so is […] the slave's own enjoyment of his/her performance: that too belongs to white people' (in Hartman 2003: 188).

References

Ahmed, S. (2014), *The Cultural Politics of Emotion*, Edinburgh: Edinburgh University Press.

Arts Council England (2016), *Analysis of Theatre in England*, London: BOP Consulting and Graham Devlin Associates.

Birch, A. (2013), *Little on the inside*, unpublished play.

Bowie-Sell, D. (2014), 'Little on the inside review', *Time Out*, 18 August. Available online: https://www.timeout.com/london/theatre/little-on-the-inside-review (accessed 12 December 2017).

Bradley, R. (2018), 'Black Cinematic Gesture and the Aesthetics of Contagion', *TDR: The Drama Review*, 62 (1): 14–30.

Brennan, T. (2004), *The Transmission of Affect*, Ithaca and London: Cornell University Press.

Caird, J. (2011), 'Breaking the Cycle', *Fest*, 19 July: 48–49.

Clean Break (2010), *Dream Pill*, Show Report 4 and 6, 17 and 20 November, unpublished company document used with permission of Clean Break (granted 17 July 2017).

Cox, M. (2014), 'Across the Festival: August 4 – Summerhall', *Across the Arts*, 6 August. Available online: http://www.acrossthearts.co.uk/news/artsblog/august-4--summerhall/ (accessed 12 December 2017).

Etchells, T. (2009), 'The Crying Game of Theatre', *Guardian*, 28 August. Available online: https://www.theguardian.com/stage/theatreblog/2009/aug/28/crying-theatre (accessed 6 September 2017).

Foucault, M. (2003), *Society Must Be Defended: Lectures at the Collège de France, 1975–76*, trans. D. Macey, New York: Picador.

Gibbs, A. (2010), 'After Affect: Sympathy, Synchrony, and Mimetic Communication', in M. Gregg and G. J. Seigworth (eds), *The Affect Theory Reader*, 186–205, Durham and London: Duke University Press.

Gillinson, M. (2013), *'Little on the inside' Review or 'Red Raw Screams in the Silence'*, 30 July. Available online: http://sketchesontheatre.blogspot.co.uk/2013/07/little-on-inside-review-or-red-raw.html (accessed 12 December 2017).

Girard, R. (1974), 'The Plague in Literature and Myth', *Texas Studies in Literature and Language*, 15 (5): 833–50.

Gould, D. (2010), 'On Affect and Protest', in J. Staiger, A. Cvetkovich and A. Reynolds (eds), *Political Emotions*, New York and London: Routledge.

Hacking, I. (2007), 'Our Neo-Cartesian Bodies in Parts', *Critical Inquiry*, 34 (1): 78–105.

Hartman, S. (2003), 'The Position of the Unthought', *Qui Parle*, 13 (2): 183–201.

Love, C. (2013), 'Little on the inside', *Exeunt*, 31 July. Available online: http://exeuntmagazine.com/reviews/little-on-the-inside/ (accessed 12 December 2017).

Massumi, B. (2015), *Ontopower: War, Powers, and the State of Perception*, Durham and London: Duke University Press.
Mbembe, A. (2003), 'Necropolitics', *Public Culture*, 15 (1): 11–40.
McAvinchey, C. (2011), *Theatre & Prison*, Basingstoke and New York: Palgrave Macmillan.
Prichard, R. (2010), 'Dream Pill', in *Charged*, London: Nick Hern Books.
Pringle, S. (2013), 'Latitude Theatre Review: Marquees and Mash-ups', *Guardian*, 22 July. Available online: https://www.theguardian.com/stage/2013/jul/22/latitude-theatre-review (accessed 12 December 2017).
Prison Reform Trust (2017), *Bromley Briefings Prison Factfile*. Available online: http://www.prisonreformtrust.org.uk/Portals/0/Documents/Bromley%20Briefings/Autumn%202017%20factfile.pdf.
Pritchard, T. (2013), 'Double Bill: Dream Pill and Little on the inside at Almeida', *Londonist*, 29 July. Available online: http://londonist.com/2013/07/double-bill-dream-pill-and-little-on-the-inside-at-almeida (accessed 12 December 2017).
Sabsay, L. (2016), 'Permeable Bodies: Vulnerability, Affective Powers, Hegemony', in J. Butler, Z. Gambetti and L. Sabsay (eds), *Vulnerability in Resistance*, 278–302, Durham and London: Duke University Press.
Scannell, R. J. (2016), 'Both a Cyborg and a Goddess: Deep Managerial Time and Informatic Governance', in K. Behar (ed.), *Object-Oriented Feminism*, 247–73, Minneapolis and London: University of Minnesota Press.
Sharpe, C. (2016), *In the Wake: On Blackness and Being*, Durham and London: Duke University Press.
Skeem, J. L. and C. T. Lowenkamp (2016), *Risk, Race, & Recidivism: Predictive Bias and Disparate Impact*. Available online: https://ssrn.com/abstract=2687339.
Slater, T. (2014), 'Little on the inside: Truth and Illusion Behind Bars', *Spiked*, 12 August. Available online: https://www.spiked-online.com/2014/08/12/little-on-the-inside-truth-and-illusion-behind-bars/ (accessed 12 December 2017).
Taylor, P. (2010), 'Charged, Soho Theatre, London', *Independent*, 17 November. Available online: https://www.independent.co.uk/arts-entertainment/theatre-dance/reviews/charged-soho-theatre-london-2135919.html (accessed 12 December 2017).
Wald, P. (2008), *Contagious: Cultures, Carriers, and the Outbreak Narrative*. Durham and London: Duke University Press.
Weheliye, A. G. (2014), *Habeas Viscus: Racializing Assemblages, Biopolitics, and Black Feminist Theories of the Human*, Durham and London: Duke University Press.
Willett, C. and J. Willett (2014), 'Going to Bed White and Waking up Arab: On Xenophobia, Affect Theories of Laughter, and the Social Contagion of the Comic Stage', *Critical Philosophy of Race*, 2 (1): 84–105.
Woddis, C. (2010), 'Charged 1 & 2, Soho Theatre', *artsdesk.com*, 14 November. Available online: http://www.theartsdesk.com/theatre/charged-1-2-soho-theatre?page=0,1 (accessed 12 December 2017).

9

Nomadic Contagion and the Performance of Infrastructure in Dale Farm's Post-eviction Scene

Lynne McCarthy

The dismantling of an unauthorized Irish Traveller settlement at Dale Farm, Essex, in 2011 showed how nomadic infrastructures are made to disappear. Thereafter, local authorities reconstituted the razed residential foundations of Dale Farm by moulding the disturbed soil of the eviction into 6-foot banks enclosing the boundaries of family plots and with the result of impeding access to those properties. Significantly, the property remained the legal belonging of the Travellers as the Dale Farm dispute was not an issue of trespass but one of planning permission. These banks, termed 'bunding', are used to stop the spread of pollutants from exposed topographies and are a legal Environmental Protection Agency mechanism used for the containment of chemical and toxic waste (EPA 2012). The only other application of 'bunding' beyond industrial waste sites is in nomadic Traveller sites where it is routinely erected to prevent access to their halting areas (Crowley and Kitchin 2007: 137). Filled by storm water, the bund-walled areas of Dale Farm floated open sewage and asbestos, insidiously exposing remaining residents to the contaminants that collected in these enclosed landscapes.

In this chapter I examine bunding as an obstruction infrastructure that discretely conducts infection to Traveller communities while enacting a cultural and environmental racism towards them. Infrastructure performs through a system of organs – quite literally through its sewage and water systems, its ventilation systems, road networks, open spaces and enclosures – to maintain public health or, its opposite, in the case of environmental racism. As I will show, infrastructure is an administrative tool of social control operating through dispersed techniques that produce easily mis-identifiable affects. I argue that bunding is representative of a state disposition towards Travellers that obliges them to act with property in ways that are punitive. In addition to the social cleansing routinely experienced by Irish Travellers in evictions, I discuss the putative hygienic use of bunding through the paradox of isolating contaminating substances while simultaneously containing Travellers, as distinctive subjects, to these areas. Containment and contamination operate as opposing principles in public health where isolation is considered a remediative public good to the menace of contagion, yet Travellers are paradoxically contained close to polluting substances and put in harm's way. I read bunding as an aesthetic infrastructure (Larkin 2013; Amin 2014) that reproduces feelings, such as being noxious, as daily affects for Traveller populations. Following thinking on infrastructure as statecraft (Easterling 2014), the aesthetic work of pollution (Douglas [1966] 2003), and pain and its contagions (Scarry 1985), I further argue that the purposeful contamination of halting sites at once attaches Travellers to literal sites of infection while performatively reinforcing metaphors of nomadic populations as contagious.

In October 2011, Basildon District Council's enforced eviction of three hundred Irish Travellers in Dale Farm, Essex, sanctioned by the Royal Courts of Justice, was carried out as a legitimate act of dismantlement. The Irish Traveller residents, once expunged, returned to the verges of Dale Farm in the weeks after the initial eviction and did so because they had not been offered alternative ethnically appropriate accommodation by Basildon District Council. Moreover, Travellers reported that on leaving Dale Farm, their caravans had been attended by police escorts who alternated duties at the boundary of each municipality the Travellers passed (Quarmby 2013 and Interview with the Author 2011). Katharine Quarmby notes that three quarters of the residents returned to the laneway adjoining Dale Farm, known as Oak Lane, with the remainder finding pitches in Cambridgeshire (2013: 152). Oak Lane was lawful Traveller property that was exempt from official enforcement notices (Puxon 2011). Residents had 'nowhere else to go' as described in one female Traveller's account of the winter spent on these verges (Interview with the Author 2011).

The land at Dale Farm had been purchased by residents in 2001 after John Major's Conservative government (1992–7) abrogated from the public provision of Travellers sites through the 1994 Criminal Justice Act. This act privatized sites by placing the onus on Travellers to buy and maintain their own private property. Although the legal owners, the Dale Farm Travellers lived on the site as an unauthorized development without planning permission. Irrespective of several planning applications made through the advocacy group, the Irish Traveller Movement in Britain, the residents faced the constant probability of eviction (ITMB 2011). Their applications, like 90 per cent of other Traveller planning applications submitted in the UK, were refused planning permission (Ryder et al. 2011). The circumstances of the Dale Farm Travellers exemplified the circumstances of Travellers across the UK who were coerced into private land purchase by the restricted and limited provision of public sites after the passing of the 1994 Criminal Justice Act. Additionally, the strengthened trespass laws in the Criminal Justice Act, which indirectly criminalized the practice of nomadism by making it illegal to stop at customary halting sites, were compounded by the closure of transit sites (temporary halting sites) under the same act. The prospect that the Dale Farm settlement would ever be authorized through retrospective planning was unlikely.

Performing nomadic contagions

The campaign led by Conservative MP Michael Howard and *The Sun* newspaper in 2005 called 'Stamp on the Camps', detailed by Tyler (2013), was a response to Traveller developments such as Dale Farm. Large settlements of 300 or more people may have seemed conspicuous and without explanation at the time but in fact arose due to the restrictive legislation of the Criminal Justice Act. A petition was lodged by *The Sun* to Downing Street outlining three demands: first, to prevent and dismantle illegal developments; second, to limit retrospective planning permission which many Traveller settlements were dependent upon; and third, to rescind human rights legislation that apparently gave minority groups more of an advantage in terms of the planning system (Tyler 2013: 136). Notably, residents of Dale Farm suffered the untrammelled prejudice that arose from this campaign when it called for sites to be abolished. At the time, Howard visited the entrance to Dale Farm to make an example of the encampments he wished to see dismantled. The present Conservative administration's (2011–) call to rescind the EU Charter of Human Rights and their policies of 'hostile environments' for immigrants and ethnic minorities (Hill 2017) appears to adhere to Howard's earlier policies in 2005 which betray a particular discrimination towards nomads but are latent to a more generalized form of ethnic discrimination.

Prime Minister David Cameron's (2010–16) response to the Dale Farm eviction that 'those people should go home' (BBC 2011) misunderstood Irish Travellers' historical attachments to nomadism in the UK for over 400 years and signalled an emerging Conservative hostility to immigrants. Such expulsions, conducted on the basis of ethnic difference, are noted in other times of austerity or crisis in English history when the Irish were expelled from Britain in 1413 under Henry V during a period of surplus labour and as a result of an earlier law in 1349, a year after the Black Death when vagrancy was outlawed (Griffin 2008: 31). The fear of contagion presented by movements of people and vagrancy is shown here to be a premodern concern, the legacy of which is still perhaps implicit in everyday British attitudes to Travellers. Polluted landscapes, dirty persons and contagious plagues are culturally regulated phenomena derived from notions that a sacred social order and its opposite, a disorderly profane exist – research distinctively explored by Mary Douglas ([1966] 2003). Over time Travellers have become associated with disorder and dirt through frequent allusions to their placing of rubbish and to their very presence as out of place. Mary Ellen Synon of the Irish *Sunday Independent* notoriously termed nomadism 'the culture of the sewers' in the mid-1990s and was later found guilty of incitement to hatred (Synon 1996). Douglas suggests that dirt is culturally perceived and a cause of fear precisely because it is something determined to be out of place with the dominant social order and thereby a threat to its stability. Although critiqued for her structuralism, Mary Douglas's thinking is apt in consideration of how contagion, not just in terms of medical materialism but in terms of culture, proliferates. The notion that something out of place poses a threat to in-common cultural production is an insight into the irrational fear and hatred often confronted by Travellers.

Christopher Griffin's anthropological work, *Nomads under the Westway* (2008), is an empathetic account of how London-based Irish Travellers have been tactically moved on by various city councils. The title refers to a small group of Travellers who consistently struggled with the borough of Kensington and Chelsea during the 1970s, the same borough, who, as I write, are accused by residents of mishandling the catastrophic fire at Grenfell Tower, a social housing high-rise where fire rapidly took hold in the summer of 2017, killing over seventy people. Local authorities attempting to abrogate from site delivery in the 1970s could apply for an exemption if 'they could prove they had no "suitable" land for the purpose' or that the territory had a 'negligible' number of Travellers (Griffin 2008: 109–10). Such an exemption was granted to Kensington and Chelsea who subsequently evicted their Irish Traveller population. This group of Travellers were eventually resited under the Westways flyover by Hammersmith and Fulham Council (Griffin 2008). However, as Griffin notes, the flyover leaked drops of lead onto trailer rooftops and the cramped open spaces of this site, which has been an ongoing source of concern for residents' health.

Placing Traveller populations near polluted sites is a means by which discrimination against them is compounded through associations with dirt and disease. 'Environmental racism', a term describing how the world's ethnic and low-income populations are routinely placed on disinvested real estate close to polluted environments, is a process of 'differentiations in social reproduction' within capitalist accumulation (Katz 2001: 711).

'Environmental racism' takes place when a 'geographical fix' is required for 'political-ecological problems, such as the siting of toxic waste repositories or the location of noxious industries (often regulated out of wealthier or more privileged locales)', and resulting in the 'social relations that encourage production in one place tapping [for instance,] a migrant workforce reproduced elsewhere' (Katz 2001: 715). In 'The Decline of Nomadism', Greenfields and Smith note such attributions to Traveller property and Travellers themselves derive from processes of 'boundary maintenance' that are upheld through categorisations of 'urban poor/Gypsy' which, give 'recourse to areas of slum housing and to marginal and derelict tracts of land thus reinforcing still further public association of Gypsies and Travellers with dirt and disorder' (2013: 3). In 2009, the Equality and Human Rights Commission (EHRC) reported that 'although conditions vary, many publicly provided sites are of poor quality with sites built on contaminated land, close to motorways, adjoining sewage works, or on other poor quality land' (Cemlyn et al. 2009: 9). Similarly, Griffin's historical tracing of the migrations of Irish Travellers in Britain observes earlier communities in Notting Dale circa 1879 where, according to a historical testimony, nomads were placed in 'the ugliest place known in the neighbourhood of London, a tract of land torn up for the Brickfield clay, half consisting of fields laid to waste in expectation of the house builder, which lies just outside Shepherd's Bush and Notting Hill' (2008: 64).

Representations of Traveller populations are conjoined with metaphors of contagion in the way that a Traveller might stand in as or personify contagion itself. Mary Ellen Synon's phrase, 'culture of the sewers', equates human waste as a stand-in for Travellers and is evocative of terms like 'defecation', 'infection', and 'disease'. These mental concepts of travelling populations as contagious have, perhaps, overworked the metaphor to the point of making it literal. When Traveller populations are geographically located near polluted sites and wastelands, ideas of contagion become literal because such sitings give an impression that Traveller lifestyles are the cause of pollution less than that the siting is symptomatic of their subjection to an environmental racism. At the same time, becoming contagious is a serious risk, if not certainty for Traveller health. Moreover, contagion and its analogues are, as Douglas ([1966] 2003) notes, culturally regulated instruments of this social order, and I argue these are shown to be arbitrated by metaphors that stick to Traveller subjectivities.

Furthermore, these states of threatening contagion lead to practices of containment. Travellers are segregated and self-segregating; they are legally restricted in the places they can reside and temporarily inhabit, and Dale Farm residents' cultural preference was to dwell in extended settlements with their kin and removed from mainstream populations. These politically ambiguous detaining and self-detaining practices suggest that containment is a performative and affective ontology for Travellers. Self-imposed and imposed detentions become performative when they train nomadic populations into an acceptance of life on the verges as punitive and restrictive. Travellers isolate themselves from what they see as their discriminatory treatment by sedentary populations only to confine themselves in the very spaces where that discrimination is executed so that it is only they who are witness. These performative situations are composed of oblique interactions as the enactors of evictions silence their addressees by obstructing any possible redress. The performative work in the edict, 'I evict' has an affective implication for its compulsory addressees, in this case a Traveller subjectivity that becomes suspended. Similarly, the affective Traveller ontologies that are at stake, like Ngai's (2005: 1) work on 'ambivalent situations' of 'obstructed agency' (32), are that negative affects become a primary mode of Traveller existence. Such 'ugly feelings' are expressed towards Travellers by producing them as 'racially marked subjects' (95) through states of 'animatedness' that evoke the 'exaggerated expressiveness of the racial stereotype' (94). For Ngai, being 'animated' has racialized affects pertaining to notions of emotional excess, surplus or the superfluous, which can line up with 'dramatizing the animation of racialized bodies for political purposes' (98). So too are Irish Travellers racially animated and dramatized through mainstream media and public discourses in the UK. On the back of Channel 4's success with *My Big Fat Gypsy Wedding* (2011) a second series was advertised across billboards in 2012 as 'Bigger Fatter Gypsier' with this text overlaid by an image of a freckled, red-haired Traveller child, amongst a campaign dominated by other deprecating imagery (Allen 2012). The use of comparative adjectives attested to the fullness of Channel 4's stereotypical animation of Travellers, and this was made all the more unforgivable by foregrounding an identifiable child as a receptor for the types of racialized tones incited by the text. The ad was censored as a result of a complaint made by the Irish Traveller Movement to the Advertising Standards Authority (ITMB 2012: 3).[1] I now elaborate on how environmental racism is enacted through infrastructure, which in turn fosters a performative relation between Travellers and their property that is obstructive.

Nomadic infrastructure

The landscape left razed at Dale Farm after the eviction attested to the destitute conditions to which the Travellers returned. Basildon District Council, the initiators of the eviction, instructed bailiffs to mount the banks of soil, known as 'bunding', further restricting Traveller use of their own property. These banks encircled and obstructed each plot in the development on a family-by-family basis. The bunding was mounted to the head height of an average adult and posed serious safety risks for the Travellers by cutting off a central collective amenity where laundry was undertaken and increasing the owners' probability of accidents (Quarmby 2013: 115). Fallen signs left by the council declared the land uneven and unsuitable for children's play when, ironically, the topography had been deliberately arranged as such by the council. These were the ways that Travellers were obstructed from undertaking their daily routines by the bunding at Dale Farm, while emphasizing racialized attitudes in the policing of Traveller property.

The local council's use of the term 'bunding' has its provenance in industrial construction where it is used as a description of a defence wall that contains 'potentially polluting substances', for instance (EPA 2012). In industrial practices and in examples given in the manual of the Environmental Protection Agency (EPA), a bund wall is deployed as a secondary defence mechanism and is typically built as a fail-safe around a structure that produces hazardous substances, such as bulk chemical stores (EPA 2012). It could be argued on the council's behalf that potentially hazardous pollutants, such as sewage pipes, could burst in the course of the eviction or that because the site had previously been used for the dismantlement of cars, upturning the soil would inevitably expose pollutants. Based on photographic evidence I recorded after the eviction, it is clear that sewage pipes were left exposed and that raw sewage ran along the channels where bunding had been constructed in parallel (Figure 9.1; EPA 2012). It suggested that the rationale for the construction of the bunding, which was to prevent contamination, was left unfulfilled by the council. Many of the hard structures including static homes had been removed by the Travellers for safety prior to the eviction, reducing the building materials that would normally produce hazardous waste in demolition work. There were valid grounds for Basildon District Council to make an effort to restrict the escape of pollutants from Dale Farm, but this effort was not completed to a standard where the pollutants were actually conducted safely away from the site and where the topography was returned to a protected state. The significance of this is that Basildon District Council had argued in the courts against the illegal use of land at Dale Farm for residential (brown belt) purposes rather than as its intended use as undeveloped green belt land.

In industrial demolition practices, it is usual to capture storm water that can carry pollutants by creating conduits or laying down a cover of peat that retains the water and, thus, pollutants (EPA 2012). In effect, the bunding did

Dale Farm's Post-eviction Scene

Figure 9.1 Open sewage flows between the bund walls at Dale Farm, 2012. Photo by Lynne McCarthy.

little to reduce the problem of pollution and BDC palpably put the owners, who had the right to use the land for green belt purposes, at health risk. The Travellers were also astonished that the very subject of the eviction – reverting the land to green belt usage – had not been followed through by the council (Puxon interview 2011).

I consider bunding as a form of municipal infrastructure that was implemented on an ad hoc basis by Basildon District Council. It is, I argue, an infrastructure that detains livelihoods and chronically limits the activities and social reproduction of Dale Farm Travellers. Typically, infrastructure is designed and implemented by states to further their goals of networks of communication, commerce and social reproduction, but infrastructure deployed as a form of obstruction shows how a state or municipality can wield geographical technologies to discontinue aspects of social life. In *Seeing like a State*, James C. Scott has questioned state schemes like planning systems that appear at face value to enact empirical and logistical programmes of state maintenance but are the utilitarian means through which social ordering, population management or social planning occurs and whose legibility is necessitated through 'state simplifications' (1998: 310). The imposition of formal order on local informal process can have disastrous consequences, like the famines resulting from Soviet Collectivisation or China's Great Leap Forward (310), which Scott notes killed local technical knowledge, initiative and 'metis' (309–20). Planning scholar Keller Easterling sees planning as 'a battery of legal restrictions constructed to disenfranchise a population through its housing or its land' (2003: 88–9). Similar strategies of obstruction infrastructure were deployed in Ireland to abolish nomadism in 1964 when the National Council on Itinerancy pursued a settlement programme for Travellers (Wickstrom 2012). Since then local authorities, who feared the permanent migration of Travellers to their areas, undertook an 'unofficial policy' of 'evicting its non-indigenous Travellers and forcing its indigenous Traveller population into large settlements (often without services) in remote areas and placing boulders and digging ditches on Travellers' traditional camping sites' (Crowley 2005: 142–4). In Maurya Wickstrom's work on Irish Travellers' theatre practices in Ireland, she notes a bureaucratic practice of building walls around Travellers' encampments as a form of containment (2012: 157). In open spaces across Ireland and England councils deploy several techniques, such as height-adjustable barriers that are electronically activated to rise as a barricade and prevent Traveller incursion onto public space, as the need arises. As a result of obstruction infrastructure Travellers are either perpetually in movement or have been hegemonically settled in a small number of authorized and unauthorized pitches.

Easterling describes in more detail how infrastructural space has become so much more than just the substructure of a city but a powerful 'medium of information' that 'resides in invisible, powerful activities that determine how objects and content are organized and circulated' (2014: 13). She has termed this phenomenon 'extrastatecraft' because it captures the 'often undisclosed activities outside of, in addition to, and sometimes even in partnership with statecraft' (15). Her central argument is that the state and its undertakings are often camouflaged through infrastructure and its systems and that infrastructures can become an enactor and 'instrument of militarism, liberalism, or universal rationalisation' (17). Infrastructural techniques, in particular free zoning (where vast tracts of urban landscapes are converted into uber-cities and have their own transnational laws and immunity to national jurisdiction, for example, King Abdullah Economic City in Saudi and Songdo City in South Korea, to name but a few), are manifest 'concentrations of authoritarian power' (22). Infrastructural forms are conduits of power that have deflected and immunized themselves to critiques of neoliberalism. She also describes how infrastructures can direct, redirect and control systems of movement whether these are physical, financial or technological, and therefore, their 'topologies are also markers of political disposition insofar as they highlight the ways in which the authorities circulate or concentrate information' (77). The political disposition of infrastructure is evident in Basildon District Council's construction of bunding as it made a clear statement that Traveller access to their land through the means of their own cultural preference was prohibited. Political information is, therefore, transmitted through the topologies created by bunding and, additionally, these politics are reinforced by the semiotic connotations implied by BDC's use of the term 'bunding' rather than, say, the term 'dyke', the former distinctly conveying a sense of the contagious. Bunding is not typically applied to domestic demolitions; rather it is used within industrial and pharmaceutical construction. Linking Travellers' domestic space to a term that is connotative of hazardous waste shows another instance of how the metaphorical association of Travellers with toxicity and contagion is literally performed through bureaucratic processes and terminology. More significantly, by embedding the logic of 'contamination' as a rationality of governance over the Travellers, the council (and by default, the state) shows a regard for nomads as subnationals with the potential to pollute or infect the sedentarist population. I maintain that infrastructure and infrastructural terminology is applied in these contexts to disguise state intolerance of nomadic populations.

Covertly deployed infrastructural techniques inhibited nomadic movement at Dale Farm and ensured that a charge of direct discrimination could not be levelled against Basildon District Council. Yet, by impeding the use rights of the Travellers, an indirect discrimination was perpetrated through property relations. The council's discriminatory acts were carried out through dissimulation; the bunding has since become a part of the natural history of Dale Farm, where grass and weeds have taken root (Figure 9.1). Typical bunding is composed of man-made materials not unlike how the foundations of a building might appear when initially laid out. This technique differed at Dale Farm because the bunding was constructed of soil making it evade the appearance of its actual purpose as a blockade. Instead, it appeared more as an incidental feature of the landscape and part of its natural history, particularly when overgrown with grass half a year later (Figure 9.2). It is in such ways that I suggest 'state violence' is exercised through objective law, not necessarily as palpable acts of lethal or brutal violence but as bureaucratic tactics that remain undeclared and that make life untenable (Benjamin 1978: 300). Neither the boulders nor the bunding are inscribed with the words 'keep travellers out', yet by implanting such infrastructure the sentiment that is carried out performs a type of state racism that permits only some groups access to property but not to others. The objective law determined that the Travellers had misused the land at Dale Farm, yet it is difficult to conceive how Basildon District Council has not equally misused objective law to stealthily enact the continued dispersal of the Travellers.

The statecraft elucidated by Scott as systems of legibility designed for the simplified management of population can also be considered in its inverse and closer to Easterling's interpretation, as deliberately illegible. The dissimulation brought about by the undisclosed function of the infrastructure at Dale Farm evinced how statecraft is reliant on stagecraft. In its theatrical context, stagecraft refers to the practical knowledge and skill required to produce a mise-en-scène by dramatizing physical space, revealing and concealing the mechanics of staging. Representations are defined through the technical visual precisions of stagecraft, emerging as this character, that community, that time or these geographies. Not all stagecraft is constructed to be duplicitous for in as much as it is historically read as pretence, it can also be illuminating. It is pertinent that the cultural meanings and ideological applications of stagecraft at any given time are distinguished. In this instance, the fact of concealing the purpose of the bunding, and its very theatrical implementation onto the Dale Farm landscape as a framing of Traveller property, attests to the critical function of stagecraft for the state proliferation of its own agendas. State agendas and stagings of democracy have everything to do with the framing of representations and in deciding which populations are to be made visible as part of that representational politics.

Figure 9.2 Dale Farm overgrowth, 2012. Photo by Lynne McCarthy.

The moulded landscape at Dale Farm suggests that not only are nomads animated as a racialized group but that their infrastructure is animated as a state response to their mobilities. Easterling's identification of the political dispositions contained in the surfaces of infrastructures is considered further here as attitudes that are animated through infrastructural form, including their theatrically covert dispositions. Bureaucracy is perceived by Travellers through infrastructures that generate negatively experienced affects. 'Tones' are set by the state in their shaping of Travellers' infrastructures inscribing attitudes that are a 'dialectic of subjective and objective feelings that our aesthetic encounters inevitably produce' (Ngai 2005: 30). Thereby, the state constructs Travellers' dispositions to infrastructure in as much as its own disposition to Travellers is communicated through its infrastructure. While on the road or in situ, nomads encounter sceneries that are composed deliberately of obstructive materials that, conversely, within an alternative sedentarist scene-scape, may appear as accidentally discarded material. Boulders and mounds of earth appear commonly to Travellers as obvious techniques of obstruction, but to sedentarists who make different use of spaces, these materials make little impact on their daily undertakings. The point that recent scholarship has posed around the visibility or invisibility of infrastructure, and to which I turn my attention, is 'not to assert one or another status as an inherent condition of infrastructures but to examine how (in)visibility is mobilized and why' (Larkin 2013: 336).

If infrastructures are the system of objects that 'undergird societies' they also 'generate the ambient environment of everyday life' (Larkin 2013: 326). In this regard, rather than analysing the declared function of infrastructure, I examine the undeclared affective and ambient indiscretions and repercussions of infrastructures' forms. Discussing the poetics of infrastructure, Brian Larkin proposes that infrastructures are 'concrete semiotic and aesthetic vehicles oriented to addressees' (2013: 326). Infrastructures become poetic when organized according to the 'material quality of the signifier' rather than its 'referential meaning' (329). Larkin's argument about infrastructures is founded on the 'palpability of the sign' and how considering infrastructure in light of the poetic means 'form is loosened from technical function' (335). The state can make you feel discretely the meaning of its infrastructure through its forms or feel meanings that are obscured by their technical function. These are feelings about the state and the state of things at quite a literal level but are affective in that their source is often difficult to identify. As a way of feeling the state, infrastructure is an apparatus through which social ordering is exercised via objects and at an arm's length from recognizable power relations. These power relations are performed discretely through a logic that 'disavows itself, seeking to organise populations and territories through technological domains that seem far removed from political institutions' (Larkin 2013: 328).

Nomadic infrastructure therefore has a duplicitous means of representing itself by making it difficult for the Travellers not to take the bunding and the boulders as social facts that cannot be overcome. The effects of obstruction infrastructure become affectively embodied for Travellers in ways similar to residents of the Brazilian favelas where:

> Hyper-visible and constantly evolving infrastructural developments make the atmosphere of place that forms the precognitive of mental, sensory and affective dispositions: the resident's experience of living in the settlement, their feelings and obligation towards each other, their attachment and responsibility towards shared public spaces, their expectations from the commons (which, range from environmental disregard and cohabitation with the makeshift to hyper cleanliness within the private compound and participating in improving communal spaces). (Amin 2014: 146)

Physical obstruction to resources, amenities, communities and kin is accompanied by the negative affects of incommodious infrastructures that bear implications for the performative reproduction of nomads in the UK. Just as Ngai understands tone to be a dialectic between subject and object, a performative relation between subject and object can be elaborated as the uses that occur, are imposed, encouraged, curtailed between people and their property. Observing and living with the bunding produced a felt condition for the Travellers that registered in despair and was also reflected and felt through illnesses. In January 2012, the United Nations unofficially gathered information for a report on the aftermath of the Dale Farm eviction and the living conditions of Travellers. When UN representatives attended the Dale Farm site, I worked with Dale Farm Solidarity to collect data on the residents' health; photographed evidence of burst sewage and water pipes from the site; and took descriptions of the long-term illnesses of the elderly and young who were without amenities, such as electricity, water and sanitation. Being in the vicinity of the bunding caused health problems for the Travellers, one of whom showed me how her hands had become swollen and infected from the open sewage – she assumed – and, although her hands were not violently maimed, her use of them to undertake daily activities, such as looking after her children, was diminished. Strikingly, this geographically enforced behaviour and relationship to her property depleted parts of her personhood by, firstly, obligating her to reroute and adjust her typical care regimes, and secondly, by invasively and infectiously putting her body in the way of harm.

I argue that the performative relations imposed between her and her property were organized to detain nomadic social reproduction.

Material feelings of illness that disrupt regular activity show how people are affected by infrastructure, how it is given priority over public health, and how it shapes the affects of users, or as the geographer Ash Amin puts it, 'how the human is imagined as adjunct to the material' (2014: 137). Scarry notably argued that a 'language of agency' (1985: 15) is given over to the inflictor of pain: 'the feeling of pain entails the feeling of being acted upon, and the person may either express this in terms of the world acting on [her] ("It feels like a knife … ") or, in terms of [her] own body acting on [her] ("It feels like the bones are cutting through")'(16). Therefore, the weakening of personhood through the weakening of agency is a plausible factor in understanding the pain of the female resident at Dale Farm. The source of pain in war is legible to Scarry through instruments of torture, and these explicitly violent situations are to her the presentations of 'fictive power' (58). Conversely, 'non-political contexts of pain' (31) are those relating to disease, old age and auto-degenerative illnesses, but I have shown here that pain caused through infection can also be deliberate at worst, neglectful at best and definitely political, including but not limited to sites of chemical warfare. Moreover, Scarry locates the sensory fabric of pain as the only state that has no object; for example and in contrast, to hear is to hear another object; to feel hunger is to be hungry for an object (1985: 161–2). Pain has no external object but is a type of sense perception that is folded back onto the subject. When pain's external location is imagined as diffuse, ambient and unattached, for instance, the object of 'torture' at Dale Farm is not immediately present, then, I argue that in searching for the location of an object that bears responsibility for pain – no one owns the microbe – the political cause of pain is often less evident. Unlike the searing violence of war, the daily endurance of pain as an irritant that vitiates life is the subject that is taken up by Lauren Berlant as a 'slow death' and a 'physical wearing out of a population in a way that points to its deterioration as a defining condition of its experience and historical existence' (Berlant 2011: 95). Reading the bunding as a type of reservoir for infection, it then becomes intelligible as an object that contributed to illness.

Conclusion

I have argued that infrastructure can obfuscate human power and responsibility by performing its functions in ways that appear natural (naturally occurring mounds or boulders) and by pursuing a type of purposeful aesthetics that seem to appear accidentally and are normatively perceived as benign. I propose that infrastructures must be read in terms of their undeclared tactical purposes by demonstrating where they are used to obstruct populations by performing an environmental racism. Whether through negligence or intent, the effect of having a population feel pain is also an effective way to communicate to them how their agency is actively being weakened. In choosing infrastructure as an object of critical focus here, it has been possible to map its relationship to contagion and social reproduction through aesthetic and performative theories. This has shown that infrastructure is obstructive and that it acts as a conduit to diffuse information and affects to populations, which in turn rise to consciousness, not just as generalized feelings but as pain. This pain is a negative affect or 'ugly feeling' that diminishes the performative possibilities and social reproduction of nomads in the UK. Travellers perceive bunding and other materials as obvious techniques of obstruction that detain life and vitiate against their social reproduction. The containment of Travellers around sites of pollution has implications for municipal and state agendas in the UK who seem tacitly unconcerned that nomadic populations are disallowed from performing their own dispositions to the social but just as significantly, are deteriorating under the performative and biological affects of an obstructive infrastructure.

Note

1 'The EHRC said, in relation to equality of opportunity, Gypsy and Traveller ethnic groups in Great Britain suffered substantial disadvantage in life chances including in health, education, employment, housing and participation in the community. They said media reporting and portrayal could have a significant impact in shaping public perceptions of Gypsies and Travellers. They said their research had found that the role of the media was a key area in the perpetuation of misunderstanding and that stereotypical images and sensational reporting frequently promoted fear and hatred in local populations. They said such problems were magnified by the absence of countervailing positive images' (ITMB 2012: 3).

References

Allen, E. (2012), '"Bigger. Fatter. Gypsier" Advertising Campaign Used by Channel 4 for Its Wedding Series Is Branded "Racist"', *Daily Mail*, 29 May.
Amin, A. (2014), 'Lively Infrastructure', *Theory, Culture & Society*, 31 (7–8): 137–161.

Anonymous Women of Dale Farm (2011), Interview with the Author. Dale Farm, Essex, 18 December. Available online: https://soildepositions.wordpress.com/.
BBC News Essex (2011), 'PM Backs Eviction of Travellers at Dale Farm', 7 September. Available online: http://www.bbc.co.uk/news/uk-england-essex-14828148 (accessed 26 November 2012).
Benjamin, W. (1978), *Reflections: Essays, Aphorisms, Autobiographical Writings*, New York: Harcourt Brace Jovanovich.
Berlant, L. (2011), *Cruel Optimism*, Durham: Duke University Press.
Cemlyn, S., M. Greenfields, S. Burnett, Z. Matthews, and C. Whitwell (2009), 'Inequalities Experienced by Gypsy and Traveller Communities: A Review', Bristol. Available online: http://www.equalityhumanrights.com/uploaded_files/research/12inequalities_experienced_by_gypsy_and_traveller_communities_a_review.pdf (accessed 22 November 2012).
Crowley, U. (2005), 'Liberal Rule through Nonliberal Means: The Attempted Settlement of Irish Travellers (1955–1975)', *Irish Geography*, 38 (2): 128–150.
Crowley, U. and R. Kitchin (2007), 'Paradoxical Spaces of Traveller Citizenship in Contemporary Ireland', *Irish Geography*, 40 (2): 128–145.
Douglas, M. ([1966] 2003), *Purity and Danger: an analysis of concept of pollution and taboo*, London; New York: Routledge.
Easterling, K. (2003), 'Subtraction', *Perspecta*, 34: 80–90.
Easterling, K. (2014), *Extrastatecraft: The Power of Infrastructure Space*, London: Verso Books.
Environment Protection Agency (2012), *Working at Construction and Demolition Sites: PPG6 (Pollution Prevention Guidelines)*, Bristol: EPA. Available online: https://www.gov.uk/government/uploads/system/uploads/attachment_data/file/485215/pmho0412bwfe-e-e.pdf (accessed 24 April 2015).
Greenfields, M. and D. Smith (2013), 'Decline of Nomadism: Enforced Settlement and Urban/Gypsy Traveller Camps in London and Its Environs', paper presented to Research Committee 21: Sociology of Urban and Regional Development, Resourceful Cities Conference, International Sociology Association, Berlin.
Griffin, C. (2008). *Nomads under the Westway: Irish Travellers, Gypsies and other Traders in West London*, Hatfield: University of Hertfordshire Press.
Hill, A. (2017), '"Hostile Environment": The Hardline Home Office Policy Tearing Families Apart', *Guardian*, 28 November.
Irish Traveller Movement in Britain (2011), 'Dale Farm: Basildon Council's Eviction of a Traveller Community'. Available online: http://irishtraveller.org.uk/wp-content/uploads/2011/09/12.09.11-21.pdf (accessed 13 June 2012).
Irish Traveller Movement in Britain (2012), *Submission by the Irish Traveller Movement in Britain to the Society of Editors Code Committee Consultation*, London. Available online: http://www.travellermovement.org.uk/wp-content/uploads/2015/09/ITMB-submission-to-the-PCC-Code-Committee-consultation-final.pdf (accessed 13 October 2015).

Katz, C. (2001), 'Vagabond Capitalism and the Necessity of Social Reproduction', *Antipode*, 33 (4): 709–728.
Larkin, B. (2013), 'The Politics and Poetics of Infrastructure', *Annual Review of Anthropology*, 42 (1): 327–343.
Ngai, S. (2005), *Ugly Feelings*, Cambridge, MA: Harvard University Press.
Puxon, G. (2011–12), Interviews with the Author, Dale Farm, Essex, October 2011, March 2012.
Quarmby, K. (2013), *No Place to Call Home: Inside the Real Lives of Gypsies and Travellers*, London: Oneworld.
Ryder, A., T. Acton, S. Alexander, P. Cemelyn, S. Van Cleemput, J. Richardson, and D. Smith (2011), 'A Big or Divided Society? Final Recommendations and Report of the Panel Review into the Coalition Policy on Gypsies and Travellers', Wales: Travellers Aid Trust.
Scarry, E. (1985), *The Body in Pain: The Making and Unmaking of the World*, New York: Oxford University Press.
Scott, J. (1998), *Seeing Like a State: How Certain Schemes to Improve the Human Condition Have Failed*, New Haven, CT: Yale University Press.
Synon, M. (1996), 'Time to Get Tough on Tinker Terror Culture', *Sunday Independent*, 28 January. Available online: http://www.indymedia.ie/article/63540?condense_comments=true&userlanguage=ga&save_prefs=true (accessed 9 October 2016).
Tyler, I. (2013), *Revolting Subjects: Social Abjection and Resistance in Neoliberal Britain*, London: Zed Books Ltd.
Wickstrom, M. (2012), *Performance in the Blockades of Neoliberalism: Thinking the Political Anew*, New York: Palgrave Macmillan.

Part Three

Conducting Emotions, Moods and Minds

10

The Paradox of Immersion: Mechanisms of Contagion and Separation in Punchdrunk's *Sleep No More*

Ana Pais

This chapter examines contagion as the transmission of affect operating through the sensorial apparatus of performance in immersive theatre. Etymologically, contagion means to get something from another through touch (*cum-tacto* or touch with). However, in the theatre, contagious phenomena may happen at a distance, or rather, by the touch of circulating affect propagated in social spaces including audiences as collective bodies.[1] By affect I mean the sensitive charges that attach to thoughts, emotions and sensations, which circulate in social spaces, in other words, felt intensities that propagate in social spaces.

I consider how *Sleep No More* (*SNM*, 2011, NYC) – the quintessential Punchdrunk production that near globalized immersive theatre and garnered the company widespread attention – is designed to impact the senses and influence individual experience through affective vulnerability. The chapter examines the role of sensorial atmospheres, in particular the role of sound design in fostering contagious moods of tension and threat. My argument is that sensorial atmospheres in *SNM* induce states of feeling that predetermine the circulation of affect and compromise the political agenda of an empowered audience. In this sense, freedom offered to the roaming spectator can be more conditioned than liberating, despite the immersive features of experience that blur the division between stage and audience. I have argued elsewhere (Pais 2017) that the audience has a crucial role in amplifying and intensifying affect, thereby producing a moving together of affect – a co-motion – that determines the sensitive quality of the performance. Such movement of affect can be more or less determined by the politics of affect of each performance and it may or may not coincide with the theatrical architecture of representation (Pais 2015). If a performance is open to the unpredictability of the theatrical encounter, that is, if it is permeable to be modulated by whatever affective contagion emerges from contact with the audience, then it potentiates emerging affect and its circulation; if a performance is contained by a scripted plan, thus unchanged by unknown affective events, then it constrains the kind of affect that will be set in motion. Both mechanisms of contagion and separation are key to understanding how affect is transmitted and how it empowers or disempowers the spectator.

Participation and audience empowerment

Felix Barrett, who co-directs Punchdrunk with choreographer Maxine Doyle, claims that the autonomy of the audience is one of the most important aspects of the company's work. The company's fundamental aim is to empower the audience by giving them the freedom of choice to create their own theatrical experience. In Barrett's words:

> A central feature of the work is the empowerment of the audience. It's a fight against audience apathy and the inertia that sets in when you're stagnating in an auditorium. When you're sat in an auditorium, the primary thing that is accessed is your mind and you respond cerebrally. Punchdrunk resists that by allowing the body to become empowered because the audience has to make physical decisions and choices, and in doing that they make some sort of pact with the piece. They're physically involved with the piece and therefore it becomes visceral. (Machon 2009: 89)

Fostering an alternative to the disciplined and passive sitting spectator, Barrett and Doyle invite the audience to engage with an empowering experience primarily anchored in the body and its visceral responses to encompassing sensorial stimuli. This kind of engagement requires a physical exploration of the space as the spectator is expected to make decisions based on instinct and impulses, as the directors further explain in the interview conducted by Josephine Machon (Machon 2009: 89). In their view, the equation is simple: if the body is actively engaged in the performance, it will grant an autonomous and empowering experience: the more visceral, the freer. Visceral experience is described in Punchdrunk's website with the following words:

> The physical freedom to explore the sensory and imaginative world of a Punchdrunk show without compulsion or explicit direction sets it apart from the standard practice of viewing theatre in unconventional locations. Although our work is necessarily structured from a practical

and safety perspective, the non-linear narrative content coupled to the high degree of viewer freedom of choice make it a singularly intense and personal experience. (Punchdrunk 2013)

This conception of audience empowerment is problematic. It implies that the sitting spectator's responses are exclusively regulated by the mind and necessarily associated with passivity as opposed to the activity aligned with the visceral experience of the roaming spectator. Yet, even in traditional theatre, the mind and the gaze are not abstract entities; rather, they are attached to bodies – that is, the theatrical experience is always mediated by the body. This rather simplistic equation aims at excluding cognition from decision and meaning-making processes and at enhancing the qualities of bodily sensorial experience as key to the spectator's freedom from theatrical apparatus and effects, thereby liberating him or her from the constraints of the Western theatrical tradition of text-based productions on a proscenium stage. In addition, identifying visceral experience with freedom neglects one crucial aspect: Punchdrunk's immersive worlds are sensorial configurations constructed to viscerally impact the spectator, determining the audience decision-making process. As the previous quote testifies, the company claims to provide freedom to explore 'without compulsion or explicit direction', to which the absence of narrative is essential. But how is the visceral materialized in Punchdrunk productions? What strategies are laid out to promote a bodily experience that is held responsible for the spectator's free choices, producing his or her unique experience of performance? How does the sensorial apparatus act upon the spectator and impact his experience?

Punchdrunk's discourse idealizes participatory models of theatre attendance and takes for granted a supposedly inherent freedom and empowerment, an issue that has been critically addressed in the last decade (Bishop 2004, 2012; Freshwater 2009; Harvie 2013, Jackson 2011). This literature claims that political empowerment is not a given in such projects but rather a romanticized vision of participation as emancipatory, which disregards both the actual contract established with the participant and the conditions of participation structuring a given project. The emphasis on audience participation as a way to create unique and potentially transformative experiences dates at least to the mid-twentieth century. As opposed to the tradition that posits theatre as a place defined by an ontological separation (the one who sees and the one who is seen), participation has been considered the only antidote for audience passivity, granting its autonomy and empowerment while neglecting the constraints of the sensorial construction of the work.

Critical approaches to participation, spectatorship, experience and labour in immersive theatre have been recently brought forth (Harvie 2013; O'Hara 2017; Santone 2014; Worthen 2012; Zaiontz 2014). For instance, Adam Alston (2016) suggests that this kind of participation immersive theatre promotes is not only far from emancipated but also dangerously close to neoliberal ideologies. In particular, Punchdrunk requires a kind of participation that is embedded in neoliberal values and ethos reflecting a hidden adoption and encouragement of participation as a risk-taking individual opportunity. Alston claims that freedom and empowerment in the company's productions is a mode of intensified 'productive participation' that he calls 'entrepreneurial', that is, a set of rules for participation in which immaterial labour and affective labour are 'co-opted as a source of capital' (2016: 16). Examining in particular how one-on-ones are exclusivist and privileged moments that demand an opportunistic risk-taking attitude that denies access to those who are, for whatever reason, unable to share it, Alston argues: 'Punchdrunk incentivize entrepreneurial participation through the production of affective experiences that are meant to be sought' (2016: 130). Hence, not only are an implicit exclusionary politics of participation at play, but the spectator's position is rendered vulnerable.

This vulnerability is enhanced by the sensorial construction of immersive worlds. Hence, the autonomy of the spectator demands to be accounted for in relation to the production's sensorial apparatus that creates the conditions of experience. I am not interested here in delving into the definition of the visceral as the fundamental quality of experiencing immersive worlds;[2] instead, I would like to examine the aesthetic mechanisms through which visceral experience is created and conditioned, configuring a contact zone with the spectator that defines, in turn, a politics of affect. What is in the balance here is the power relation that defines the conditions of experience and the way by which they determine that same experience. How permeable is the spectator to the aural, the visual or the tactile orchestration of the space of performance? What is the role of sensorial atmospheres in inducing affective contagion and shaping the experience of the audience? How do the politics of affect determine or potentiate free and singular aesthetic experience, thus producing an empowered spectator?

Contagion and separation are two key mechanisms of audience engagement that ensure the politics of affect of *SNM*. If participation is the model used by Punchdrunk to reduce theatrical distance represented by the paradigm of nineteenth-century Wagnerian darkened auditorium and its disciplined audience trained to sit in silence, the experience of the spectator is still ruled by built-in aspects of that shared space. As Lepecki and Banes remind us, in every performance there is a political economy of the senses that draws a dividing line between the perceptible and the imperceptible (Lepecki and Banes 2007: 3), what is offered to be seen or not, to be valued or not, to circulate or not. To each system of presence of the body on stage there is a corresponding system of perception. Thus, if the political economy of senses defines ways of perceiving it also engenders a politics of affect that can grant more or less freedom to what the spectator might feel. In the case of Punchdrunk aesthetics, the overwhelming sensorial apparatus contaminates the perception of the spectator because it is designed to produce effects, that is to instil a specific type of affect that mediates the whole experience, which, in fact, is not so far from the effects produced by the machine of the proscenium theatre. As Barrett himself describes, the emphasis on the production of effects (of affect) is crucial to ensure the spectator feels the same as he did when exploring the space in the early stages of the creative process (Machon 2009: 92). Hence, while dissipating divisions between fiction and reality, performers and audience members, sensorial immersion entails mechanisms of contagion and separation that need to be accounted for in the purposeful ecology of immersive productions.

An atmospheric version of *Macbeth*[3]

Since 2000, Punchdrunk has been staging classical texts (like *The Duchess of Malfi* (2010) and *Faust* (2006), amongst other projects) in laborious, sophisticated and unmatched scenographic immersive worlds where the spectator can roam freely. The meticulous and refined visual treatment of the space produces highly impacting atmospheres, mastered by light and sound design. These powerful atmospheres envelop the spectator, operating at the level of his bodily and affective responses to the environment and to the performers. A well-known feature of Punchdrunk productions, the mask confers the spectator with anonymity, reinforcing the supposedly inherent freedom of a roaming experience, although not necessarily granted by interactive features (Biggin 2017: 74). At times closer to a cinematographic experience (Maples 2016: 124), the spectator is like a voyeur within the movie.

Sleep No More is an atmospheric version of *Macbeth*, an immersive performance-installation that transforms the tragedy of Shakespeare into visual, tactile and sonic environments, to the beat of a Hitchcockian thriller. Not a word from the original text is spoken; all its emotional tonalities materialize intense and almost palpable atmospheres that pervade different spaces. Dramatic conflicts – ambition and morality, the individual and the nation, power and justice – are turned into intense choreographies of performers, repeated in loops of scripted actions (one complete loop is around one hour and the show runs for four hours daily, eight on the weekend). We are left with emotional shades, insanity and the ghosts of Macbeth's hideous crimes. Contrary to a performance in a proscenium theatre, where stage lighting directs the audience's attention, *SNM*'s whole scenic building is dimly lit: three old warehouses in Chelsea compose the fictitious McKittrick Hotel, named after a scene in the movie *Vertigo*. Devised by Livi Vaughan, Felix Barrett and Beatrice Minns, the impressive scenography was implemented with the help of two hundred unpaid volunteers, who over the course of four months built and decorated the whole environment (Piepenburg 2011).[4] All five floors configure the entirety of the scenic area (including a secret sixth floor) without borders between performers and audience. The spectator is invited to roam freely, exploring and engaging all the senses: smell (in the woods, rooms with plants); touch (opening drawers and touching objects); vision (reading letters, peeking in rooms, following performers); and even taste (eating candy in the candy shop). As sound is omnipresent and greatly influential it will be addressed later in detail. There are one hundred rooms to explore all over five floors.

The first thing the spectator steps into is a semi-lit labyrinth that leads to the bar, where he or she is warmly welcomed, although pressured to join the tour. At this point, spectators are told the rules of the game and given a mask. In groups of five to ten, they go up in an elevator and are separated randomly at different floors. Instructions are clear and sharp: one cannot talk or take off the mask during the whole show. Yet individual experience and tactile curiosity are encouraged: one can touch props, open drawers, pursue the performers through corridors or linger in some rooms more than in others in search of exciting events or encounters. Tactility as a form of close contact is stimulated in order to give the spectator a feeling of empowerment while affective contagion creeps up the body unnoticed. Differently from conventional theatre, audiences are inside the theatrical space, deciding where to go, what to touch and look at, but their embodied experience is predetermined by the immaterial immersive atmosphere of the production. Contagion here does not ensue via touch but rather via the subtle transmission of affect generated by sound design, as it will be examined later in detail. A slightly different phenomenon happens with the performers. However close in space to the audience, as there is no line of separation between stage and audience, the contact established between performers and spectators is reduced to zero, except in one-on-one scenes. Even if one might be standing five inches away from performers, one does not feel close as they ignore the audience.

None of the performers can have a global perception of the rhythm of the show. Immersion demands from them a strong discipline in performing the script surrounded by unpredictable crowds, which requires an ability to adapt – physically, mentally and emotionally – to audience behaviour insofar as it comes their way. As there is no backstage, performers are always exposed to the gaze of the audience but, although they are not supposed to interact with the performers, spectators affect the unfolding of the performance in the most elementary ways. For instance, gregarious movement of performers and audience is central to the aesthetics of the production. In Maxine Doyle's words, spectators inhabit scenic space and frame the scenes becoming part of the 'choreographic landscape' (Machon 2009: 58). The spectator's experience is, thus, aestheticized in a play of effects as a consequence of the 'imperative to be productive as a condition of affective audience engagement' (Alston 2016: 21). In turn, performers need to develop skills to deal with the moving landscape.

Apparently contradicting the spirit of immersion, performers are mainly self-absorbed in fulfilling their tasks, except for brief and exceptional privileged moments when they engage with individual spectators out of sight. Proximity and contact with the audience risks losing control of the performance. For Tori Sparks, one of the 2011 NYC performers, a '360° sensibility' is needed for the job. To her mind, the audience can disturb the unfolding of the show, easily behaving disrespectfully, precisely because the separation of spaces and the distinction between immersive and interactive theatre is not equally clear for everyone (Sparks 2012; see also Biggin 2017: 74). At the same time, admits Sparks, the blurring between spaces and actions produces the most gratifying results 'because it's so visceral and it's raw and it is acting but everybody's so close that it's beyond acting' (Sparks 2012; see also Biggin 2017: 74). If one can say that audiences re-affect the stage by the collective atmosphere they create in the room, in immersive theatre such circulation can dramatically challenge the performer's delivery. Due to physical proximity in immersive theatre, audiences push performers to the limit precisely because there is no border between spaces. They can re-affect the performers to a point of putting at risk both doing dramatic actions and keeping acting in the zone, as they say. Hence, immersion can become a trap for performers if spectators become too autonomous or ill disciplined. In such cases, traditional theatrical forms of affective contagion from actors to spectators shift direction and hit the performers. Ignoring the audience is, thus, a safe way to conduct the show because it contains unpredictable behaviour and excessive contact.

Not looking directly at spectators is a rule in Punchdrunk performances, as British performer Mathew Blake confirms (2012). When performers swiftly move around the space followed by crowds of spectators or when they act out a scene that demands more attentive listening, they make clear that the audience is separated, ignoring them. Although performers can be so close they can literally touch spectators, they bypass the latter as if they weren't there or if they were invisible (White 2012: 233), which reinforces their voyeur status. Although the performance provides an immersion in sensorial atmospheres, the mask situates the audience in a place of observation not so different from more conventional formats. Hence, the spectator is inside the movie but simultaneously peeping from behind a window.[5]

Sound atmospheres: Mechanisms of contagion

A crucial aspect to the distinctive sensorial atmospheres that feature strongly in Punchdrunk productions is sound design. It is key to understanding affect contamination. Contributing to a cinematographic and unsettling sense of suspense, sound fills all rooms and floors encompassing the audience in a rhythmic background. To the beat of Herrmann's 'visceral' scores (Sullivan 2006: 229), Stephen Dobbie, an associate of the company since 2002, adds layers of big band jazz songs from the 1930s and 1940s in remixed tracks blended with electronic sonorities. This amalgamation suggests a general atmosphere of expectation, and produces the tension of a thriller, peppered with Wagnerian romanticism like in Herrmann's compositions. According to director Felix Barrett (Punchdrunk 2013), the hallmark of the *SNM* soundscape is the suspense of a thriller, which is more influenced by Bernard Herrmann's musical scores than by Hitchcock movies themselves. Musical sections of *Vertigo*, *The Man That Knew Too Much* or *Psycho* can be easily identified in the musical remix of *SNM*. The repetition of these sections supports a rhythmic background against which individual thrilling experiences can happen.

Sound design is overwhelming, invading and omnipresent. Sound is impossible to escape, and its source impossible to discern, as Glenn Ricci points out (Ricci 2012), which resonates with the politics of affect of the performance. The more it dissipates in a familiar continuum, the more it infiltrates the experience of the spectator, intoxicating it and undermining his or her empowered autonomy.[6] Through the dark, one responds cautiously, reducing the speed of movements. Even after adjusting one's eyes to the light, reduced visibility in many areas activates all the senses: we feel the space to be able to move through it, which sometimes seems to be reduced to a gigantic cabinet of curiosities. While on the one hand, darkness calls on tactile perception to know what is not visible to the eye, on the other hand, it produces sensations of insecurity, hesitation and vigilance. While stimulating the skin – the largest organ covering the whole body – as a primary source for engaging with the work, *SNM* activates the porosity of a surface that opens up to a space between the inside and outside of the work.

Gareth White problematizes this idea of performance interiority. Referencing the seminal studies on metaphor and its mediations by Lakoff and Johnson, White shows that immersion implies the condition of separation between subject and object (White 2012: 225 and following pages). He gives the example of the swimmer who, immersed in the water, is still distinct from it. If being immersed is being completely surrounded by something, then that something is necessarily external to him or her (White 2012: 228). In this sense, the concept of immersion brings forth a paradox for the spectator: as visceral experience that envelops the whole body, it entails separation from the surrounding environment, which contributes to his or her status as cinematic voyeur. Soundscape operates by subliminally instilling subtle states of tension; it invades bodies, which has consequences at a physiological level. The use of suspensive musical compositions, perhaps the genre with the strongest physical impact on the body, as the backdrop of sound design shows how contagion works through sound to propagate affect. Instilling an immersive atmosphere of threat and tension by a rhythmic background of suspense, *SNM* disseminates an ecology of fear that hits the audience via felt rhythms, frequencies and intensities. Hence, sound's 'politics of frequency' mobilizes and modulates affect in social spaces (Goodman 2010: xvii and *passim*), a strategy that film soundtracks have long been using. According to Goodman, 'certain frequencies can produce an affective tonality of fear in which the body is left posed in anticipation, expectant of incoming events: every pore listens for the future' (Goodman 2010: 189). And whatever future events happen they are filtered by tension and fear.

Distinguished in Hollywood for his compositions, Bernard Herrmann's unique soundtracks have a fundamental role in the narrative of Hitchcock movies, spraying emotional tonalities to enhance intended effects in the narrative, frustrating expectations, which is one of the distinctive strategies of the genre. Suspense movies fabricate effects to reach specific goals: stimulate terror, fear, anxiety or disturbance in the spectator through increasing states of tension that produce sharper contrasts between what is seen and what is not seen, between the expected and the unexpected. Audiences are permanently the targets of manipulation. Graham Bruce refers to the refinement of Herrmann's unique style pinning down the strategies that generate a correspondence between suspense narrative and its musical analogue that underlines the story told (Bruce 1985: 218), such as minor major seventh chords invoking affects of restlessness and dissatisfaction inflicted by the suspension of harmony; dissonance and polytonality, deviations of harmony used to extend discomfort; chromaticism, rhythmic sequences repeated to create ambiguity and tension; repetitive devices, such as the *ostinato*, whose persistent reiteration reinforces states of tension (Bruce 1985: 118–33). In conclusion, states Bruce, Herrmann uses detours from conventional harmony as a force to suspend narrative expectations so that 'the denial or delay of the expected is the source of the affective power of these scores' (Bruce 1985: 137).

It is precisely in this forceful power of suspense that *SNM* anchors mechanisms of contagion, producing tension by instilling an affective tonality of fear and threat. In combination with dimly lit areas, sound design purposefully encourages states of tension, discomfort and disturbance that provoke instinctive physiological states associated with fear or self-preservation. Such reactions are triggered by a sense of threat by primary processes of the nervous system that bypass cognition (Ledoux 1996). Free-roaming through space, the spectator sinks into an aural environment that acts efficiently at the most imperceptible levels of conscious experience: the chilling tones of violins, the dazzling figures of *glissando*, the repetition of rhythmic series and the *crescendo* that makes tension escalate, enveloping the body of the spectator and arousing states of agitation, tension, restlessness and disturbance. Moreover, these states reflect a typology of reactions of bodily discomfort with varying intensities at the level of our breathing system (breathlessness, pain in the chest area, difficulties breathing) and cardiovascular system (cardiac and blood circulation acceleration, palpitations). They all stress the body.

Scientifically proven and used in therapeutic practices, the effects of music over physiological states indicate the existence of a direct correspondence between the system of organization of music and that of the body, though running in a different circuit than that of cognition: 'music communicates with the body by speaking the language of physiology'; therefore, it has a direct impact on it (Schneck and Berger 2006: 24). Likewise, sound design in *SNM*, anchored in the rhythmic scores of Herrmann's suspense, has concrete effects on the physiology of the spectator. It creates tension, expectation and anxiety. Yet the adrenaline that those states produce does not necessarily translate into emotions, thoughts or behaviours shared by spectators. (They know they are in a fictional, thus relatively safe, environment.) While for some adrenaline will produce discomfort, for others it will instigate curiosity and the pleasure of playing. What spectators share, however, are the conditions of experience that, far from free and empowered, are cultivated by a sensorial and affective atmosphere of intensities to which the body is vulnerable. In this sense, suspense materializes a contact zone with the staged world in a particularly constrained way that reveals a conflicting reality: spectators are encouraged to freely explore the space and create their own singular theatrical experience but the pervading sound design creates a strongly conditioned embodied experience as it is dominated by unconscious physiological processes. If these inform decision-making, as the company desires, how can spectators be empowered and have free choice? And how is this experience different from a theatre tradition of illusionary effects that directs audience engagement? Affective contagion and compulsory participation are fundamentally manipulative: spectators are free to choose as long as they accept being part of the system and engage with the economy of affects at play.

If spectators are free to pursue performers and explore the space, they cannot, however, escape the rhythmic background of tension that, in turn, follows them everywhere. It is interesting to note that *SNM* reproduces one of the most relevant facets of aural perception in current times: the musical background disseminated through the majority of global societies' public spaces, especially, those associated with commercial activities (cafes, bars, stores). As Anahid Kassabian reminds us, this prevalent musical infiltration has consequences on the way we listen. We have developed a 'ubiquitous listening', a mode of listening simultaneous to the performance of other activities, hence, becoming a secondary activity that is responsible for the production of 'distributed subjectivity' (Kassabian 2013: 9). This subjectivity constitutes a field in which power is irregularly and unpredictably distributed. Familiar and imperceptible, this kind of listening promotes the efficiency of affective manipulation. Such is the case of *SNM*. The performance does not require an investment in attention to listen. On the contrary, soundscape is listened to 'ubiquitously' producing distributed subjectivities of roaming individual spectators so that effects on the body be more efficient: the tension, the restlessness and anxiety that it instils powerfully manipulate visceral experience. Instead of a permeable contact zone, soundscape engenders a mechanism of contagion that constrains the possibilities of a visceral exploration of space.

The spectator-voyeur: Mechanisms of separation

As the actor is the one traditionally wearing a mask, Punchdrunk problematizes this tradition by allowing the spectator to enjoy the privilege of masquerading, which suspends the usual codes of behaviour while offering protection from social judgements. Masks grant the spectator's anonymity, generating a carnavalesque freedom to become another, both stimulating the exploration of space and inhibiting contact between spectators. Such anonymity hides faces and their expressions as the most immediate form of communication; it diminishes the possibilities of interaction between spectators, allowing for deviant behaviour as well as a voyeuristic gaze. Simultaneously, spectator-explorers are deprived of the possibility of bonding, connecting and sharing with other spectators, which reinforce the intention of an isolated individual experience. In other words, interaction between spectators does not bring forth contagion directly, but it reinforces a contained individual experience which, in turn, will give more room to the work of sound. Masks as a mechanism of separation contribute to a strong sense of threat by weakening social engagement.

Masks in *SNM* are a device of separation that shape bodies as unreachable, affectionless and even scary others. Masks materialize the skin as border. In addition, the gregarious roaming of masked spectators produces an intensification of the atmosphere that reinforces the other as distant and untrustworthy. As Sara Ahmed suggests, intensification is the performative process by which emotions and sensations produce the surface of bodies and shape attitudes of distance or proximity (Ahmed 2004). They materialize affective borders on the body of others orienting attitudes of distance or proximity, making bodies as objects of positive or negative affects. Ahmed argues that such processes form the basis of racist beliefs and behaviour, for instance. She discusses the concept of 'affective economies' (2004: 44) to define the circulation of objects of emotion and signs that produce affective value by accumulation: the more objects of emotion circulate, reiterated by the repetition of social and cultural narratives, the highest value they accumulate. Ahmed's argument displaces the subject from the centre of emotional processes to a nodal point in affective economies. The subject is neither the origin nor the goal of the economy but a point of impact of its trajectories (2004: 46). Immersed in the circulation of affect in public space, he or she is part of a permanent flux of exchange that mediates his or her contact with the other.

Hence, one can argue that the mask in *SNM* works as a surface that shapes the body of other spectators as enclosed and separated from the others. Sensorial atmospheres produce this intensification, in particular, sound design that contaminates states of tension and anxiety as well as adrenaline and translates into an 'entrepreneurial participation', an obligation to explore the space to actually be able to attend the performance. The mask is the materialization of such intensification that, ultimately, shapes the other as an opponent, a competitor and an untrustworthy rival (see Zaiontz 2014 on competition in audiences), who will, potentially, have the best experiences, find the best angle of a scene or have the privilege of a one-on-one. Here is someone to keep both at a distance but also an eye on; inviting a sort of suspicious surveillance, especially if you wish to avail of the best opportunities the show has to offer. More importantly, contrary to the claims of Punchdrunk directors, masks do not guarantee spectators an empowering and free experience because while they are contained in a body surface of intensified affect they are instilled with the rhythms and the frequencies of a threatening ecology of sound. Contagion is, thus, enhanced by this mechanism of separation.

Conclusion

Considering the affective economy of *SNM*, the spectator is a point of impact of predetermined sensitive charges associated with states of tension induced by the soundscape that he or she amplifies and disseminates. Sound mediates experience and conditions both the decisions of the spectator and the atmosphere the audience creates and feeds. In this sense, affect in *SNM* is largely predetermined, reinscribed and reproduced by the show's ostensibly immersive strategies.

What is, then, the paradox of immersion in *SNM*? Offering and denying the spectator a fully empowered experience of participation. *SNM* invites the roaming spectator to follow his or her (visceral) instinct but not without impacting bodies with a contagious atmosphere of threat and tension. Propagated by a saturated soundscape, affect conditions the audience's embodied experience. Furthermore, the mechanism of separation used in many Punchdrunk productions (masks and self-absorbed performers) works against the ostensible immersive aim of changing the status of the spectator from voyeur to participant. Paradoxically, the audience engages with a movie-like experience that is already contaminated by a threatening atmosphere of sound affect.

Notes

1 Examples of studies on crowd behaviour and others can be found in the chapter 'Transmission in Groups' (Brennan 2004).
2 For in-depth definitions of the visceral see Machon 2009; Biggin 2017.
3 In this text, I will be referring to the NYC production, which premièred on 7 March 2011 at the McKittrick Hotel, Chelsea.

4 It is worth noting that the production has been running since 2011 with a huge commercial success that allows the company to invest in other large-scale projects (Healy 2013).
5 For a relevant examination of Punchdrunk's intimacy experiences as sexual voyeurism see Gordon 2012 and Maples 2016.
6 For an approach to positive intoxication see Alston 2012: 203–5.

References

Ahmed, S. (2004), *The Cultural Politics of Emotion*, New York: Routledge.
Alston, A. (2012), 'Funding, Product Placement and Drunkenness in Punchdrunk's The Black Diamond', *Studies in Theatre and Performance*, 32 (2): 193–207.
Alston, A. (2016), *Beyond Immersive Theatre. Aesthetics, Politics and Productive Participation*, Houndmills: Palgrave.
Biggin, R. (2017), *Immersive Theatre and Audience Experience*, Houndmills: Palgrave Macmillan.
Blake, M. (2012), Interview with Mathew Blake, by Ana Pais, 8 April.
Bishop, C. (2004), 'Antagonism and Relational Aesthetics', *October* (110): 51–79.
Bishop, C. (2012), *Artificial Hells. Participatory Art and the Politics of Spectatorship*, London and New York: Verso.
Brennan, T. (2004), *The Transmission of Affect*, Ithaca, NY: Cornell University.
Bruce, G. (1985), *Bernard Herrmann: Film Music and Narrative*, Michigan: Umi Research Press.
Freshwater, H. (2009), *Theatre & Audience*, Houndmills: Palgrave.
Goodman, S. (2010), *Sonic Warfare. Sound, Affect and the Ecology of Fear*, Cambridge and London: MIT.
Gordon, C. (2012), 'Touching the Spectator: Intimacy, Immersion, and the Theater of the Velvet Rope', *Borrowers and Lenders. The Journal of Shakespeare and Appropriation*, VII (2): n.p.
Harvie, J. (2013), *Fair Play. Art, Performance and Neoliberalism*, Houndmills: Palgrave Macmillan.
Healy, P. (2013), 'A London Troupe Thrives with Ambitious Free-Range Theater', *New York Times*, August: C1.
Jackson, S. (2011), *Social Works: Performing Art, Supporting Publics*, London and New York: Routledge.
Kassabian, A. (2013), *Ubiquitous Listening*, Berkeley and Los Angeles: University of California Press.
Ledoux, J. (1996), *The Emotional Brain: The Mysterious Underpinnings of Emotional Life*, New York: Touchstone.
Lepecki, A. and S. Banes (2007), *The Senses in Performance*, New York: Routledge.

Machon, J. (2009), *(Syn)aesthetics Redefining Visceral Performance*, Houndmills: Palgrave Macmillan.
Maples, H. (2016), 'The Erotic Voyeur: Sensorial Spectatorship in Punchdrunk's The Drowned Man', *JCDE*, 4 (1): 119–33.
O'Hara, M. (2017), 'Experience Economies: Immersion, Disposability, and Punchdrunk Theatre', *Contemporary Theatre Review*, 27 (4): 481–96.
Pais, A. (2015), 'From Effect to Affect: Narratives of Passivity and Modes of Participation of the Contemporary Spectator', *STUDIA UBB DRAMATICA*, LX (2): 123–49.
Pais, A. (2017), 'Almost Imperceptible Rhythms and Stuff Like That', in D. Kapchan (ed.), *Theorizing Sound Writing*, 233–50, Middletown, CT: Wesleyan University Press.
Piepenburg, E. (2011), 'Stage Is Set. Ready for Your Part?', *New York Times*, 20 March. Available online: http://theater.nytimes.com/2011/03/20/theater/sleep-no-more-from-punchdrunk-transforms-chelsea-warehouses.html?_r=0 (accessed 7 March 2019).
Punchdrunk (2013), 'Punchdrunk'. Available online: https://www.punchdrunk.org.uk (accessed 15 December 2013).
Ricci, G. (2012), 'Tracking the Scottish Play: The Sounds of *Sleep No More*', *Borrowers and Lenders. The Journal of Shakespeare and Appropriation*, VII (2): n.p.
Santone, J. (2014), 'The Economics of the Performative Audience', *Performance Research*, 19 (6): 30–6.
Schneck, D. and D. Berger (2006), *The Music Effect. Music Physiology and Clinical Applications*, London and Philadelphia: Jessica Kingsley.
Sparks, T. (2012), Interview with Tori Sparks, by Ana Pais, 16 March.
Sullivan, J. (2006), *Hitchcock's Music*, New Haven and London: Yale University Press.
White, G. (2012), 'On Immersive Theatre', *Theatre Research International*, 37 (3): 221–35.
Worthen, W. B. (2012), '"The Written Troubles of the Brain": Sleep No More and the Space of Character', *Theatre Journal*, 64 (1): 79–97.
Zaiontz, K. (2014), 'Narcissistic Spectatorship in Immersive and One-on-One', *Theatre Journal*, 66 (3): 405–25.

11

Outer and Inner Contagions

Mark Pizzato

Theatre artists know when a performance is connecting with its audience by the concentration given at serious moments. Yawns, coughs and sneezes minimize (with their potential for contagion). Squirming in seats ceases. Eyes focus. Mouths open in awe. Or, in comic moments, laughter erupts, rippling across the field of minds and bodies with actors waiting for its peak before continuing, energized by the collective joy.

But how are brains onstage, as they re-present characters' minds, connecting with those in seats? What are the mechanisms of such contagion – with distinct variations in each person, especially regarding the emotions of melodrama, comedy and tragedy? This chapter will explore how outer theatre elements reflect (and affect) inner theatre elements of the brain's staging of consciousness with 'stagehands' signalling between brains. It will draw upon neuroscience discoveries about our animal-human heritage, pleasure/pain and arousal/quiescence systems, mirror-neuron simulations, malleable body images, and projective identifications in relation to 'emotional contagion' (Hatfield et al. 2009) between actors – or characters they present – and spectators, shaped by dramatic modes and performance choices. It will also consider ancient and modern theories of such experiences, from Aristotle, Bharata Muni and Abhinavagupta to Antonin Artaud and Bertolt Brecht, developing an interdisciplinary and intercultural approach to theatrical contagion.

Recent research shows that laughter itself has social and health benefits, even if simulated (Mora-Ripoll 2011). But mockery in real life can be hurtful. So can concentrated emotions. In theatre, how does contagious passion and laughter, as a 'shared manifold' (Gallese 2001), become insightful and therapeutic, as well as entertaining, in changing minds collectively? How might it backfire?

Inner theatre elements, a Trojan horse and quiescence/arousal

The 'staging of consciousness' in each of our brains (Baars 1997) involves a balancing act, shaping the pleasure/pain and arousal/quiescence of emotional contagion in outer performances. The left hemisphere (neocortex) of the brain, including its frontal and parietal lobes, has many distinct functions from the right (detailed by McGilchrist 2009 and charted in Pizzato 2016). We all use both hemispheres, to some degree, all the time. But the left's dominance with abstract rules, verbal thought and objective focusing (in 90 per cent of people) leads me to call it the inner *scriptwriter/critic*. The right cortex, on the other hand (with each cortex tied to the opposite side of the body), plays a 'Devil's Advocate' role, 'to question the status quo and look for global inconsistencies' (Ramachandran and Blakeslee 1998: 136–7). It is often inhibited by the left cortex, which has 'Freudian defense mechanisms to deny, repress, or confabulate – anything to preserve the status quo' (Ramachandran and Blakeslee 1998: 136–7). This becomes extreme with hemi-neglect and denial patients who ignore the left side of the body, or deny they are paralysed, or even that the left limbs are part of them, after a right-hemisphere stroke, with the left cortex as overdominant.

With its holistic, contextual, visuospatial openness to alternatives, I call the right cortex an inner *mime-improviser/scene-designer*, complimenting various functions of the left. But the right- and left-cortical functions compete as well as cooperate, especially with the right's stronger ties to the subcortical limbic system, deeper in the brain, involving emotions and primal drives as mostly conforming, yet sometimes trickster *stagehands* (the Freudian 'id'). In the theatres of everyday life, as in the art of theatre, each inner theatre of artist and spectator draws on a shifting balance of left, right and subcortical functions, prior to and during the performance of Self for Other in the collective show. ('Self' is capitalized here as the fiction of a complete ego; 'Other' means the social or metaphysical network, as superego, for which the Self performs.)

The left-cortical *scriptwriter/critic*, which evolved from animal circuits for focused, objectifying predation, but with added human skills of language and rationality, filters the broader awareness of the right-cortical *improviser/ designer*, evolved from potential prey anxieties and mating, nurturing bonds. The inner *scriptwriter/critic* analyses with strong beliefs, competitiveness and conscious agency, while the *improviser/designer* intuits with empathetic care, cooperation and unconscious socio-environmental influences. The left cortex examines parts in a linear, categorical way, focusing on cause and effect. The right comprehends more of the whole in a cyclical, contextual way, involving paradoxical, poetic associations with ambiguous meanings and ironic humour (McGilchrist 2009: 82). There is also evidence that the left forebrain connects with *quiescent* feelings of familiarity and safety with appetitive, approach behaviours, through the body's parasympathetic nervous system, and the right with *arousal* emotions of danger and withdrawal through the sympathetic nervous system (Craig 2005; McGilchrist 2009: 69). Thus, the left-cortical *scriptwriter/critic* cues the body's parasympathetic quiescence for *concentrated attention*, while the right-cortical *improviser/designer* opens it to sympathetic arousal, especially with disruptive passions or ironic laughter.

The inner theatre of Self and Other consciousness also involves the lateral prefrontal cortex (LPFC) on each side of the brain, activated when a subject looks in a mirror. So I call this neural awareness of one's appearance to others the *inner character* network – with the mask of Self hinged at those lateral hubs. The lower part of the LPFC on one side, the right ventrolateral prefrontal cortex (rVLPFC), is active for impulse and attitude control, as the *inner sound/light operator*, regarding imagined, potential and performed actions in relation to limbic moods. The rVLPFC is especially involved in Devil's Advocate challenges to left-cortical dominance: overcoming prior beliefs and impulses through a *shift* to new perspectives (Lieberman 2013: 212–15).

The inner Other, as framework for the Self, involves a *director* network, with its hub in the dorsomedial prefrontal cortex (DMPFC), the upper part of the forehead between the eyes. This 'mentalizing' network simulates the perspectives of other minds. It is also called the 'default' network, active when the subject is not given a task during a brain scan. Thus, the 'Theory of Mind' ability in our highly social species became crucial to personal and group survival, especially as our ancestors evolved from small, hunter-gatherer bands to agricultural communities with territorial hierarchies to huge cities and global media. This also extends to the current 'moral contagion' of social media (Brady et al. 2017) with frontal-lobe identities, especially in developing teenage brains, often dependent on Facebook 'likes' and Instagram 'selfie' performances – as people of all ages form ideological 'filter bubbles' – in being directed by others' views.

The Other within also involves a *stage/production manager*, monitoring current behaviours. This network, with a hub in the ventromedial PFC, the lower part of the forehead between the eyes, connects with the deeper limbic system to give us a feeling of doing the right thing or not in our performances for others around us. Such moral appraisals are tied to reward networks that operate for both social and physical pleasure/pain, thus relating also to playful, rebellious, trickster (id) desires of subcortical *stagehands* – working against, as well as with, superego norms.

Balancing with these networks is the *inner actor* of the medial PFC with the DMPFC above and VMPFC below. The MPFC is active when a subject in the brain scanner is asked which adjectives apply to one's Self. Yet its activity also predicts the influence of an experimenter's message (in a video about the health benefits of using sunscreen or quitting smoking) better than the subject's conscious plan to follow such advice in the future. Thus, the MPFC network, as 'Trojan horse self', absorbs social influences 'without realizing where these foundational worldviews came from' (Lieberman 2013: 196–200, 235). This connection – between the private, Trojan horse self and external, mimetic-messaging Other – shows the contagious power of theatricality, through stage and screen media (such as the health video), affecting the *inner actor* into the future, beyond one's conscious awareness.

The inner sense of Self, as moment-to-moment consciousness, also performs for and draws on the support of an *inner audience*, as the ghosts of past influences, in cooperating and competing neural circuits, 'cheer' and 'boo' what appears onstage (Pizzato 2006). Temporal-lobe memory traces, intuitions and predictions (specific to each person) project what the Self might expect and do in each external situation – or reflect further creative possibilities through fantasies and dreams. Indeed, this inner, temporal-lobe audience plays a key role in sympathetic *arousal* and parasympathetic *quiescence*. Within the temporal lobes on each side of the brain, at the temples near the ears, the hippocampus forms and reconstructs long-term memories. It is also a key 'diplomat' of the limbic system, with the nearby amygdala, regulating the neural flow of arousal or quiescence in relation to emotional images, memories and learning (Newberg et al. 2002: 45–6).

As the spectator relaxes safely in the theatre and feels drawn into the drama onstage, perhaps in a dreamlike way, the parasympathetic nervous system of quiescence activates. This involves the temporal-lobe *audience* of personal associations, focusing contagious concentration through the left-cortical *scriptwriter/critic*. During the play sympathetic arousal also activates, through the right temporal-lobe *audience*, evoking contagious passions of identification with the hero's struggles onstage – perhaps blurring self/other, spectator/actor/character boundaries. Yet right-cortical *improviser/designer* networks can shift from aroused anxiety to sudden quiescent relief, through comic twists onstage (or farcical violence without serious injury), resulting in collective laughter, also involving temporal-lobe *audiences* (Wild et al. 2003). This comes from the action onstage, identifications of audience members with the characters and plot, and the sounds and sights of bodily changes in fellow spectators,[1] as the laughter spreads – with *inner stagehands* signalling between brains.

Mirror neurons, allegiances and inter-subject correlations

Mirror neurons were initially discovered in monkey brains with the same brain cell firing when the monkey watched or made a specific goal-directed action, such as picking up a peanut. Auditory mirror neurons were also discovered at typical goal-oriented, action sounds, such as the cracking of a peanut, heard or performed. Canonical neurons were found, too, for objects of goal-directed actions, viewed or interacted with. Corresponding mirror-neuron areas have also been found in humans. For example, canonical mirror neurons become active in the ventral premotor cortex, an area that signals actions, when someone simply views a tool, vegetable, clothes or a sexual organ (Freedberg and Gallese 2007: 200).

Experimenters discovered that dancers who watch videos of others dancing have mirror-neuron activation as if they were dancing themselves – and more so with styles they have performed (Calvo-Merino et al. 2005). This also happens with musicians listening to music (Hyman 2012). Thus, kinaesthetic experience and interest filters the automatic activation of mirror neurons in humans (Sheets-Johnstone 2012), exciting or inhibiting the inner simulations of action scenes observed. Neurons send mimetic signals to feel the movement, yet not complete the action, in what is commonly called 'identification' with a performer onstage – as an initial, automatic mechanism of motor and emotional contagion.

Film theorist Murray Smith (1999) explores various aspects of spectator identification with characters onscreen.[2] He uses the term 'alignment' for a cognitive connection with the character's perspectives and actions – or 'allegiance' as emotional participation with them, sometimes involving 'perverse allegiances' with mixed feelings regarding morality. In my view, the inner theatre model summarized above, along with mirror-neuron experiments, further refines such terms. A spectator's left-cortical *scriptwriter/critic* aligns with the plot and main character onscreen (or onstage). The right-cortical *improviser/designer* feels further allegiances, moral or ambiguous, consistent or changing, through the melodramatic (good versus evil) or tragicomic (more complex) goals, obstacles and conflicts of the hero – plus the stirring music, other characters as allies or villains, and action scenes. But there is also a bottom-up process of the spectator initially sharing in the goal-oriented actions within scenes through mirror-neuron simulations producing potential allegiances with inner *stagehand* and *audience* circuits of drives, affects and personal associations, involving pleasure/pain and arousal/quiescence. These are filtered through the higher-order awareness of cognitive alignments with consistent or perverse allegiances – as a contagious blurring of other with self in the shifting 'spotlight' of consciousness (Baars 1997).

Studies by Uri Hasson and his colleagues (2008) discovered that 45 per cent of the neocortical activity of five subjects was synchronized as they watched the opening thirty minutes of the Sergio Leone film *The Good, the Bad, and the Ugly* (1966) – and that their eyes mostly tracked the same areas of the screen. This 'inter-subject correlation' (ISC) was much higher than when watching a video of ordinary life in a park (5 per cent). It was also higher than with an episode of the Larry David television sitcom, *Curb Your Enthusiasm* (18 per cent). And yet, when subjects watched an episode of the television series, *Alfred Hitchcock Presents*, called 'Bang! You're Dead' (1961), the ISC was even higher (65 per cent), perhaps because they watched the entire thriller in contrast to the action film.

Film and television can evoke a great deal of emotional contagion, measured as synchronous neocortical activity, even when watched individually, inside an fMRI brain scanner. Potentially, spectators at a live theatre event experience as much or more emotional contagion in subcortical areas, too, as they share space and time with each other and the actors. Indeed, experiments show that mirror-neuron activation in humans and monkeys is stronger with live action than video (Risko et al. 2012).

But there are risks with theatrical contagion, as Artaud said about his 'theatre of cruelty'.[3] Too much ISC of animal emotions between spectators' inner *stagehands* may evoke the merging of self with other towards dangerous behaviours. This can happen even with an artfully constructed play or film, depending on the spectator's personal associations and choices, as with Oliver Stone's *Natural Born Killers* (1994). It influenced the Columbine High School killers in Colorado and various other viewers who performed copycat crimes. For example, two teenagers, male and female, watched the film a dozen times in Oklahoma, while taking LSD, and then went on a road trip to other states, like the film's anti-heroic couple, mimicking its violence by shooting strangers (Pizzato 2005). Contagious violence has occurred in theatre history, too, such as the copycat plays and many suicides after a popular kabuki piece by Chikamatsu, *Love Suicides at Sonezaki* (1703), until such plays were banned twenty years later. Melodramatic fear, sadness and vengeful rage (depending on viewers' personal associations and desires) may focus allegiance towards the sacrifice of self and others as objects, for an imagined audience, outside the theatre.

Poses and faces, beauty and body swapping

Scientists researching emotional contagion continue to debate how automatic it is and how early the cognitive dimension of 'contextual appraisal' becomes involved in human empathy (De Vignemont and Singer 2006) – as a cathartic alternative to copycat violence. The current consensus is that mirror-neuron simulation of observed actions creates 'empathy' between the spectator and performer, in the brain's sensorimotor, posterior parietal (kinaesthetic), inferior frontal (goal-coding) and superior temporal (visual description and sensory matching) areas. Faceless, full-body poses in photographs also evoke contagious empathy through the amygdala (part of the temporal-lobe *audience*) and orbital-frontal cortex (part of the VMPFC *stage manager*), especially regarding primal emotions, such as fear and happiness. Indeed, fear expression, even without object-directed movement, evokes emotion-action (flight) networks in the viewer, through mirror-neurons, like but more than a happiness pose evokes that emotion (de Gelder et al. 2004). Thus, current neuroscience reveals what theatre in various cultures has explored for centuries: the power of contagious emotions through the actor's body onstage, as with kabuki *mie* (poses at emotional peaks), Delsarte's acting method (with characteristic gestures) and modern stage and screen melodramas (with stereotyped figures and actions).

Likewise, the viewing of facial expressions evokes emotion through mirror-neuron and temporal-lobe networks, such as fear via the amygdala and disgust via the insula (van der Gaag et al. 2007). The insula is also a key hub for the mirror-neuron 'relay from action representation to emotion' (Carr et al. 2003), as part of the *inner audience*, lobbying for what appears onstage in consciousness. But such primal empathy is filtered by advanced (developing later in evolution and childhood) 'mentalizing' networks with cognitive perspective-taking in the temporal lobes and DMPFC (*inner director*): understanding the other person's 'intentions, goals, and beliefs' (Singer 2006). This relates to the cathartic backfire of copycat crimes, especially in teenage viewers, because our prefrontal networks do not fully mature (with myelin coating) until our mid-twenties.

Paul Ekman and his colleagues have produced decades of evidence that similar facial expressions occur across many human cultures for six basic emotions: fear, disgust, anger, sadness, happiness and surprise (Levenson et al. 1990). They have defined the precise muscle movements for each of these in a Facial Action Coding System (FACS). They find that people trained in that system, whether actors or scientists, when making voluntary facial expressions, feel the corresponding emotion with sympathetic nervous system activation, measured by heart rate and skin sweat levels. A related experiment using computer-generated 'avatar' faces shows that viewers automatically mimic happy and angry expressions with their own facial muscles, involving mirror-neuron areas (Likowski et al. 2012). Thus, a spectator watching an actor mimics facial expressions (perhaps more so with film close-ups) through the right-cortical *mime-improviser/scene-designer* to the degree that the left-cortical *scriptwriter/critic* allows, while mirroring emotions and actions internally.

The spectator's automatic, yet filtered mimicry of facial expressions, along with inner simulations of gestures and poses, while sitting quiescently in the theatre, increases 'liking' and 'affiliation'. But such 'imitation' is primed by the performer's physical attractiveness, whether female or male, even without the viewer's awareness of beauty playing a role (van Leeuwen et al. 2009). Experiments have also shown that cross-modal sensations can increase such liking and affiliation (or alignment and allegiance, in Smith's terms). The simultaneous touching of a viewer's face and a video face evokes self/other merging, in 'enfacement' experiments, depending on the viewer's empathy and the other face's beauty (Sforza et al. 2010). Thus, beauty onstage or onscreen evokes contagious affiliation, idealizing the viewer's inner mirror of *character*.

One's body image can also be extended to a rubber hand through simultaneous stroking of it, while feeling one's hand being stroked in the same way. And then, the experimenter sticking a needle into the rubber hand evokes a startle response with arousal system activation, measured by increased sweat levels (Ehrsson 2012: 778). Further experiments with a subject wearing a video device that gives the visual perspective of being the head on a manikin's body also *projects* the viewer into that bodily position, evoking arousal when a knife is plunged into that other body, where the Self has merged. This can even produce an 'out-of-body' illusion when one views one's body through a camera behind it, while a rod approaching to touch the area below the camera is felt on the viewer's body. Such experiments can create the illusion of shaking one's own hand, also relating to robotic-hand and virtual-reality theatres (784–8).[4]

These experiments suggest the power of theatrical media, even without touch, through mirror-neuron empathy and emotional contagion to transform viewers with the face and body expressions of performers, onstage or onscreen. This involves a collective allegiance, especially with beautiful heroes and victims, against ugly villains, or with romantic love objects – whether through ancient masks or modern typecasting, make-up, attractive costumes and close-ups. But how do contagious emotions evoke tragicomic catharsis or melodramatic backfire, collectively and individually?

Primal emotions, rat laughter, reappraisals and theatre theories

In the affective sciences, there are competing theories for defining emotions on a spectrum from basic, universal ones to automatic 'appraisals' with degrees of cognition to psychologically structured feelings interpreted from core affects to socially constructed feelings (Gross and Barrett 2011). Akin to Ekman's six emotions in universal facial expressions (contested by Barrett 2017), Jaak Panksepp defines seven primal emotions after decades of mapping the brain circuits of animal behaviours. He writes these in capital letters: SEEKING from invertebrates to humans; RAGE, FEAR, and LUST in reptiles, mammals and humans; and CARE, SADNESS/GRIEF/PANIC, and JOYFUL PLAY in mammals and humans (Panksepp and Biven 2012). Along with the core affects of arousal/quiescence and pleasure/pain, interpreted by the human brain's top-down cognitive networks as psychologically and socially constructed feelings (Barrett 2017), I find Panksepp's bottom-up, evolutionary dimensions to be insightful regarding theories of emotional contagion in theatre history.

Viewed in light of Panksepp's work, Aristotle's ancient theory of 'catharsis' (purification of emotions) suggests the most primal emotion of SEEKING as key to the contagious engagement of spectators (or readers) with tragic poetry. The spectator SEEKS through sympathy with the admirable, yet flawed, hero to follow his fate in the plot through twists (*peripeteias*) and recognition moments (*anagnorises*), 'producing love or hate' between the characters, as that builds to a climax and then resolves the philosophical and emotional conflict (*agon*). This also involves reptilian-mammalian FEAR as the spectator identifies with the fated and flawed hero through mammalian CARE as sympathy. Increasingly, the JOYFUL PLAY of participating in the fictional realm onstage with a LUST for new experience and knowledge, as well as beauty, and RAGE at antagonists and injustice leads the spectator through the reversals and recognitions of the plot to the climax of tragic SADNESS/GRIEF/PANIC. The suffering of the hero offers spectators a cathartic challenge to learn from the play – and *not repeat* his errors contagiously (although suggesting that danger). Through purified emotions, viewers may have a better chance of survival and reproduction, practising bio-culturally evolved skills as in dreams (Valli and Revonsuo 2009).

Thus, the audience shifts back and forth between a quiescent, left-cortical *scriptwriter/critic* focus in plot SEEKING (with dopamine, 'wanting' circuits activated) and aroused, more right-cortical *improviser/designer* engagements with various character passions (via noradrenaline, alertness circuits), through mirror-neuron simulations signalling between unconscious *stagehands*. This process includes diverse cognitive appraisals in the theatres of the minds watching through core affects evoked collectively in their bodies. Different personal associations involve inner *actor, director, stage manager* and *character* networks with specific memory *audiences*, identifying with and against the characters onstage. Yet this may evoke a contagious, 'spillover effect' (Newberg et al. 2002) of quiescent and aroused, pleasurable (opioid 'liking') and painful brain circuits in the ecstatic Self/Other merging of spectators with outer actors, characters and scenes, especially towards the tragic climax.

The other side of such merging, in the spectator's sympathy for the hero's tragic alienation, relates to a survival mechanism in mammalian young (Pizzato 2016: 45–6). Rat pups will squeal briefly for a missing mother and then resort to a prolonged, frightful *freeze* – apparently akin to human alienation with depressive, yet anxious withdrawal, in a *negative* spillover of quiescence and arousal circuits, as primal SADNESS/GRIEF/PANIC. If the mother returns soon enough and licks the pup with CARE, then the infant's cortisol networks become stronger in handling stress later in life. But a prolonged absence of the mother (like trauma in human childhood) leads to hypersensitive arousal with excessive anxiety and less ability to handle stress in adulthood, causing similar withdrawal behaviours.

All of us experience some degree of primal alienation through our normal prematurity of birth as humans, compared with other primates, and our highly complex brains. We are extremely dependent on others in infancy as we become reborn into their symbolic realm (with a 'lack of being', according to Lacanian psychoanalysis). So theatre offers a way for us to re-experience the terror of such alienation with primal anxiety in tragedy (or specific fears in the horror genre) through the hero's contagious abjection. But we also re-emerge, connected to others, with *collectively* real, imaginary and symbolic insights.

Panksepp (2005) finds that contagious, JOYFUL PLAY in humans relates to the laughter or 'chirping' of rats at high frequencies when tickled by the experimenter. The rats return again and again for more tickling and become better able to socialize later through this and other forms of play. Yet Panksepp suggests a 'dark side' to human humour with the objectifying of others expressing hierarchical dominance or 'eminency' (according to philosopher Thomas Hobbes). Likewise, I would argue that theatrical tickling improves socialization, especially through tragicomic insights. But laughter in theatre may also involve contagious scapegoating, expressing hierarchical dominance through the melodramatic or farcical objectifying of certain types of people as villains and fools.

There are many variations and alternatives to Aristotelian plot structure, evoking spectator quiescence/arousal and different emotions along the playful course of the performance. Action movies, for example, typically have a 'hot' beginning, arousing FEAR and CARE, and then proceed with quiescent backstory introductions, perhaps with SADNESS at prior and potential losses – as the first act (first half hour) develops the hero's commitment to action. Such initial tragic reflections arouse RAGE and action commitment in a series of melodramatic conflicts of the hero against the villain(s) along with comic (PLAYFUL JOY) and romantic (LUST) twists. This SEEKING of revenge after damages with further threats to victims reaches a climax of courage and JOY (in the last half hour) as good triumphs over evil. Some plays, movies and television shows have multiple, intertwining, episodic plots, each with peaks of crisis, rising to the overall climax and resolution. For example, Shakespeare's *The Tempest* has a hot start with the storm splitting a ship and its people through the melodramatic vengeance of Prospero. Yet its episodic conflicts eventually develop towards tragicomic mercy, mixing RAGE, FEAR and LUST with SADNESS, CARE and JOY.

FEAR is a crucial element in various genres, evoking audience CARE, not just in tragedy as Aristotle specified but in melodrama, horror, mystery, thriller, well-made play (with dangerous secrets), comedy, farce and romance. Likewise, social animals, such as dogs and primates, exhibit 'subordination displays' of FEAR, which evoke 'affiliative and appeasing' behaviours of 'approach' in dominant others (Marsh et al. 2005). This arouses CARE towards cooperation more than, yet through, competition. Experiments found this in humans, too, with fearful and angry expressions in photographs, as viewers pulled a lever more with fearful ones, as approach, and pushed more with angry ones, as avoidance – responding more quickly to fearful and female faces. Thus, fear expressions appear to viewers 'as rounder, kinder, warmer, more submissive, and more babyish than anger expressions ... Indeed, evidence exists to suggest that fear and other distress-related emotions like sadness and anxiety elicit not only the desire for affiliation but also caregiving from members of the social group' (122). This suggests that the RAGE contagion in many theatrical genres, onstage and onscreen, needs a FEAR element first (often involving a female or child victim) to evoke CARE in the viewer with approach then as a stronger pull than avoidance.

But how does contagious fear and care become compassion, even towards the villain, rather than a rage for revenge? Researchers on mindful compassion, as 'cognitive reappraisal', have scanned subjects' brains while asking them to view aversive, sad or erotic photos and film clips – and then to 'interpret' their response, mentally talking themselves through it, *or* to reimagine it as a 'detached observer' (Beauregard 2007; Ochsner et al. 2002; Schwartz et al. 2004). Brain activity shifts towards the left lateral prefrontal cortex (*inner character*) with a verbal *reinterpretation* of the emotional effect or to the right LPFC with a detached *reimagining* of it, which also involves the right anterior cingulate and right orbital frontal cortex (*inner stage manager*). These experiments relate to the modern theatre theories of Brecht, with alienation effects distancing the spectator towards verbalized, critical reappraisal of (Aristotelian) emotional contagion, and Artaud, evoking the spectator's participation in the 'cruelty' onstage, yet also a mindful reimagining of it. These differing dimensions of Brechtian distancing and Artaudian resonance also relate to Barrett's evidence for psychologically and socially constructed interpretations of core affects – as a critique of Panksepp's primal emotions and Ekman's universally shared facial expressions. In my view, the entire spectrum of these approaches is valuable, not just one side or the other, especially regarding theatre theories of emotional contagion.

Also insightful is the ancient Indian *Natya-Shastra* tradition of Bharata Muni and others, which started about two thousand years ago. Eight emotions (*bhavas*) and their corresponding 'flavours' (*rasas*) are defined: fear, sadness, anger, lust/love, humour/joy, disgust, heroic courage and awe/surprise – with each Sanskrit play focusing on one *rasa* as primary and another as secondary to 'resonate' with the spectator yet be 'tasted' at a distance. This cultivates 'good taste' in the audience through performers' face, body and hand (*mudra*) expressions as an artful sign language. A ninth *rasa*, 'peace', added by Abhinavagupta about a thousand years ago through the influence of Buddhism, becomes an enlightening refinement of the others. Such mindful attentiveness aims at union with the divine (*Brahman*) through communion with other humans (*tanmayibhavana*) in calmness beyond sensual attachments or what might be called the 'spillover effect' of arousal with quiescence.

Many of the nine *rasas* relate to Aristotle's theory of tragic catharsis: the spectator's sympathetic *sadness* through *fear* as the *awe*-inspiring hero's *disgusting* flaw is revealed through *courageous* struggles, involving *love* or hateful *rage*, eventually producing *calm purification* in the viewer. The nine *rasas* also relate to various theories of emotion in neuroscience and social psychology (Pizzato 2016).[5] Thus, it becomes most useful to build an interdisciplinary, intercultural theory of emotional contagion, as dangerous or beneficial, regarding melodramatic and tragicomic modes of theatre across various genres and media.

A *rasa*-cathartic effect might be evoked with ironic, tragicomic twists, even in popular melodramas. As 'cognitive reappraisal' experiments show, the left-cortical *scriptwriter/critic* can verbally *interpret* subcortical *stagehand* and limbic *audience* passions, especially regarding LPFC *character* attitudes. In Brecht's sense, quiescent 'distancing effects' might encourage viewers' reinterpretation of contagious emotions, provoking the left-cortical *scriptwriter* to critically address social problems – through right-cortical networks of ironic laughter and its inverse. 'The epic theatre's spectator says ... I laugh when they weep, I weep when they laugh' (Brecht in Willett 1957: 71). Yet performance elements that shift viewers' brains towards right-cortical *improviser/designer* networks (especially the right LPFC) can also arouse them to *reimagine* infectious passions through alternative, holistic, detached contexts. As Artaud suggests, a greater awareness of plague-like cruelty, reimagining sacrificial perspectives, may help spectators with their own scapegoating temptations: to *not* act out the 'violence of the thought' (Artaud [1938] 1958: 82).

For example, *Mother Courage and Her Children* (1939), by Brecht and Margarete Steffin, evokes quiescent, left-cortical *interpretations* with its brief summaries at the start of each scene (as signs or narrations onstage), its epic leaps in plot, and its critical, distancing moments, such as a soldier saying that a town needs war to restore moral order, Courage losing her first son to the military while haggling for a sale, and her subsequent biting of a gold coin. But Courage's silent scream when her second son is executed and her daughter's sacrificial death at the climax, with Courage then pulling her business wagon alone – along with many other details of the family's plight and periodic songs with ironic lyrics – stir aroused, right-cortical passions and yet the detached *reimagining* of contextual relations between war, business and migration. Such tragicomic shifts between emotional resonance and *rasa*-cathartic (dis)tastes are vital to the current insights and motivations for change that spectators might gain through parallels in a war from the 1600s.

Conclusion

Emotional contagion acts powerfully upon viewers' inner theatres through automatic, mirror-neuron, goal-imitating empathy and vicarious body swapping. Evoked by gestures, poses, anticipated actions, facial expressions and plot devices, it is also filtered by personal associations and desires. Inter-subject correlations may occur in a majority of viewers' neocortical networks. This happens especially through stage or screen displays of melodramatic stereotypes, in-group/out-group allegiances, and primal emotions of FEAR, RAGE and LUST for vengeance, along with romantic objects of mimetic rivalry. Yet with tragicomic twists and ironic humour, depending on each viewer's inner-theatre orientation, left- and right-cortical shifts may create laughter and compassion, as Brechtian and Artaudian, *rasa*-cathartic mindfulness.

This is a key neuro-performance issue. Our melodramatic, mass and social media often project what is flawed, disgusting or fearful in one's Self or in-group onto others, objectifying them as villains. Such self and group purifying projections of righteous rhetoric and polarizing imagery – in theatre, movies, television shows and online sites – provokes some viewers towards the cathartic backfire of hate speech, collective marches and personal violence. However, *rasa*-cathartic compassion can be rehearsed through our various theatrical media, within and between brains, with subtle effects rippling far beyond mimetic entertainment. Attitude changes and impulse controls might be increased through the right VLPFC *operator* along with other inner-theatre networks, regarding animal-human drives and emotional contagions in everyday life. Such an awareness of (and ability to make personal choices about) outer and inner contagion is crucial today, especially with the power of our highly politicized, hyper-theatrical, social and mass media – and yet the potential of theatre artists and spectators, working together, to counteract such copycat dangers.

Notes

1 Provine (1992) found that just the sound of a 'laugh box' could produce smiles and laughter in a class of undergraduates, although the effect degraded and became 'obnoxious' to many by the tenth trial. See also Hatfield et al. (2009: 23–4) on emotional contagion through 'sound feedback' in speech, involving intonation, vocal quality, rhythm and pausing. This might occur with the inner voices of spectators during dialogue between characters.
2 See Coplan (2006) for further theories of emotional contagion in film viewing.
3 'There is a risk. But ... though a theatrical gesture is violent, it is disinterested ... [and] theatre teaches precisely the uselessness of the action which, once done, is not to be done, and the superior use of the state unused by the action ... which, *restored*, produces a purification' (Artaud [1938] 1958: 82).
4 See, for example, www.crewonline.org or the many Oculus VR videogames.
5 See also Schechner (1988) for a brief comparison of rasa facial expressions and Ekman's six faces for primal emotions.

References

Aristotle ([c. 335 BCE] 2013), *The Poetics of Aristotle*. Available online: https://www.gutenberg.org/files/1974/1974-h/1974-h.htm (accessed 24 September 2018).
Artaud, A. ([1938] 1958), *The Theatre and Its Double*, trans. M. C. Richards, New York: Grove.
Baars, B. J. (1997), *In the Theater of Consciousness: The Workspace of the Mind*, Oxford: Oxford University Press.
Barrett, L. F. (2017), *How Emotions Are Made*, Boston, MA: Houghton.

Beauregard, M. (2007), 'Mind Does Really Matter', *Progress in Neurobiology*, 81: 218–36.

Brady, W. J., J. A. Wills, J. T. Jost, J. A. Tucker and J. J. Van Bavel (2017), 'Emotion Shapes the Diffusion of Moralized Content', *PNAS*, 114 (28): 7313–18.

Calvo-Merino, B., D. E. Glaser, J. Grèzes, R. E. Passingham and P. Haggard (2005), 'Action Observation and Acquired Motor Skills', *Cerebral Cortex*, 15: 1243–9.

Carr, L., M. Iacoboni, M. Dubeau, J. C. Mazziotta and G. L. Lenzi (2003), 'Neural Mechanisms of Empathy in Humans', *PNAS*, 100 (9): 5497–502.

Coplan, A. (2006), 'Catching Characters' Emotions', *Film Studies*, 8: 23–38.

Craig, A. D. (2005), 'Forebrain Emotional Asymmetry', *Trends in Cognitive Sciences*, 12 (9): 566–71.

de Gelder, B., J. Snyder, D. Greve, G. Gerard and N. Hadjikhani (2004), 'Fear Fosters Flight', *PNAS*, 101 (47): 16701–6.

De Vignemont, F. and T. Singer (2006), 'The Empathic Brain: How, When and Why?' *Trends in Cognitive Sciences*, 10 (10): 435–41.

Ehrsson, H. H. (2012), 'The Concept of Body Ownership and Its Relation to Multisensory Integration', in B. E. Stein (ed.), *The New Handbook of Multisensory Processing*, 775–92, Cambridge: MIT Press.

Freedberg, D. and V. Gallese (2007), 'Motion, Emotion and Empathy in the Esthetic Experience', *Trends in Cognitive Science*, 11 (5): 197–203.

Gallese, V. (2001), 'The Shared Manifold Hypothesis', *Journal of Consciousness Studies*, 8: 38–9.

Gross, J. J. and L. F. Barrett (2011), 'Emotion Generation and Emotion Regulation', *Emotion Review*, 3 (1): 8–16.

Hasson, U., O. Landesman, B. Knappmeyer, I. Vallines, N. Rubin and D. J. Heeger (2008), 'Neurocinematics', *Projections*, 2 (1): 1–26.

Hatfield, E., R. L. Rapson, and Yen-Chi L. Le (2009), 'Emotional Contagion and Empathy', in J. Decety and W. Ickes (eds), *The Social Neuroscience of Empathy*, 19–30, Cambridge: MIT.

Hyman, I. (2012), 'Listening to Music and Watching Dance Using Mirror Neurons', *Psychology Today*, 9 August.

Levenson, R. W., P. Ekman and W. V. Friesen (1990), 'Voluntary Facial Action Generates Emotion-Specific Autonomic Nervous System Activity', *Psychophysiology*, 27 (4): 363–384.

Likowski, K. U., A. Mühlberger, A. B. M. Gerdes, M. J. Wieser, P. Pauli and P. Weyers (2012), 'Facial Mimicry and the Mirror Neuron System', *Frontiers in Human Neuroscience*, 6 (214): 1–10.

Lieberman, M. D. (2013), *Social*, New York: Crown.

Marsh, A. A., N. Ambady and R. E. Kleck (2005), 'The Effects of Fear and Anger Facial Expressions on Approach- and Avoidance-Related Behaviors', *Emotion*, 5 (1): 119–24.

McGilchrist, I. (2009), *The Master and His Emissary*, New Haven, CT: Yale University Press.

Mora-Ripoll R. (2011), 'Potential Health Benefits of Simulated Laughter', *Complimentary Therapies in Medicine*, 19: 170–7.
Newberg, A., E. d'Aquili and V. Rause (2002), *Why God Won't Go Away: Brain Science and the Biology of Belief*, New York: Ballantine.
Ochsner, K. N., S. A. Bunge, J. J. Gross and J. D. E. Gabrieli (2002), 'Rethinking Feelings', *Journal of Cognitive Neuroscience*, 14 (8): 1215–29.
Panksepp, J. (2005), 'Beyond a Joke', *Science*, 308: 62–3.
Panksepp, J. and L. Biven (2012), *The Archaeology of Mind*, New York: Norton.
Pizzato, M. (2005), *Theatres of Human Sacrifice*, Albany: State University of New York Press.
Pizzato, M. (2006), *Ghosts of Theatre and Cinema in the Brain*, New York: Palgrave.
Pizzato, M. (2016), *Beast-People Onscreen and in Your Brain*, Santa Barbara, CA: Praeger.
Provine, R. R. (1992), 'Contagious Laughter', *Bulletin of the Psychonomic Society*, 30 (1): 1–4.
Ramachandran, V. S. and S. Blakeslee (1998), *Phantoms in the Brain: Probing the Mysteries of the Human Mind*, New York: William Morrow.
Risko, E. F., K. E. W. Laidlaw, M. Freeth, T. Foulsham and A. Kingston (2012), 'Social Attention with Real versus Reel Stimuli', *Frontiers in Human Neuroscience* 6 (143): 1–11.
Schechner, R. (1988), *Performance Theory*, New York: Routledge.
Schwartz, J. M., H. P. Stapp and M. Beauregard (2004), 'The Volitional Influence of the Mind on the Brain, with Special Reference to Emotional Self-Regulation', in M. Beauregard (ed.), *Consciousness, Emotional Self-Regulation, and the Brain*, 195–238, Amsterdam: John Benjamins.
Sforza, A., I. Bufalari, P. Haggard and S. M. Aglioti (2010), 'My Face in Yours', *Social Neuroscience*, 5 (2): 148–62.
Sheets-Johnstone, M. (2012), 'Movement and Mirror Neurons', *Phenomenology and the Cognitive Sciences*, 11: 385–401.
Singer, T. (2006), 'The Neuronal Basis and Ontogeny of Empathy and Mind Reading', *Neuroscience and Biobehavioral Reviews*, 30: 855–63.
Smith, M. (1999) 'Gangsters, Cannibals, Aesthetes, or Apparently Perverse Allegiances', in C. Plantinga and G. M. Smith (eds), *Passionate Views*, 217–38, Baltimore: Johns Hopkins University Press.
Valli, K. and A. Revonsuo (2009), 'The Threat Simulation Theory in Light of New Empirical Evidence', *American Journal of Psychology*, 122 (1): 17–38.
van der Gaag, C., R. B. Minderaa and C. Keysers (2007), 'Facial Expressions', *Social Neuroscience*, 2 (3–4): 179–222.
van Leeuwen, M. L., H. Veling, R. B. van Baaren and A. Dijksterhuis (2009), 'The Influence of Facial Attractiveness on Imitation', *Journal of Experimental Social Psychology*, 45: 1295–98.
Wild, B., F. A. Rodden, W. Grodd and W. Ruch (2003), 'Neural Correlates of Laughter and Humor', *Brain*, 126: 2121–38.
Willett, J., ed. and trans. (1957), *Brecht on Theatre*, New York: Hill and Wang.

12

Theatre, Appification and VR Apps: Disability Simulations as an Intervention in 'Affective Realism'

Liam Jarvis

'When is a gun not a gun ... ?'

... the answer, according to neuroscientists Lisa Feldman Barrett and Jolie Wormwood, is when it is a smartphone. Drawing on statistics released from the US Department of Justice that analysed eight years of shootings by Philadelphia police officers, Barrett and Wormwood observed that 15 per cent of those shot were unarmed. In half of those cases an officer misidentified a 'nonthreatening object', such as a phone, as a weapon. Barrett and Wormwood's claim was that a psychological phenomenon called 'affective realism' might explain some of these fatalities – the way in which feelings can influence what you see, 'not what you think you see, but the actual content of your perceptual experience' (Barrett and Wormwood 2015). The Chekhovian trope that the presence of a gun onstage necessitates its firing in the following act is an argument for stories to obey their causal logic. Affective realism rather draws attention to the way in which feelings write our inner 'scripts' and how we act upon them in a similar cause and effect way. According to Barrett, scientific studies have suggested that the brain is a 'predictive organ' and that 'neural guesses' shape what we perceive, leading to the counterintuitive assertion that 'believing is seeing', rather than vice versa. Philosopher in cognitive neuroscience, Mark Miller, argues that if this hypothesis is accurate it has a 'dark side' because the past will not simply bias how you are in the present but 'your experiences in the past constitute your present experiences ... you are experiencing the world as though you are remembering the present' (Miller 2016).[1] This understanding creates new concerns as the purported 'misidentification' of a gun could also provide a convenient cover story for conscious and unconscious biases; one recent study drawing on police shootings data from 2015 suggested that black civilians were more than twice as likely to have been unarmed than white suspects (Nix et al. 2017). According to Barrett and Wormwood, affective realism, far from an alternate explanation, may actually be a way in which a phenomenon such as racial bias expresses itself.

If we accept this predictive model of the brain – that the enmeshment of past experience, affect, perception and bias plays a critical part in making 'neural guesses' about reality – how do we read and respond to bodily otherness for which our experiences can provide no correlate? For example, individuals whose perception of the world has been altered by a neurological condition. Through the lens of affective realism, it is conceivable that the lived conditions of others are particularly susceptible to misidentification, misunderstanding and, consequently, intolerance. In this chapter, I will examine a virtual reality (VR) smartphone app developed by Alzheimer's Research UK (ARUK) and digital developer Visyon called *A Walk Through Dementia* (*AWTD*) (2016), which positions users within a series of first-person simulations of pathological phenomena (e.g. symptoms associated with dementia). Drawing on my embodied participation, I will examine the affective insights yielded and the underlying ethical considerations that individualistic technologies might inadvertently smuggle inside empathic, downloadable and self-generating experiences. What might a user think they 'know' when exiting the app and what gets lost through the vehicle of transmission?

It is my contention that apps of this kind are best examined as theatrical spaces – interfaces that offer a platform for users to perform identities with remote third-person inaccessible perceptual experiences of their world. Such spaces intersect with notions of 'contagion' because the phenomenological experiences replicated exist independent from their bodies of origin in such a way that they can propagate online – spreading and generating affective learning among participating downloaders in an attempt to mobilize the transmission of ineffable knowledges associated with altered forms of consciousness. Using the example that began this introduction as a point of departure, might apps of this kind provide a valuable intervention by reframing smartphones from misidentified weapons to empathy tools that enable their users to make more informed 'neural guesses' about different perceptual experiences of otherness?

A Walk Through Dementia: Augmented subjectivities

The desire to take up the position of fragile, ineffable and neuro-non-typical bodies courtesy of immersive simulation has emerged from various different domains. But of particular relevance to this chapter are both theatre makers and app developers who make no claim to be 'theatre makers', working in collaboration with third-sector organizations. For example, the *Autism Too Much Information (TMI) Virtual Reality Experience* (2016) app reconstructs the sensory overload of a ten-year-old autistic boy in a shopping centre, while *A Walk Through Dementia* illustrates everyday challenges associated with the symptoms of dementia in three 360° VR films. Other apps such as *The Wayback* (2017) are less oriented on communicating complex bodily experiences through simulation and more concerned with ameliorating the lives of those living with Alzheimer's by providing an ever-growing 'virtual reality memory bank' – the resurrection of past cultural events such as the Queen's Coronation in 1953 is intended to trigger happy personal memories, which is consistent with the long-standing applied approaches of reminiscence theatre pioneers such as Age Exchange.

The three VR films that comprise *A Walk Through Dementia* were developed through workshops coordinated by the charity with individuals living with Alzheimer's disease contributing to the writing process.[2] 'On the Road' positions the app's user as a woman walking home in the company of her son, Joe. She gets lost, becoming disoriented when she sees the face of her son on the body of a stranger and perceives threats in the surrounding environment, such as a puddle that looks like a sinkhole in the pavement (Figure 12.1). These visual misperceptions are accompanied by negative affective responses, such as anxiety represented through increased breathlessness and a quickening heartbeat. Occupying the first-person perspective is a narrative focalization tactic to make visible anomalies of perception that necessitate possessing a body that is undergoing the kinds of changes imposed by Alzheimer's as a progressive disease. But at three minutes and twenty seconds in duration, this experience provides little information about the back history of the virtual and unseen body we are cast within (represented only by subjective camera or point-of-view shot), we have no access to their memories, and our character remains unnamed throughout except through possessive nouns that indicate 'our' relationship to others in the film. Beyond the voice-over of our character's inner thoughts (recorded by actress Dame Harriet Walter, who lost both parents to dementia) and the assemblage of post-production effects that simulate disturbances of perception to prompt the downloader-experiencer to guess the virtual world incorrectly, the user ultimately steps into a hollow body.

In relation to video gaming, Slavoj Žižek has argued that games interpellate the gamer into a specific mode of subjectivity – immersion in the 'undead' space of video games offers an 'obscene immortality' in which

Theatre, Appification and VR Apps 189

Figure 12.1 Screenshots from 'On the Road', in the *A Walk Through Dementia* app. Courtesy of Alzheimer's Research UK.

after every destruction the player can return to the beginning and start again (Žižek 2017). While charity empathy apps are not video games, first-person engagement in enveloping video/CGI environments is a subjectivity that originates from the medium of gaming. For Žižek, the subjectivity that video games produce is not confined to onscreen interactions, since for him we live in an always already augmented reality ('Slavoj Žižek on Video Games' 2017) – affective realism adds a new dimension to Žižek's claim in respect of the way in which past feelings can augment perception of our present reality. Furthermore, ideologies from gaming can resurface in our real-world interactions. Žižek uses the example of people treating their love life like a video game, discarding one partner for another because through the logic of obscene immortality one can endlessly return to the beginning and start again. The intention with VR apps like *AWTD* is to increase our capacity to care for virtual others and carry across our learning into our real-world encounters. But does the paradoxical embedded logic of an 'undead' virtual identity that is both touched by illness but simultaneously impervious to death diminish or greaten our sense of responsibility for the hollow body whose position we take up?

Pervasive theatres, online virality and appification

'Pervasive theatre' is an umbrella term for practices that incorporate pervasive digital media, a defining feature of which is the integration of information processing in the world of everyday objects and environments (Coyne 2010: ix). Pervasive theatres are inherently transmedial with layered interactions that can span offline and online worlds and make diverse use of the technologies that audience members carry in their pockets, for example, prompting interactions via text messaging (e.g. Proto-type Theater's *Fortnight* 2011–15)[3] or using a smartphone's in-built global positioning system for audio walks in designated site-specific locations (Kneehigh's *Walk with Me* 2017–18).[4] The term 'appification' is a neologism that refers not only to the proliferation of smartphone applications that create or modify an existing service but to 'fundamental shifts in how we access and use information and media' (O'Brien and Van Deventer 2015: 417). Accordingly, what I am terming as 'app theatre' is a subset of wider developments in pervasive theatre making that use digital interfaces to create self-generating or participatory structures. App theatres combine the benefits of downloadable media with aspects of phenomenological liveness through user interactions that cannot be propagated by means other than human inputs/processes. Apps are enabling theatre makers to reach online audiences and generate new kinds of encounters, such as the distribution of cinematic and interactive audio participatory structures (Circumstance's *A Hollow Body* 2014),[5] as a form of intercontinental social networking (e.g. Invisible Flock (UK) and Quicksand's (India) *Duet*),[6] or mixing gaming and storytelling in the form of a pseudo-'life coach' app that elicits the user's data for subsequent psychological profiling (Blast Theory's *Karen* 2013).[7] Charity VR empathy apps such as *AWTD* are occurring in tandem with these developments, but they are non-relational one-on-none experiences (as opposed to the intimate 'one-on-one' face-to-face encounters associated with immersive theatre making); 'one-on-none' in the sense that the app's user will never come into contact with the individuals whose experiences inspired the mediatized representation. Remote participation means it is not only difficult to capture the precise learning that anonymous users take away but that specific instances of participation occur unknown to the app's maker.

It's notable that the effects of mediatization on theatre have been historically described by commentators such as Philip Auslander using the pathological language of contagion. For example, the notion that theatre is not 'immune from contamination by ... mediatized forms' (Auslander 1999: 7). In media archaeology, Jussi Parikka has argued that beyond the metaphorical, both biological and computer viruses illustrate ways in which bodies and environments 'infect each other' (2007: 270). One 'infecting' influence that a diversifying digital marketplace is having on theatre spectatorship is that it is widening participation and shifting the emphasis for audiences from the primacy of 'liveness' to economics and convenience. A 2016 audience survey in Live-to-Digital work – which encompasses 'event cinema', streaming/ downloading online, and television broadcasts – shows that motivations for streaming include accessing work at convenient times, avoiding travel costs and buying cheaper tickets. Furthermore, this survey evidences that streamers tend to be younger and more diverse than live theatre and event cinema audiences (AEA Consulting 2016).

A cursory search using the keyword 'theatre' in the Apple App store on 4 January 2018 retrieved results that indicate the most common uses for apps in the sector – of the first 100 apps listed, 47 per cent were non-theatre related (e.g. cinema listings), 34 per cent were theatre ticketing apps, 5 per cent were online databases/event listings and the remaining results included apps offering theatre building tour guides (3 per cent),[8] show-specific apps for musicals (2 per cent),[9] technical theatre apps (2 per cent) and a variety of other apps that each accounted for 1 per cent of the online search (pertaining to theatre-related job listings, industry news, etc.). These results imply that the primary usage of apps is as an interface to sell theatre tickets or provide an auxiliary function to the live event – the framing of an app as the theatrical event *in itself* remains a minority practice. Nonetheless, I argue that convergences between performance practices, VR film-making and the internet means that the subject of 'contagion' in the context of this discussion intersects with studies in virality and memetics online, commonly examined in the fields of media studies, marketing and political communication.

The medical definition of 'contagion' involves the 'passing of disease from a sick person to others' (Sell 2012) – the word 'contagion' is from the late Middle English denoting a contagious disease, which originates etymologically from the Latin *contagio*(n-), from *con-* 'together with' + the base of *tangere* 'to touch'. 'Contagion' in the context of a third-sector empathy app is paradoxical; it is an interface that enables users to perform a desirable, if virtual, boundarylessness between one's own 'healthy' experience and that of another who has been touched by ill health. The promise is to better understand another's experiences but in the absence of any direct contact, and the vehicle of transmission in question is a fictional character. Whereas internet 'memes' entail the propagation of 'jokes, rumours, videos and websites from person to person via the internet' (Shifman 2014: 2), VR apps such as *AWTD* entail a different kind of user engagement, since they require a Google cardboard headset to undertake the full immersive experience and carry the embedded promise within the medium of VR of empathic acts of perspective-taking. Whereas internet memes tend to prompt user-generated derivatives promoting the self-mediatization of the uploader's body as 'emblems of strategic self-commodification' (2014: 30) (e.g. selfies, 'planking', the 'Harlem Shake'), downloadable apps such as *AWTD* afford affective insights into the reconstructed experiences of others to a dispersed online community. The aim is to raise awareness of the lesser-known symptoms through reproducible simulation as a kind of positive social, or asocial, contagion in digital culture – 'asocial' on account of a VR app's disaggregated 'audience'.[10] Correspondingly, in ARUK's survey of the app's users, 68 per cent of participants reported undertaking the experience alone without sharing the experience or passing it onto others (Brisbourne 2018).

Both the emergence of pervasive theatres and my critical reading of VR film through a theatre studies lens might provide a basis for contestation among some cultural commentators. Despite theatres' centuries-old entanglement with technology, there has always existed a steady strand of discourse on theatre that conceptualizes the practice as a site of technological relief. For example, playwright Ayad Akhtar recently argued that a living actor before a living audience – or what he terms as the 'situation of all theatre' – is an 'antidote to digital dehumanization' (Akhtar 2017). More than this, Akhtar sees theatre as a site of resistance to what he describes as the 'great lie of American individualism – that my experience is the most important thing, and should be protected and enabled at all costs' (Akhtar 2017). In light of this critique, might the technologized notion of 'app theatre' carry within it the very logic of narcissistic neoliberal 'individualism' that Akhtar critiques here? Referring back to my earlier survey, the majority of 'theatre' apps operate functionally as a remote box office for the live event. Akhtar argues that in a world 'increasingly lost to virtuality and unreality – the theater points to an antidote' (Akhtar 2017). But through the lens of affective realism, even non-mediatized face-to-face encounters cannot be assumed to be the 'antidote' to the 'unreal' tout court because predictions based on the past may be prioritized over what is actually taking place if 'believing is seeing'. Philosopher of mind Andy Clark similarly proposes that we see the world by 'guessing the world' (2016: 5), which renders perception itself as a kind of virtual reality. Furthermore, there is a growing corpus of scientific knowledge that is demonstrating the role that remembered sensations play in predicting our world and influencing our behaviour at an unconscious level; from hungry judges perceiving defendants to be worthier of harsher sentences *before* lunch (Danzigera et al. 2011), to perceiving a hill as a steeper gradient when wearing slippery shoes (Miller 2016). This knowledge raises new questions about the role that downloadable simulations might play in training unconscious responses towards various kinds of bodily difference and how longer-term behavioural impacts might be evidenced.

'There's an app for that'* – the trademarked slogan originating from Apple's iPhone 3G commercial in 2009 – rapidly became an ironic meme, remixed by internet users to parody the empty promise of limitless app-based solutions to life's complex and innumerable problems.[11] Scholarly critiques have surfaced examining how apps are deployed in different cultural spheres and the human-to-human services that they might inadvertently, or intentionally, displace. For example, in women's studies, Rosalind Gill and Ngaire Donaghue have critiqued the 'appification' of well-being in higher education. Health-related mindfulness apps have been promoted by universities to help workers and students cope with multiplying demands and increasing stress levels. They argue that these individualized coping tools 'turn attention away from political and structural interventions towards increasing work on the self' (2016: 98). Put differently, these apps consign their users to isolation by making *them* responsible for solutions to more systemic failures as 'ideal neoliberal subjects' (98). Correspondingly, experiential apps could be critiqued as a kind of 'self-service' theatre, emerging at a time when neo-liberalism is firmly passing on the responsibility for the purchase of goods and services to consumers. While *AWTD* is not an app that is intended to offer health solutions to work-related problems, it is categorized by the charity under 'Health & Fitness' in online app stores, as opposed to other searchable categories (e.g. Education, Entertainment). In a press release, ARUK state their aim to 'encourage the public to think beyond "memory loss" as a key symptom' ('Virtual Reality App Offers Unique Glimpse into Life with Dementia' n.d.) and help people to recognize a greater range of the telltale signs of dementia. The app's purpose as a symptom awareness-raising interface could lead to earlier recognition, diagnosis and treatment, so the intended wider reaching benefits in relation to 'health' and well-being are clear.

Simulations and the transfer of affect offline/online

On ARUK's website for the project, the organization poses the question above the 'download' button, 'how would it feel to face these challenges every day?' The implication is that the app might provide affective insights, operating under the logic that 'feeling' itself might be transmitted with the virality of an internet meme. Teresa Brennan in *The Transmission of Affect* (2004) examined '*how* one feels the others' affects' (2004: 1), focusing on affective transfer in psychiatric clinics and the prevalence of psychogenic illness in contemporary life. She argued that in psychology 'the healthy person is a self-contained person' with 'established boundaries' (24). But Brennan challenged this idea in relation to phenomena such as entrainment

– a form of transmission of affect that brings a group's nervous or hormonal systems into alignment, making them more 'alike' (9), for example, chemical entrainment associated with unconscious olfaction that can produce hormonal interactions (9–10). The notion that 'something from without' can enter one's body complicates both the boundaries of discrete individuals and the broader notion that boundarylessness is necessarily associated with ill health alone. Whereas for Brennan affective transmission is 'social in origin, but biological in physical effect' (3), it is the virtualized 'leakage' of another's affective experiences that underpin the desire of empathy apps such as *AWTD* – correspondingly, simulated first-person experience might be conceptualized as a productive kind of virtual contamination to better understand eccentric forms of perception through their reconstruction. The potency of this kind of contactless spread of affect has been demonstrated in studies that have shown that emotional contagion can occur not only through real-world social networks (Fowler and Christakis 2008; Rosenquist et al. 2011) but also through online social networking without any direct interactions with others (Kramer et al. 2014). But the affects associated with social media can also be addictive. Former Apple engineer Chris Marcellino has said that the attention economy 'incentivises the design of technologies that grab our attention … in so doing, it privileges our impulses over our intentions' (Lewis 2017). It is this logic, in part, that has contributed to the sensationalizing of news/politics, clickbaiting and addiction to affirmations on social media such as retweets or 'likes', which the inventor of Facebook's 'like' button, Justin Rosenstein, has described as 'bright dings of pseudo-pleasure' (Lewis 2017).

Paul Bloom has argued that 'VR is far from the moral game changer that some make it out to be' (Bloom 2017). He contends that disability simulations can give a false and frightening impression of some physical experiences that can be awful in the short term, but over longer durations individuals have the capacity to 'habituate and adapt'. But where dementia differs considerably from other impairments that Bloom discusses (e.g. blindness) is that it is a progressive condition that worsens over time, producing disturbances in 'perception, cognition and emotion' (McNally 2011: 213). In an article reviewing disability scholarship on the effects of disability simulations of blindness, Arielle Michal Silverman has argued that simulations can be misleading on a number of grounds. Firstly, they cannot capture the long-term effects of an impairment and tend to highlight the 'initial trauma' rather than the ongoing realities. Secondly, simulated impairments are escapable. According to this reasoning, a self-administered VR experience cannot hope to provide an answer to how it would feel to face the challenges of Alzheimer's 'every day' – but equally, an inescapable simulation would be an unethical one. Finally, personal experience is crucial in shaping a person's beliefs about conditions, so if a participant is given 'an experience marked by fear, frustration, and incompetence, they will be apt to conclude that people's lives are similarly marked by fear, frustration, and incompetence' (Silverman 2015).

Data gathered by ARUK from thirty-two users in response to the app indicate that on average respondents rated it highly, particularly in terms of its perceived emotional engagement and the extent to which it provided a deeper insight into the challenges faced by people with dementia (Figure 12.2). But I would argue that the delivery mechanism creates not only new possibilities in terms of its perceived impacts and reach (*AWTD* had received 12,593 installs as of 12 January 2018 (Brisbourne 2018))[12] but new tensions in terms of ethics. How can VR simulations resist the techno-fetishization of a virtual other whose constructed experiences are assimilative from the first person and reducible to 'my' experience? In Emmanuel Levinas's discourse on ethics, 'alterity' encompasses the insistence that an 'other' always remains irreducible to either representation or to oneself – the other is characterized as a 'dimension of separateness, interiority, secrecy' that escapes comprehension (Critchley and Bernasconi 2002). But avatars in gaming are not so much 'others' as an extension of the self in a virtual world. It is a subjectivity that is problematizing Levinas's distinction. Furthermore, while AZUK's app situates the downloader-experiencer within a range of symptoms, they can only experience a single character's 'affect disposition'. Affect dispositions are 'stable traits that have an affective quality' (Scherer 2005). For example, some individuals may be generally more happy or anxious than others and respond differently to similar sets of symptoms. As the example that started this chapter serves to evidence, affect can contribute to damaging predictions about reality (e.g. seeing a phone as a gun). Similarly, if executed without due care, simulations can result in the disproportionate assumption of another's helplessness and consequently 'paternalistic discrimination' (Silverman 2015).

VR's promise is different to watching a play because it 'operates under the logic of transparency' (Bolter and Grusin 1999: 162) – in other words, it purports to offer first-person access to simulated phenomena using wearable technologies that seek to bring about their own disappearance. This promise introduces an inevitable epistemological tension – that the medium's ontology reaffirms its inevitably false promise that users can ever truly 'know' individual experiences of AD via a fixed simulation, which arguably plays to our sensations rather than rationality (hence, the charity's aforementioned question, 'how would it *feel* … ?'). Much as we know little about our avatar beyond the sets of constructed symptoms, knowing precisely *what* affects are elicited through

196   *Theatres of Contagion*

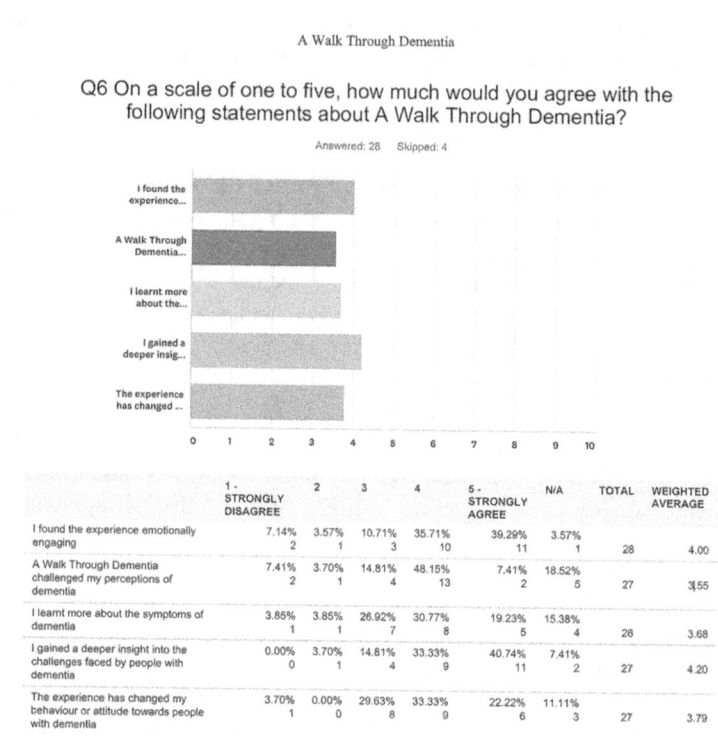

Figure 12.2 Data gathered from Alzheimer's Research UK's survey of *A Walk Through Dementia* app user. Reproduced courtesy of Alzheimer's Research UK.

this experience's web of atomized online users is difficult to discern. But we do know that through the lens of affective realism, our sensations – our personal store of feelings in memory – provide the basis for our unconscious anticipations. Apps such as *A Walk Through Dementia* may play an important role in shaping better informed predictions (e.g. recognizing a greater range of symptoms, offering insights into the potential affective quality of symptoms) as to the challenges those living with Alzheimer's face.

Conclusion

VR charity apps are making important interventions by attempting to reimagine individualistic technologies as affordances through which users might better relate to a virtual other. In *A Walk Through Dementia*, the 'other' is an unseen avatar that bridges our presence to the virtual environment – a chimera-like identity constituted from collected testimonies of those with Alzheimer's that contributed to the development process. The desire is for simulated symptoms of other's mis-perceptual experiences to enter into circulation as a digital export, allowing us to inhabit anxieties and challenges associated with recreated experiences of Alzheimer's in everyday scenarios. *AWTD* is not offered as self-administered 'cure' to more endemic cultural problems (as per Gill and Donaghue's (2016) critique of well-being apps), but instead forms part of a broader awareness-raising campaign – it instantiates virtual scenarios that users can experience as their own by standing in place of the avatar. But arguably, simulations in VR apps smuggle in other unintended ideologies that are co-present in the very vehicle of transmission – for example, the undergirding logic that we might take possession of another's bodily experiences as a kind of disability tourism, the reducibility of the other to the self through virtual means and the paradox of vulnerability experienced through an 'obscene subjectivity'. Disability simulations raise distinct sets of ethical challenges as to precisely what is being transmitted, especially as a result of their tendency to communicate the initial trauma of *becoming*, rather than the *being* of a condition (Silverman 2015). But much as through the logic of affective realism remembered feelings can change 'the actual content of your perceptual experience' (Barrett 2015), *AWTD* seeks to make a mediatized intervention to expose users to challenges that are otherwise beyond their perceptual grasp. Data gathered by the charity evidences the value that participating users had perceived in using apps to gain new affective insights into the challenges AD symptoms can pose – with 92 per cent of users in ARUK's survey indicating that they would like to see more scenarios developed for the app ('A Walk Through Dementia: Data' n.d.). Correspondingly, the charity is developing new approaches to training around the online app and gathering user input to inform this activity.

Through the lens of affective realism, sensations influence subsequent action when faced with similar sets of circumstances, and the brain only checks whether its predictions were correct *after* the fact. Studies are increasingly evidencing the capacity of online media to spread emotional contagion, and this knowledge is coinciding with new mediatized expressions that potentially isolating felt experiences of neurological disorders might be shared and distributed using VR apps. The simulation of complex and unknowable forms of altered consciousness always enters into a tension between a desire to reach towards the unreachable, while recognizing the impossibility of the endeavour. As such a constructed virtual other that experiences perceptual phenomena independent of a body can only ever provide a falsification of another's experience – everything rests on whether this falsification might be valuable to create better predictions about the felt states of others by agitating our habitual ways of perceiving the world. App theatre and downloadable VR empathy apps raise urgent new questions about what can enter into virulent circulation online and how developers can care for the experience of a user whom they will likely never meet.

Notes

1. Miller is quoting American biologist Gerald Edelman whose theory of consciousness was published in *Remembered Present: A Biological Theory of Consciousness* (1989).
2. Alzheimer's Research UK's launch film provides insights into the contributors to the app's research and development process ('A Walk Through Dementia – Launch Film' 2016).
3. Proto-type's *Fortnight* was a two-week-long treasure hunt involving participants who received text messages, emails, phone calls and letters to create a fictional world that 'encouraged audiences to interact with each other and their surroundings' ('Fortnight by Proto-type Theater' n.d.).
4. Kneehigh's *Walk with Me* app documents stories and memories collected from people that artist Anna Maria Murphy and friends met while walking in Cornwall on the company's Rambles Programme. The six stories can be listened to while rambling in the relevant locations via GPS mode ('Walk with Me: App Project 2017–2018' n.d.).
5. Circumstance's *A Hollow Body* (2014) is described by the company as an 'interactive mobile app with specially composed music score and narration' that 'guides you and a companion on a journey through the City of London' (*A Hollow Body* 2014). The app was commissioned by the Museum of London as part of their Sherlock Holmes exhibition programme.
6. DUET is a collaboration between Invisible Flock and Quicksand, funded by Arts Council England and the British Council. The app invited participants in India and the UK to develop an anonymous relationship with someone on the other side of the world by answering one question a day – each participant built a gradual picture of their partner and their surroundings through these shared responses ('DUET' n.d.). The messages received were presented as an animated visualization both online and in location-specific contexts.
7. Blast Theory's *Karen* is an app developed with National Theatre Wales in 2013 in which users interact with an onscreen 'life coach'. *Karen* explores big data and technological intrusion with a dramaturgy emerging from the user's answers to multiple choice questions formulated through research into psychological personality tests/appraisals (*Karen* 2013).
8. For example, the *Shakespeare's Globe 360* app (enabling users to explore a virtual 3D model of The Globe theatre).
9. For example, *Hamilton: The Official App* and the *fabulous wonder.land* VR app.

10 Social contagion concerns the idea that sociocultural phenomena can spread from person to person like biological phenomena. The notion of contagion as a descriptive device for social, and not just biological, phenomena can be traced to the late nineteenth-century France in the work of social psychologists such as Gabriel Tarde's discourse on 'imitation' in *Les Lois Sociales (Social Laws*, 1898) and Gustave Le Bon's investigation of crowd psychology in *The Crowd: A Study of the Popular Mind* (1895).
11 *Wired* reported in an article on the trademarking of the slogan that countless 'There's an app for that' jokes were appearing in blog posts (Chen 2010).
12 Of these downloads, 5,691 were on iOS and 6,902 were on Android devices.

References

AEA Consulting (2016), 'From Live-to-Digital: Understanding the Impact of Digital Developments in Theatre on Audiences, Production and Distribution', Commissioned by Arts Council England, UK Theatre and Society of London Theatre. Available online: https://www.artscouncil.org.uk/sites/default/files/download-file/From_Live_to_Digital_OCT2016.pdf (accessed 22 April 2018).

A Hollow Body (2014) [App], Circumstance. Available online: http://www.ahollowbody.com (accessed 5 January 2018).

A Walk Through Dementia (2016) [App], Great Abington: Alzheimer's Research UK. Available online: http://www.awalkthroughdementia.org (accessed 5 January 2018).

'A Walk Through Dementia: Data' (n.d.), Great Abington: Alzheimer's Research UK.

'A Walk Through Dementia – Launch Film' (2016), [video] *YouTube*, 2 June. Available online: https://www.youtube.com/watch?time_continue=188&v=nW1Y3Fnv7Mw (accessed 5 January 2018).

Akhtar, A. (2017), 'An Antidote to Digital Dehumanization? Live Theater', *The New York Times*, 29 December. Available online: https://www.nytimes.com/2017/12/29/theater/ayad-akhtar-steinberg-award-digital-dehumanization-live-theater.html (accessed 3 January 2018).

Auslander, P. (1999), *Liveness: Performance in a Mediatized Culture*, London: Routledge.

Barrett, L. F. and J. Wormwood (2015), 'When a Gun Is Not a Gun', *The New York Times: Gray Matter*, 17 April. Available online: https://www.nytimes.com/2015/04/19/opinion/sunday/when-a-gun-is-not-a-gun.html (accessed 12 November 2017).

Bloom, P. (2017), 'It's Ridiculous to Use Virtual Reality to Empathize with Refugees', *The Atlantic*, 3 February. Available online: https://www.theatlantic.

com/technology/archive/2017/02/virtual-reality-wont-make-you-more-empathetic/515511/ (accessed 8 January 2018).

Bolter, J. D. and R. Grusin (1999), *Remediation: Understanding New Media*, Cambridge, MA and London: MIT.

Brennan, T. (2004), *The Transmission of Affect*, Ithaca, NY: Cornell University Press.

Brisbourne, R. (2018), Email from the Author (containing ARUK's download data for *A Walk Through Dementia*), 12 January.

Chen, B. X. (2010), 'Apple Registers Trademark for "There's an App for That"', *Wired*, 10 November. Available online: https://www.wired.com/2010/10/app-for-that/ (accessed 3 January 2018).

Clark, Andy (2016), *Surfing Uncertainty: Prediction, Action, and the Embodied Brain*, Oxford: Oxford University Press.

Coyne, R. (2010), *The Tuning of Place: Sociable Spaces and Pervasive Digital Media*, Cambridge, MA: MIT Press.

Critchley, S. and B. Robert (2002), *The Cambridge Companion to Levinas*, Cambridge: Cambridge University Press.

Danzigera, S., J. Levav and L. Avnaim-Pesso (2011), 'Extraneous Factors in Judicial Decisions', in *Proceedings of the National Academy of Sciences of the United States of America*, 108 (17): 6889–92.

'DUET' [App]. Available online: http://duet-app.com (accessed 5 January 2018).

'Fortnight by Proto-type Theater' (n.d.), Bristol: Watershed. Available online: https://www.watershed.co.uk/ished/theatresandbox/projects/2010/fortnight/ (accessed 5 January 2018).

Fortnight (2011–15), Proto-type Theater. Available online: http://proto-type.org/projects/past/fortnight/ (accessed 5 January 2018).

Fowler, J. H. and N. A. Christakis (2008), 'Dynamic Spread of Happiness in a Large Social Network: Longitudinal Analysis over 20 Years in the Framingham Heart Study', *British Medical Journal*, 337 (5 December): A2338.

Gill, R. and N. Donaghue (2016), 'Resilience, Apps and Reluctant Individualism: Technologies of Self in the Neoliberal Academy', *Women's Studies International Forum*, 54: 91–9.

'Help Us Spread the Word about Dementia' (n.d.), Great Abington: Alzheimer's Research UK. Available online: https://www.alzheimersresearchuk.org/orange/ (accessed 4 January 2018).

Karen (2013), Blast Theory. Available online: https://www.blasttheory.co.uk/projects/karen/ (accessed 21 October 2017).

Kramer, A. D. I., J. E. Guillory and J. T. Hancock (2014), 'Experimental Evidence of Massive-scale Emotional Contagion through Social Networks', *Proceedings of the National Academy of Sciences of the United States of America*, 111 (24): 8788–90.

Lewis, P. (2017), '"Our Minds Can Be Hijacked": The Tech Insiders Who Fear a Smartphone Dystopia', *Guardian*, 6 October. Available online: https://www.

theguardian.com/technology/2017/oct/05/smartphone-addiction-silicon-valley-dystopia (accessed 18 October 2017).

McNally, R. J. (2011), *What Is Mental Illness?*, Cambridge, MA: Belknap Press of Harvard University Press.

Miller, M. (2016), 'Mark Miller – "Affective Realism": The Light and Dark Side of Seeing-with-feeling', [Video] *Vimeo*. Available online: https://vimeo.com/165309118 (accessed 18 October 2017).

Nix, J., B. A. Campbell, E. H. Byers and G. P. Alpert (2017) 'A Bird's Eye View of Civilians Killed by Police in 2015', *Criminology & Public Policy*, 16 (1): 309–40.

O'Brien, D. G. and M. McDonald Van Deventer (2015), 'The Appification of Literacy', in *Handbook of Research on the Societal Impact of Digital Media*, 417–36, Pennsylvania: IGI Global.

'Optimizing for App Store Search', [Website] *Apple Developer*, https://developer.apple.com/app-store/search/ (accessed 4 March 2018).

Parikka, J. (2007), *Digital Contagions: A Media Archaeology of Computer Viruses*, New York: Peter Lang Publishing.

Rosenquist, J. N., J. H. Fowler and N. A. Christakis (2011), 'Social Network Determinants of Depression', *Molecular Psychiatry*, 16 (3): 273–81.

Scherer, K. R. (2005), 'What Are Emotions? And How Can They Be Measured?', *Social Science Information*, 44: 693–727.

Sell, R. et al., eds. (2012), 'Contagion', in *Dictionary of Medical Terms*, 6th edn, Hauppauge, NY: Barron's Educational Series. Available online: http://ezproxy01.rhul.ac.uk/login?url=http://search.credoreference.com/content/entry/barronsm/contagion/0?institutionId=8498 (accessed 23 September 2017).

Shifman, L. (2014), *Memes in Digital Culture*, Cambridge, MA and London: MIT Press.

Silverman, A. M. (2015), 'The Perils of Playing Blind: Problems with Blindness Simulation and a Better Way to Teach about Blindness', *Journal of Blindness and Research*, 5 (2). Available online: https://nfb.org/images/nfb/publications/jbir/jbir15/jbir050201.html (accessed 9 January 2018).

'Slavoj Žižek on Video Games' (2017), [Video] *YouTube*, uploaded on 26 October. Available online: https://www.youtube.com/watch?v=8EqSAER0wbo (accessed 21 March 2018).

'Virtual Reality App Offers Unique Glimpse into Life with Dementia' (n.d.), *St Pancras International*. Available online: https://stpancras.com/media/162562/walk_through_dementia__launch_release.pdf (accessed 9 January 2018).

'Walk with Me: App Project 2017–2018' (n.d.), Cornwall: Kneehigh. http://www.kneehigh.co.uk/list/walkwithme-app.php (accessed 5 January 2018).

Žižek, S. (2017), 'The Obscene Immortality and Its Discontents', *International Journal of Žižek Studies*, 11 (2). Available online: https://zizekstudies.org/index.php/IJZS/article/view/1016 (accessed 21 October 2017).

Index

Abhinavagupta 170, 181
affect/affective expressions in music
    affective frequencies 41–2, 47, 49, 51–3
    affective potential 44, 49
    Langer on 42, 47
    Massumi on 42
    motor-intentional 44
    sonic 44–5, 49, 53
    vibrational affects 43–6, 49
affect disposition 195
affectio/affection 44–5, 49
affective contagion 16, 45, 77, 81–5, 155–6, 161
affective economies 166
affective realism 186–7, 189, 192, 197, 198 n.2
affective transmission 11, 16, 78, 155–6, 194
affectus 44–5
Ahmed, Sara 129, 166
AIDS/HIV crisis 4, 13, 23–4, 31, 33
    audience/performer's concern on 30
    Davidson on effects of 34
    Dean on unprotected sex 34–5
    records of 25
Akhtar, Ayad 192
Alfred Hitchcock Presents (TV series) 175
Alhazen 58
Almeida Theatre 23, 37 n.2
    dressing room 122–4
Almond, Marc 29
Alston, Adam 158
Alzheimer's Research UK (ARUK) 187, 193, 195–7
Amin, Ash 149
Ammaniti, M. 100

amphitheatres 65
Anatomy of a Suicide (Birch) 92
Angels in America (Kushner) 24, 33–4, 89
Animal Magnetism (Inchbald) 14, 74
animal magnetism/mesmerism 14, 100
anti-Oedipal subjectivity model 12
anti-theatricality/antitheatricalists 10
    Gosson's arguments on 66
    treatises 56
    in *Twelfth Night* 66–8
anti-theatrical prejudice 90, 99
appification 190–3
Apple App store, 'theatre' in 191
Appleby, Alex 82
app theatre 190, 192, 197–8
Archer, William 94
Architettura (Serlio) 64
Aristotle 31, 170
    catharsis theory 178, 181
    Poetics 11
Artaud, Antonin 15, 89–90, 93–4, 170, 180, 182
    The Theater and Its Double 12, 98–9
    'The Theatre and Culture' 98
    theatre as plague 12–13
Arts and Humanities Research Council (AHRC) 133 n.6
As You Like It (Shakespeare) 14, 56, 60–2, 68
atmosphere
    Bohme's perception of 81–2
    contagious 82–5, 167
    sound 162–5
Atmosphere as the Fundamental Concept of a New Aesthetics (Bohme) 81

Index

audience/spectators 50, 71
   affective contagion 82–4
   and aural environment 164
   consciousness (*see* brain (staging of consciousness))
   emotional engagement of 83
   experiencing discomfort 83–4
   faintness of (*see* faintness/fainting of audience)
   feedback/response from 78, 80, 83
   identification 174
   masks (masked spectators) 166–7
   participation and empowerment 156–9
   and performers 160–2, 165
   responses to Grand-Guignol 106–8
   Russell-Smith and 82–3
   in scenarios of criminalization 125
   spectator-voyeur 165–7
   survey 191
   temporal-lobe 173
auditory contagion 43
auditory mirror neurons 173–4
augmented subjectivity 187–9
Auslander, Philip 190
Autism Too Much Information (*TMI*) *Virtual Reality Experience* app 188
Averell, William 8
A Walk through Dementia (*AWTD*) VR app 17, 187–94
   ARUK's survey 196
   'On the Road' in 188–9
Ayrton, Maxwell 73

Bacon, Francis 63
Bailey, Lucy 15, 105, 113, 115
Banes, S. 158–9
'Bang! You're Dead' (*Alfred Hitchcock Presents*) 175

Bans, Shani 14
Barish, Jonas 89
   anti-theatrical prejudice 90
Barrett, Felix 156, 159–160, 162
Barrett, Lisa Feldman 181
   affective realism 187
   study on brain 186
Barrett, Wilson 96
Barrough, Philip 59–60
Barthes, Roland 5–6
Bartlett, Neil 3–4
Bashford, Alison 64
Basildon District Council (BDC) 141–2
   bunding construction 145
   discriminatory acts of 145
   eviction of Irish Travellers in Dale Farm 137
   against illegal use of land 142
basilisk/cockatrice (mythical beast) 58–9, 61–2
Bataille, Georges 11–12
Beale, Simon Russell 26
Beau, Dickie 13, 24, 34
   and Charleson 36
   dramaturgy of 31, 36
   dressing/undressing mannequins 29
   and Hamlet 33
   lip-synching by 28, 36–7
   main productions of 25
   playback theatre 25
   queer cultural transmission and 37
   Re-Member Me 23–5, 31, 33–7, 37 nn.1–2
behavioural contagion 77
Bennett, Jane 6
Berlant, Lauren 149
Bermondsey Artists' Group 73
Bernstein, Leonard 43–4
Bharata Muni 170, 181
Bibliothèque nationale de France 106
Binet, Alfred 106, 112

Bio Inc – Biomedical Plague game
        (DryGin Studios) 93, 102
Birch, Alice 92, 122–3, 125–6, 129–31
Black Death 138
Black movement 130
Blackouts: Twilights of the Idols
        (Beau) 25
Blake, Mathew 161
blood-injury-injection (BII) phobia,
        Grand-Guignol's 110–12, 116
Bloom, Paul 194
Boaden, J. 74
body-to-body/bodily transmission
        102
Bohme, Gernot 81–2
Boilly, Louis Leopold 109
Bollen, Jonathan 101
Bower, Gavin James 114
Bradley, Rizvana 130
brain (staging of consciousness) 170–1
    activity 180
    DMPFC 172, 176
    inner sound/light operator 172
    LPFC 172, 180–1
    mime-improviser/scene-designer
        171–4, 178, 181
    MPFC 172–3
    Other consciousness 172, 179
    rVLPFC 172
    scriptwriter/critic 171–2, 174, 181
    Self consciousness 171–3, 179
    stage/production manager 172
    VMPFC 172
Branagh, Kenneth 26
Brathwait, Richard 58
Brecht, Bertolt 170, 180–2
Brennan, Teresa 11, 128, 193–4
Brexit and US migration policies 8
Brieux, Eugène 11, 15, 89, 96
Britain, migration of Irish Travellers
        in 140
Bruce, Graham 163–4
Buchanan, H. 111
Burton, Richard 31

Cacioppo, John T. 16
Callard, Felicity 101
Camera Lucida (Barthes) 5–6, 25
Cameron, David 18 n.3, 138
Camus, Albert 3–4
Carlson, Marvin 28, 37, 95
catharsis theory 178, 181
Cat on a Hot Tin Roof (Williams) 26
causal theory of contagion 77
Chalk, Darryl 66–7
changgeuk (Korean opera) 48
Charleson, Ian 13, 23–4, 31, 34
    and Beau 23, 36
    Coke on 27
    Eyre on 27
    as Hamlet 23, 26–8, 30, 36
    illness and death of 26–8
    and McKellen 27–8, 38 n.9
    Peter's review on 36
    recognition from audience 27
Chekhov's gun 186
Chikamatsu 175
Christensen, Allan Conrad 15
Churchill, Winston 133 n.5
Clark, Andy 192
Clean Break Theatre Company 15–16
    guts and algorithms 129–32
    prison theatre 132
    tearjerking 126–9
    threat and compassion 122–6
Cleansed (Kane) 115
cognitive reappraisal 180–1
cohesion, principle of 90
Coke, Judith 27
*A Comparative Discourse of the
        Bodies Naturall and Politique*
        (Forset) 8
contagion-based gaming 93
contagion, medical definition of 191
contagious affect 49, 71–2, 76, 84, 126
contagious crime/criminal behaviour
        121
Contagious Diseases Acts 15, 96, 102
contagious dramaturgies 31, 72

contemporary musicals 52
contextual appraisal 175
Cooke, Jennifer 90
Coulson, N. 111
Craig, Edward Gordon 94
crime epidemics 121, 133 n.1
crime mapping software 130
Criminal Justice Act 137–8
criminal justice system 122, 133 n.5
Critchley, Simon 31
cross-disciplinary 101
cross-modal sensations 177
The Crowd: A Study of the Popular Mind (Le Bon) 76
The Crucible (Miller) 14
cultural-biological feedback loop 128
culture as containment 98–100
'The culture of the sewers' (Synod) 139–40
Cummings, Alan 26
Cunningham, Andrew 77
Curb Your Enthusiasm (David) 175
Cymbeline (Shakespeare) 58

Dale Farm, Essex 136–8
 infrastructure (*see* infrastructure, nomadic)
 overgrowth of 146
 Travellers (nomadic) (*see* Irish Travellers (nomadic))
 UN representatives on site 148
Damaged Goods (Brieux) 96
dance music 42, 48
danso (end-blown vertical flute) 49
David, Larry 175
Davidson, Gordon
 analysis of Charleson 38 n.11
 on effects of AIDS 34
Davies, S. 41
Day-Lewis, Cecil 34
Day-Lewis, Daniel 26, 34, 38 n.7
Dean, Tim 34–5
de Certeau, Michel 72–3

The Decline of Nomadism (Greenfields and Smith) 140
De Contagione et Contagionis Morbis et eorum Curatione Libri Tres (Fracastoro) 8
default network 172
Definitional Excursions: The Meanings of Modern/Modernity/Modernism (Friedman) 90
de Jongh, Nicholas 38 n.13
Dekker, Thomas 10
Deleuze, Gilles 12
de Lorde, André 106, 108, 112
Devil's Advocate (role) 171–2
Diamond (Hoyle) 24
Dido, Queen of Carthage (Marlowe) 72
Dilston Grove 14, 71–2, 78, 81
 performance space at 79
 places and spaces of 73
Discourses of the Preservation of the Sight (Laurentius) 58
disease transmission 76, 96, 121
 humoral theory of 8, 18 n.1
 ocular metaphors of 14, 56
distributed subjectivity 165
Dobbie, Stephen 162
The Doctor's Dilemma (Shaw) 96–7
Dolan, Jill 90
A Doll's House (Ibsen) 15, 97
Donaghue, Ngaire 193
dorsomedial prefrontal cortex (DMPFC) 172, 176
Douglas, Mary 139–40
 Purity and Danger 12
Doyle, Maxine 156, 161
dramatic art, power of (Bataille) 11
dramatic conflicts 159–60
Dream Pill (Prichard) 16, 126, 129, 131–2
 AHRC-funded research for 133 n.6
 audience–performer relationship 123, 125

black subjectivity 125, 127
  innocent-carceral environment 124
  response from audience 126
  sex-trafficking 122–3, 127–8
dreamthinkspeak (theatre company) 81
DUET app 198 n.6
Dumaniant (Antoine-Jean Bourlin) 14
Dundy, Elaine 111
Duse, Eleanora 94
dynamic axis of bodies (Spinoza) 80–1

Easterling, Keller 144–5, 147
Edelman, Gerald 198 n.1
Edelman, Lee 34
The Effect of Melodrama (painting by Boilly) 109
Ekman, Paul 176, 178
Elam, Keir 65
Elizabethan theatre 89
embodied simulation (ES) 100
emotional contagion 6, 16, 41, 57, 122, 127, 170–1, 174–7, 180–2, 183 n.1, 197
emotional mobility 126
emotions
  basic 176
  bhavas and *rasas* 181
  mudra (artful sign language) 181
  primal (*see* primal emotions)
empowerment of audience 156–9
Endemic: Essays in Contagion Theory (Nixon and Servitje) 90
An Enemy of the People (Ibsen) 97
entrepreneurial participation 158, 166
Environmental Protection Agency (EPA) 136, 142
environmental racism 136, 139–41, 150
epidemics 12, 15, 76, 95–6, 121, 133 n.1

epidemiological modelling 121–2, 130
Equality and Human Rights Commission (EHRC) 140, 150 n.1
erotohistoriography 35
Esposito, Roberto 7, 9
Essaies upon the Five Senses (Brathwait) 58
Etchells, Tim 126–7
The Ethics (Spinoza) 80
Ethics; and, on the Correction of Understanding (Spinoza) 42
EU Charter of Human Rights 138
eugenics 92–3
Euripides 10
Europe, plague in 3, 8–9
external agents 8–9
extramission theory of sight 58, 60, 62, 68
'extrastatecraft' (Easterling) 144
Eyre, Richard 23, 25
  on Charleson 27
  Hamlet of 38 n.7

Facial Action Coding System (FACS) 176
facial expressions (emotions) 175–8
faintness/fainting of audience
  BII phobia 110–12, 116
  as marketing tool 115–16
  at Théâtre du Grand-Guignol 105, 108–10
  vasovagal syncope 105, 108, 110, 115, 116
The Falling (Morley) 110
fear of contagion, concept 106–7
Felski, Rita 90
Felton-Dansky, Miriam 12
Ferrand, Jacques 63
Fiennes, Ralph 26
The First and Chief Groundes of Architecture (Shute) 65
Fitzgerald, Des 101

Fool for Love (Shepard) 26
Forset, Edward 8
Fortnight (Proto-type Theater) 190, 198 n.3
Foucault, Michel 9, 127
Fracastoro, Girolamo 8
Freeman, Elizabeth 35
Friedman, Susan Stanford 90

Gallese, V. 100
Galsworthy, John 133 n.5
Ganggangsullae (Korean ritual dance) 49–51
Garner, Stanton B., Jr. 13, 94–5
gay 24–5
    actors played role of 13, 26
    McKellen on 33
    performer's concern on AIDS 30
    Public Health England reports on 38
    research by Tatchell 32
germ theory 8, 13, 15, 95
Ghosts (Ibsen) 93–4
Ghosts and Gibberings (Archer) 94
Gibson, Mel 26
Gielgud, John 25–6, 33–4
Gill, Rosalind 193
Girard, René 11, 125
A Global Doll's House (Holledge, Bollen, Helland and Tompkins) 101–2
global positioning system 190
Goodman, S. 163
The Good, the Bad, and the Ugly (Leone) 174
Gordon, Mel 106, 114
gore/gory spectacle 109, 113–15
Gosson, Stephen 66
Gould, Deborah 127
Grand-Guignol 115–16
    audience responses to 106–8
    BII phobia 110–12
    contagious legacy of 116–17
    faintness of audience at 105, 108–110
    gory effects of 113–14
Great Leap Forward (China) 144
Great Plague of London (1665-6) 8, 29
Greenblatt, Stephen 98–9, 101
Greenfields, M. 140
Green, Julius 15
Griffin, Christopher 139–40
groove (music) 44–6
Guattari, Félix 12
Guignoleurs 107–8
Gut (Korean ritual) 48
Gypsy and Traveller ethnic groups 140, 150 n.1

habeas viscus (Weheliye) 130–1
Hacking, Ian 131–2
haemophobia 110, 112, 115–16
Hamlet (Shakespeare) 10, 13
    Carlson on 28
    Charleson as Hamlet 13, 23, 26–8, 30, 36
    contagion and 29–30
    Critchley on 31
    Eyre's 38 n.7
    homosexuality and 33
    Icke's production of 23, 31, 37 n.2
    impact on plague 30
    Mallin on 30
    queerness and 13, 26, 33–4
    Traversi on 30
    Webster on 31
    Wooster Group's 31
Hammond, Aubrey 111
Hand, Richard J. 106–7
Haraway, Donna 9
Hardt, Michael 8
Hare, David 3–4
Hart, Eric 114
Hartman, Saidiya 124
Hasson, Uri 174
Hatfield, Elaine 16

hazardous pollutants 142, 145
health-related mindfulness apps 193
Helland, Frode 101
heredity 15, 92, 95, 99
Herne, James A. 15, 96
Herrmann, Bernard 162–3
    Bruce on 164
    soundtracks for Hitchcock movies 163
Hippocrates 18 n.1
Hippolytus (Euripides) 10
Hitchcock, Alfred 162–3
HIV/AIDS crisis. *See* AIDS/HIV crisis
Hockney, David, exhibition of 24
Holledge, Julie 101
A Hollow Body (Circumstance) 190, 198 n.5
Homosexual Acts 38 n.4
homosexuality 31–3, 38 n.9
Hooker, Claire 64
horror genre 105–7, 112
'house doctor,' Grand-Guignol 111–12, 115
Howard, Michael 138
Howells, Adrian 81
Hoyle, David 24
Huguenot Protestants 71, 74–5, 78
humoral theory of disease transmission 8, 18 n.1

iatrophobia (fear of doctors) 112
Ibsen, Henrik 8, 89
    A Doll's House 15, 97
    An Enemy of the People 97
    Ghosts 93–4
    The Lady from the Sea 95
    The Master Builder 97
Icke, Robert 23, 31, 37 n.2
'ideal neoliberal subjects' 193
'imaginary experience of music' 51
imitation/imitative contagion 11, 31, 36, 76, 84–5
    Tarde on 77
Thrift on 80
violence through 76
immersive theatre 81, 85, 116–17, 155, 158, 161
immunity and defence 9
Inchbald, Elizabeth 77, 80, 84
    Animal Magnetism 14, 74
    The Massacre (see *The Massacre* (Inchbald))
Infectious Ideas: Contagion in Premodern Islamic and Christian Thought (Stearns) 76
infectious sights, Shakespeare's 56
    As You Like It 56, 60–2, 68
    King Henry VI Part 2 57–60, 62, 68
    Twelfth Night 56, 61–4, 68
infrastructure, nomadic 136–7, 141–9
    bunding 136, 142–3, 145, 148–9
    bureaucracy 147
    defence wall 142
    free zoning 144
    hazardous pollutants 142, 145
    height-adjustable barriers 144
    obstruction 148, 150
    poetics of 147
    political disposition of 145, 147
    resident's pain 149–50
    sewage pipes 142–3
    statecraft 137, 144, 146
    UN representatives' visit to Dale Farm 148
in-group behaviour 78–80, 84
The Inheritance (Lopez) 24
inner actor network 172–3
Inner Experience (Bataille) 11
inner theatre elements 170–3
integral performative texts 43
interactive mobile app 198
intercontinental social networking 190
intercultural theatre 42–3, 51–2
interdisciplinarity 101–2

Interdisciplinarity Inc. 102
intergenerational transmission 6–7
internet memes 191–3
inter-subject correlations (ISC) 173–5, 182
intertheatricality 101–2
intimate theatre 81
intromission theory of sight 58, 63
Ionesco, Eugène 3–4
Irish Traveller Movement in Britain (ITMB) 137, 141
Irish Travellers (nomadic) 136
   Cameron's response to eviction of 138
   and contagion 138–41
   containment of 137, 140–1, 144, 150
   Douglas's research on 139
   environmental racism 136, 139–41, 150
   eviction in Dale Farm 137
   infrastructure (*see* infrastructure, nomadic)
   Oak Lane 137
   objective law and 145–6
   planning applications 137
   settlement of 144
   urban poor/gypsy 140

James I, King 65
James, Simone 123
Jarvis, Liam 16–17
Jean Hennuyer, the Bishop of Lizieux or the Massacre of St Bartholomew 74
Jones, Henry Arthur 96
Jones, Inigo 64–5
Jonson, Ben 64–5
Jowitt, Deborah 46
Julius Caesar (Shakespeare) 10

Kane, Sarah 115
Karen app (Blast Theory) 198 n.7
Kassabian, Anahid 165

Kensington Gore 114
Kepler, Johannes 58
Keston, Fi 114–15
kinaesthetic contagion 130
kinetic axis of bodies (Spinoza) 80–1
King Henry VI Part 2 (Shakespeare) 14, 56–60, 62, 68
Kirkwood, Lucy 91–2, 100
kkoktu kaksi (Korean ritual) 48
kkwaenggwari (brass gong) 50
Korean rituals (dance/music)
   danso (end-blown vertical flute) 49
   Ganggangsullae 49–51
   Gut 48
   kkokdoosue 50
   kkoktu kaksi 48
   kkwaenggwari (brass gong) 50
   notdari bapchi (treading on roof tiles) 50
   p'ansori 48, 51
   play-within-play sequence 50
   pungmul nori 48, 53 n.3
   Romyo and Juri 48
   samul nori 48–9, 51, 53 n.3
   shaman 42
   talchum 48
Kushner, Tony 24, 34
   Angels in America 89

The Laboratory Revolution in Medicine (Cunningham) 77
The Lady from the Sea (Ibsen) 95
Langer, Susanne 42
   affect as feeling of 47–8, 51
Langley, Eric 63, 68 n.1
language of agency 149
Larkin, Brian 147
The Last Man (Shelley) 93
lateral prefrontal cortex (LPFC) 172, 180–1
Laurentius, Andreas 58–61
Laws of Imitation (Tarde) 77

Le Bon, Gustav 14, 76–7, 80, 84, 199 n.10
Legacies of Plague in Literature, Theory and Film (Cooke) 90
Le Médecin Malgré Tout le Monde (Dumaniant) 14
Leone, Sergio 174
Lepecki, A. 158–9
Les Remplaçantes (Brieux) 96
Levinas, Emmanuel 195
LGBTQ culture 24, 36
Lister, Joseph 95
Little on the inside (Birch) 16, 122–6, 129–32
  behavioural contagion 131
  guilty-carceral of adult women 124
  racism 123–5
  response from audience 126
Live-to-Digital work audience survey 191
Lobanov-Rostovsky, Sergei 59
Local Government Act 1986 32
Lodge, Thomas 62
  Treatise of the Plague 8
London
  -based Irish Travellers 139
  bookers data in 133 n.2
  crime epidemics in 133 n.1
  theatres shut down of plague 10, 30
London Grand Guignol season 108–9, 111
Lopez, Matthew 24
Lost in Trans (Beau) 25
Love's Labours Lost (Shakespeare) 63
Love Suicides at Sonezaki (Chikamatsu) 175

Macbeth (Shakespeare), atmospheric version of 159–62
Machon, Josephine 156
make-up artists, theatrical 113–14, 117

Mallin, Eric S. 30
Man and His Makers (Barrett and Parker) 96
The Man That Knew Too Much (Hitchcock) 162
Marcellino, Chris 194
Margaret Fleming (Herne) 96
Marlowe, Christopher 72
Mas, Émile 108
Mason, Tallulah 73
The Massacre (Inchbald) 14, 71, 73, 74, 84
  contagious affect 76
  killings of Huguenot Protestants 74
  and negative contagion 74–6, 78
  violence 75–6
Massumi, Brian 42, 126
  accounts on *affectus* 44–5, 53
The Master Builder (Ibsen) 97
Masterpiece of the Oral and Intangible Heritage of Humanity 51
Mathias, Sean 25
Maurey, Max 106, 108, 111–12, 115–16
Maxa, Paula 111
Mbembe, Achille 121–2, 129
McCarthy, Lynne 12, 16
McCutcheon, Rebecca 14, 85 n.1
McKellen, Ian 25–6
  and Charleson 27–8, 38 n.9
  on homosexuality 33
McPhee, Molly 15–16
medial PFC (MPFC) 172
mediatization on theatre 190
A Mervailous Combat of Contrareties (Averell) 8
Mesmer, Franz Anton 14, 74, 100
mesmerism 14, 100
Méténier, Oscar 106
The Method of Phisick (Barrough) 59–60
Mew, Charlotte 99–101

micro-environment 82–4
A Midsummer Night's Dream
  (Shakespeare) 64
migrants 3, 9
  Trump on Mexican migrants 8–9,
    18 n.2
Miller, Arthur 14
Miller, Mark 186, 198 n.1
mind–body continuum 91–2
mind-to-mind contagion 102
Minns, Beatrice 160
mirror neurons 173–6
  activation 174–5
  auditory 173–4
  canonical 174
  facial expressions 175–7
  insula 176
  scientific studies of 6
mise-en-scène 43, 51, 146
mob behaviour, effect of 14, 71
moment-to-moment consciousness
  173
moral contagion 172
Moretti, Franco 102
Morley, Carol 109–10
Mosquitoes (Kirkwood) 91
Mother Courage and Her Children
  (Brecht and Steffin) 182
motor-intentional affect 44
Munday, Anthony 56, 66, 68
Murphy, Anna Maria 198
music 52
  abstraction 47
  affect (*see* affect/affective
    expressions in music)
  contemporary musicals 52
  dance music 42, 48
  Davies on expressiveness of 41
  groove 44–6
  'imaginary experience of music' 51
  in/as ritual 47, 50
  simplicity and predictability 53 n.5
  sonic continuum 43, 45
  sound and 41–3

musical theatre 43
My Big Fat Gypsy Wedding (TV
  series) 141

National Changgeuk Company of
  Korea 42
National Theatre 13, 23–4, 26, 36,
  115
National Theatre Archive 38 n.8
Natural Born Killers (Stone) 175
Natya-Shastra tradition of Bharata
  Muni 181
necropolitics of contagion 121, 129
negative contagion 74–6, 78, 84–5
Negri, Antonio 8
neoliberalism 193
neural guesses 186–7
neuroscience 5, 16, 107–8, 115, 170,
  176, 181
Ngai, S. 141, 148
1984 (Broadway production) 115
nineteenth-century theatre 15, 90
  engagements of 89
  and heredity 15, 92, 95
  with medical discourse 94
  and neurological sciences 107–8
Nixon, Kari 90, 100
nomadic contagions 138–41
Nomads under the Westway (Griffin)
  139
Nordlund, Marcus 58
Northam, Jeremy 26
notdari bapchi (treading on roof
  tiles) 50

Oak Lane (Traveller property) 137
ocular anatomy 60
Oedipus Rex (Sophocles) 10, 89
'On Affect and Protest' (Gould) 127
online virality 190–3
Orgel, Stephen 64
O'Toole, Peter 26
outer theatre elements 170
out-group behaviour 78–80, 84

Pais, Ana 10, 16
Panksepp, Jaak 178-9, 181
p'ansori (musical storytelling) 48, 51
Paracelsian theory of contagion 62
Parker, Louis N. 96
Park, Robert 121
participatory models of audience 157-8
Pasteur, Louis 13, 94
Pennington, Michael 26
permeable alliances 125, 129
pervasive theatre 190-3
perverse allegiances 174
Peter, John 36
physical mobility 126
The Physician (Jones) 96
Pierron, Agnès 106, 110, 111
plague
    and contagion 10
    in Europe 8
    Hamlet's impact on 30
    history of 7-9
    in London 10
    theatre as plague 12-13
    in *Twelfth Night* 61-4
The Plague (Bartlett) 3-4
Plague Inc. game (Ndemic Creations) 93, 101-2
Plague over England (de Jongh) 38 n.13
Plato 6, 11
playback theatre 25
playhouse, architecture of 65-6
Poetics (Aristotle) 11
political-ecological problems 140
predictive policing 121, 130, 132
pre-exposure prophylaxis (PrEP) medication 25, 35
Prichard, Rebecca 122-3, 128, 130-1
primal emotions 176-82
    distress-related emotions 180
    Ekman's 178, 181
    fear 180
    in mammals 178-9

Panksepp's 178, 181
    in rats 179
'The Prince of Terror' (de Lorde) 106
productive contagion 101-2
proscenium theatre 160
Provine, R. R. 183 n.1
'proximate discipline' 101
Pryce, Jonathan 26
pseudo-'life coach' app 190
Psycho (Hitchcock) 162
psychoanalysis 6
    Girard on 11
    psychoanalytic sense of death 31
Punchdrunk (theatre company) 81, 155-6
    Alston on entrepreneurial participation 158
    neoliberal values 158
    participatory models of audience 157-8
    separation, mechanism of 165-7
    visceral experience 156-8
pungmul nori tradition (Korean folk music) 48, 53 n.3
Purity and Danger (Douglas) 12

Quarmby, Katharine 137
Queer British Art 1861-1967 (exhibition) 24
queer culture 24-5, 31-2
    Beau and 37
    and *Hamlet* 13, 26, 33-4
    HIV/AIDS records 25
    LGBTQ 24
Queer Theatre 24
Quigley, Karen 110
Quinn, Damian 85 n.1

Rainolds, John 10
Rapson, Richard L. 16
rasa-cathartic effect 181-3
Ratineau, Paul 114
Ravenhill, Mark 29
reciprocal affinity 125

Rees, Roger 26
Re-Member Me (Beau) 13, 23–5, 31, 33–7, 37 nn.1–2
Republic (Plato) 6, 11
Rethinking Interdisciplinarity (Callard and Fitzgerald) 101
Rhinoceros (Ionesco) 3–4
Ricci, Glenn 162
Richard III (Shakespeare) 58
Rickman, Alan 26
right ventrolateral prefrontal cortex (rVLPFC) 172
risk assessment algorithms 130
ritual dance. See Korean rituals (dance/music)
Robbins, Jerome 43
Robins, Elizabeth 97
Roholt, Tiger 44, 46–7
Romeo and Juliet (Shakespeare) 10, 13, 52
  'All are punish'd' 53
  curse of Mercutio 41
  and Romyo and Juri (see Romyo and Juri (Sun-Whan))
  and West Side Story (see West Side Story (Robins))
Romyo and Juri (Sun-Whan) 42, 47–51
  affect in 48–51
  feelings in 48–9, 51
  rituals in (see Korean rituals (dance/music))
Rosenstein, Justin 194
Round Dance (Schnitzler) 72
Rousseau, Jean-Jacques 124
Royal Shakespeare Company (RSC) 114, 116
Russell-Smith, Kate 82–3, 85 n.1
Rylance, Mark 26

Sabsay, Leticia 125
same-sex marriage, legislation for 38 n.14
Sampson, Tony D. 16

samul nori tradition (Korean folk music) 48–9, 51, 53 n.3
Scannell, R. Joshua 130
Scarry, E. 149
Schechner, R. 183 n.5
Schneider, P. E. 107, 111
Schnitzler, Arthur 72
Scott, Andrew 26
Scott, James C. 143–4
  on statecraft 146
A Second and Third Blast of Retreat from Plays and Theatres (Munday) 56–7
Sedgwick, Eve Kosofsky 38 n.3
Seeing like a State (Scott) 143
separation, mechanism of 165–7
Serlio, Sebastio 64–5
Servitje, Lorenzo 90, 100
Sexual Offences Act 1967 23–4, 32–3
Shakespeare's Globe 15, 105, 113, 115
Shakespeare's Globe 360 app 198 n.8
Shakespeare, William 10
  As You Like It 14, 56, 60–2, 68
  Cymbeline 58
  infectious sights (see infectious sights, Shakespeare's)
  Julius Caesar 10
  King Henry VI Part 2 14, 56–60, 62, 68
  Love's Labours Lost 63
  A Midsummer Night's Dream 64
  ocular metaphors of transmission 14, 56
  Richard III 58
  Romeo and Juliet (see Romeo and Juliet (Shakespeare))
  spectators' awareness of plague 30
  The Tempest 180
  Titus Andronicus 15, 105, 111, 113
  Twelfth Night (see Twelfth Night (Shakespeare))
  The Winter's Tale 59

Sharpe, Christina 131
Shaw, George Bernard 8
  The Doctor's Dilemma 96–7
  Too True to Be Good 97–8
Shelley, Mary 93
Shepherd-Barr, Kirsten E. 15
Shepherd, Sam 26
Shunt (theatre company) 81
Shute, John 65
The Silver Lotus (Robins) 97
Silverman, Arielle Michal 194
Silverstone, Catherine 32–3
Simpson, Sir John 73
site-based practice/practitioner 72
  dreamthinkspeak 81
Sleep No More (*SNM*) (Barrett and Doyle) 16, 155, 158–60, 162–4
  affective economy of 167
  masks in 166–7
Slinger, Jonathan 26
Smith, D. 140
Smith, Matthew Wilson 107, 115
Smith, Murray 174
social antagonisms 125
social contagion 121–2, 124, 132, 199 n.10
social contract, Rousseau's 124
social disease 89
social media 194
Soho Theatre 24
Sondheim, Stephen 43
sonic affect 43–5, 49, 53
Sontag, Susan 10
Sophocles
  Oedipus Rex 89
  Women of Trachis 10
sound atmospheres 162–5
Soviet Collectivisation 144
Sparks, Tori 161
spillover effect 178
Spinoza, Baruch 42, 85
  on nature of bodies 80–1
stagecraft 16, 146
stagehands 170–5, 178, 181

'Stamp on the Camps' (Tyler) 138
Stearns, J. K. 76
Steffin, Margarete 182
Stone, Oliver 175
Strindberg, August 15
The Sun (newspaper) 138
Sun-Whan, Park 48–9, 51
survey
  of app's users, ARUK's 192, 196–7
  audience 191
Symons, Arthur 94
Synon, Mary Ellen 140
syphilis 8, 89, 94, 96, 107
Syphilis, or, A Poetical History of the French Disease (Fracastoro) 8

talchum, Korean dance 48
Tan, Marcus Cheng Chye 13–14
Tarde, Gabriel 14, 77, 80, 84, 199 n.10
Tatchell, Peter 32
Taylor, Millie 43
telegony 95
The Tempest (Shakespeare) 10, 180
temporal-lobe networks 173, 176
Ten Plagues (Ravenhill) 29
A Testimony and a Silence (McCutcheon) 14, 71–2
  in-/out-groups behaviour in 78–80
The Theater and Its Double (Artaud) 12, 98–9
'The Theater and the Plague' (Artaud) 12
'The Theatre and Culture' (Artaud) 98
'theatre' apps 192
theatre, derivation of 56
Théâtre du Grand-Guignol. *See* Grand-Guignol
theatre makers 3, 5, 7, 112–13, 116, 188, 190
Theatre of Cruelty 94
theatrical genre

dangers of (Mas) 108
  by Maurey and de Lorde 112
theatrical spaces 187
theatrical/stage blood 113–15
  formula 113, 115
  Gordon on 114
  noted brand (Kensington Gore) of 114
  by Ratineau 114
  types of 114
'Theory of Mind' 172
Thrift, Nigel 80, 85
Thucydides 10
Timon of Athens and *King Lear* (Shakespeare) 10
Tinegate, John 114
Titus Andronicus (Shakespeare) 15, 111
  Bailey's production at Shakespeare's Globe 15, 105, 113
  faintness of audience 105
  by RSC 116
Tompkins, Joanne 101
Too True to Be Good (Shaw) 97–8
tragic poetry 11
transmission, mechanisms of
  breastfeeding 96, 99
  microbial agents 95
  prostitutes 96
The Transmission of Affect (Brennan) 11, 193
Travellers (nomadic). *See* Irish Travellers (nomadic)
Traversi, Derek A. 30
Treatise of the Plague (Lodge) 8
trigger warnings 115
Trump, Donald 18 n.3
  on Mexican migrants 8–9, 18 n.2
Twelfth Night (Shakespeare) 14
  antitheatricality in 66–8
  infectious sights in 56, 61–4, 68
Tyler, I. 138
Tynan, Kenneth 111

Understanding the Affective Spaces of Political Performance (Thrift) 80
universal contagion 8

Van Den Bosch, Jan-Willem 23
vasovagal syncope (fainting) 105, 108, 110, 115, 116
Vaughan, Livi 160
ventromedial PFC (VMPFC) 172
Vertigo (Hitchcock) 160, 162
vibrational affects 43–6, 49
video games, Žižek on 188–9
violence, contagious 175
Viral Performance: Contagious Theaters from Modernism to the Digital Age (Felton-Dansky) 12
virtual reality (VR)
  charity apps 196
  films 188, 192
  memory bank 188
  self-administered experience 194–5
  simulations 195
  smartphone app 187, 190–2, 197
visual contagion 56
Visyon (digital developer) 187
Vrettos, Athena 15

Wald, Priscilla 6, 131
Walk with Me app 198 n.4
Warner, Marina 113
The Wayback app 188
Webster, Jamieson 31
Weheylie, Alexander 125
Weismann, August 95
Wells, Elizabeth 43–4
Western literature, Greenblatt on 98–9
West Side Story (Robins) 42–7, 53
  affectio/affection 44–5, 49
  affective contagion 45
  affective frequencies 47, 49, 52

affectus 44–5
finger-snapping 44–6, 49
groove 44–6
Jets/Sharks 45–7
Jowitt on 46
musical numbers 44–6
vibrational affect 44–6, 49
Wells on 43–4
Whishaw, Ben 26
White, Gareth 163
A White Night (Mew) 99–100
The Whore of Babylon (Dekker) 10
Wickstrom, Maurya 144
Wilderson, Frank 133 n.7
Williams, Tennessee 26
Wilson, Michael 106–7
The Winter's Tale (Shakespeare) 59
Wokoma, Susan 123
Women of Trachis (Sophocles) 10
Wormwood, Jolie 1 86
  affective realism 187

Young Vic Theatre 24

Zen and the Art of Motorcycle
  Maintenance (Pirsig) 91–2
Žižek, Slavoj 188–9

www.ingramcontent.com/pod-product-compliance
Lightning Source LLC
Chambersburg PA
CBHW052039300426
44117CB00012B/1884